The Martians
Have Landed!

The Martians Have Landed!

A History of Media-Driven Panics and Hoaxes

ROBERT E. BARTHOLOMEW
AND BENJAMIN RADFORD

McFarland & Company, Inc., Publishers
Jefferson, North Carolina, and London

A companion title by Robert E. Bartholomew: *Little Green Men, Meowing Nuns and Head-Hunting Panics: A Study of Mass Psychogenic Illness and Social Delusion* (McFarland, 2001)

LIBRARY OF CONGRESS CATALOGUING-IN-PUBLICATION DATA

Bartholomew, Robert E.
    The Martians have landed! : a history of media-driven panics and hoaxes / Robert E. Bartholomew and Benjamin Radford.
       p.   cm.
    Includes bibliographical references and index.

    ISBN 978-0-7864-6498-2
    softcover : 50# alkaline paper

    1. Mass media — Psychological aspects.   2. Hoaxes in mass media.   3. Mass media — Influence.   I. Radford, Benjamin, 1970–   II. Title.
P96.P75B37 2012
302.23 — dc23   2011037370

BRITISH LIBRARY CATALOGUING DATA ARE AVAILABLE

© 2012 Robert E. Bartholomew and Benjamin Radford. All rights reserved

No part of this book may be reproduced or transmitted in any form or by any means, electronic or mechanical, including photocopying or recording, or by any information storage and retrieval system, without permission in writing from the publisher.

On the cover: (foreground) Orson Welles (CBS Radio/Photofest); background © 2012 Shutterstock

Manufactured in the United States of America

McFarland & Company, Inc., Publishers
   Box 611, Jefferson, North Carolina 28640
   www.mcfarlandpub.com

Table of Contents

Preface   1

Section One : It Came from the Airwaves — Radio

1. The London Riot Hoax   13
2. Radio Daze — The Martian Invasion Broadcast   16
3. The Martians Return   23
4. Infamous Disc Jockey Hoaxes   27
5. Playing with Fire: Nuclear Scares   30

Section Two : It Came from the Small Screen — Television

6. "This Just In..." NBC Frightens Viewers   37
7. "Look! Up in the Sky!" Asteroid Panic   40
8. Pokémon Panics and Creepy Crawley Scares   44
9. The "Documentary" That Fooled England   49
10. Hurricane Katrina Mythmaking   53
11. Chicken Little and the Bird Flu Panic   59
12. The Russians Are Coming!   64
13. The Video Nasties Scare *(Peter Hassall)*   67

Section Three : It Came from Ink — Newspapers

14. The Batmen on the Moon Hoax   79
15. The Central Park Zoo Panic   84
16. The Halley's Comet Scare of 1910   87
17. How the Press Created an Imaginary Terrorist   92

18. The Hook Hoax	98
19. The Ghost Slasher of Taiwan	101
20. The Phantom Clown Panic	105

Section Four : It Came from Cyberspace—The Internet

21. Chemtrails and Conspiracies	113
22. Morgellons: The First Internet Disease?	117
23. Katrina Evacuee Myths	120
24. The E-mail Virus Panic *(Bill Ellis)*	123

Section Five : It Came from a Friend of a Friend — Media-Spread Urban Legends

25. Urban Legends and the Media	131
26. The Curse of the Crying Boy *(David Clarke)*	134
27. Photos of the Gods *(David Clarke)*	146

Section Six : It Came from Everywhere

28. The Satanic Cult Scare	157
29. Halloween Panics	162
30. Stranger Danger and the Predator Next Door	170
31. The School Safety Panic	176
32. "Out of the Water!" Media Shark Frenzy	179
33. The Great Puerto Rican Chupacabra Panic	182
34. YouTube, Popcorn and the Killer Cell Phones	187
35. Someone Stole My Kidney! Organ Theft Scares	192
36. Killer Vaccines *(Felicity Goodyear-Smith and Helen Petousis-Harris)*	197

Notes	213
Bibliography	229
Index	241

Preface

The mass media shape public opinion like no other force in society. Radio, television and newspapers have a long history of causing undue alarm. The newcomer on the block — the Internet — is rapidly gaining a similar reputation. From the 1835 "batmen on the Moon" hoax to recent bird flu scares and Hurricane Katrina myths, this book presents a number of colorful case studies that highlight the impact of the media on our lives and its tendency to sensationalize. Most accounts are from the United States, while others are from Europe, Asia, Africa, South America, Australia and New Zealand. Some are global in scope. A single shark attack on a popular beach may generate headlines for weeks, yet each day over 40,000 people — mostly women and children — die of starvation and poverty-related diseases — and it rarely makes the news. Such is the nature of the media with its focus on the unusual and the sensational, that it often paints a distorted picture of the world.

At the dawn of the twenty-first century, unprecedented amounts of information cross international boundaries of our global village in the blink of an eye. As we grow more reliant on the media in our everyday lives, we must also be wary of its potential — be it intentional or unconscious — to transmit erroneous images of the world we live in. George Santayana once wrote: "Those who do not heed the mistakes of the past are condemned to repeat them." The cases in this book are a good starting point from which to understand the nature of the media, which is ultimately a business aimed at selling a product, and the many instances where it has created public fear and unrest, either inadvertently or by design. Make no mistake: no matter how educated or experienced, we are all potential victims.

Chapter 1 looks at the events of January 1926, when the British Broadcasting Corporation stunned listeners by reporting on a worker revolt in London. It was said that an angry mob of unemployed workers were running riot through the city, lynching, burning and looting everything in sight. In reality, they were hearing a radio play. In the opening segment, Ronald Knox announced that the upcoming stories were fictional, but many listeners in England and Ireland missed the disclaimer and took the show at face value.

In Chapter 2, the infamous Martian "invasion" is examined. On October 30, 1938, over a million Americans became frightened after listening to a live radio drama about a Martian invasion in the New Jersey marshlands. In Trenton, twenty families fled their homes, covering their faces with wet handkerchiefs to protect themselves from the "poison gas." At St. Michael's Hospital in Newark, fifteen people were treated for stress. Phone lines jammed as police and newspaper offices were swamped by callers desperate for information on the Martian "gas raids." *The New York Times* alone logged 875 phone inquiries. In Indiana, a woman burst into a church service, shouting: "New York destroyed; it's the end of the world. You might as well go home and die. I just heard it on the radio." Years later, the show's producer, Orson Welles, said he did it on purpose to boost his ratings, but was surprised by the scale of the response. How did the 23-year-old actor pull off what is arguably the greatest hoax of the 20th century, and why are we vulnerable to similar hoaxes today?

Since the infamous Welles broadcast, other radio dramas have sparked similar scares. Chapter 3 looks at two of episodes from South America. On the night of November 12, 1944, pandemonium erupted in Chile after a nationwide broadcast of the *War of the Worlds*. Some people barricaded themselves in their homes; others fled to the hills. One provincial governor mobilized artillery units to repel the "Martians." Five years later there was an even greater uproar in Quito, Ecuador, after a radio drama about invading space aliens. Upon realizing it was a play, angry residents began rioting. A mob marched on the radio station and burned it to the ground, killing fifteen, including the drama's mastermind.

Disc jockey hoaxes are the subject of Chapter 4. KIKX-FM in Tucson, Arizona, staged a kidnapping of their morning DJ in 1974, reporting the incident as a news item — even giving descriptions of the suspect's vehicle. Other outrageous antics include claims that a talk host had been shot. What was the public reaction? What has the Federal Communications Commission done to prevent future episodes?

Several radio broadcasts have featured hoaxes about a nuclear accident or attack. Chapter 5 documents several such incidents. Southern Sweden was the scene of a panic in 1973 after a fictitious radio announcement that a nuclear power plant had suffered an accident. Nine years later, a radio station in Illinois broadcast a pre-recorded play about a leak at a nearby nuclear power facility, telling listeners that a radioactive cloud was drifting toward Springfield. On August 11, 1984, prior to his weekly radio address, President Ronald Reagan was testing his microphone to see if it was working when he quipped: "My fellow Americans, I am pleased to tell you today that I've signed legislation that will outlaw Russia forever. We begin bombing in five minutes." Soviet leaders were not amused, placing their military on alert. In 1991, Don Ulett of KSHE-FM in Crestwood, Missouri, suddenly interrupted music with a recorded announcement that the U.S. was under a nuclear attack, adding: "This is not a test." A deluge of phone calls from worried listeners jammed phone lines. The Federal Communications Commission fined the station $25,000 and Ulett was temporarily relieved of his duties.

Chapter 6 examines the role of television in triggering scares about a terrorist attack with a bogus nuclear device. On the evening of March 20, 1983, hundreds of Americans became frightened during a broadcast of the NBC Sunday night movie *Special Bulletin*, about a news team covering a group of terrorists who were said to be threatening to detonate a nuclear device in South Carolina. The movie won an Emmy for its realism, but prompted a barrage of irate calls from viewers who felt they had been duped.

An asteroid scare prompted by a TV movie is the subject of Chapter 7. In October 1994, the CBS Sunday night movie *Without Warning* resulted in numerous phone calls to station affiliates by viewers fearful that an asteroid cluster was about to strike the earth. The film was broadcast as a news program, causing confusion. After an initial warning that many viewers missed, the program began like an ordinary Sunday night movie but was interrupted by news bulletins. Adding to the realism was veteran TV journalist Sander Vanocur, who anchored the news desk as he switched to "live" footage of impact sites.

Chapter 8 examines the infamous Pokémon panic of 1997, when a relatively small group of schoolchildren suffered seizures after watching rapidly flashing lights during a Pokémon cartoon segment. Japanese TV reported the reactions in dramatic style. Soon 12,000 more children began complaining of strange symptoms that were also blamed on the show: headaches, difficulty breathing, nausea, vision problems and weakness. Doctors attributed the second wave of illnesses to mass hysteria, triggered by sensational media coverage of the initial cases of epilepsy.

In 1992, the British Broadcasting Corporation aired *Ghostwatch* as an estimated eleven million viewers were told they were seeing a live, on-the-scene investigation of Britain's most haunted house. In reality, it was a scripted drama that led many viewers to believe the reporters were being attacked by an evil spirit. Chapter 9 explores the firestorm of controversy which ensued as 20,000 phone calls and letters swamped BBC offices in protest. Many children were emotionally distraught, as two of the reporters being "attacked" were hosts of popular children's TV shows in England. Physicians writing in the *British Medical Journal* documented cases of post-traumatic stress disorder in some children, while at least one suicide was linked to the show.

Chapter 10 scrutinizes media claims in the days after Hurricane Katrina ravaged Louisiana and Mississippi during September 2005. There were sensational reports of mob rule across New Orleans, including a surge in rapes, murders and looting, and gangs terrorizing and killing dozens of evacuees taking refuge in the Superdome. There were also accounts of toxic drinking water and claims that Katrina had been an unprecedented super storm that was created by global warming. Checks of police records and subsequent interviews with witnesses at the scene and with experts in meteorology portray a very different picture. The early accounts were riddled with misinformation and reflected stereotypes of how the poor in New Orleans were expected to react and about the nature of global warming.

The bird flu scare of 2005 and the likelihood that an outbreak of avian influenza could create a global pandemic on a scale of the Great Spanish Flu of 1918–1919 is the subject of Chapter 11. While a bird flu outbreak involving human-to-human transmission is possible, many prominent scientists have criticized the sudden fear of a pandemic in 2005 and beyond as alarmist, arguing that the likelihood of an outbreak is no greater than in previous years—with the difference being sensational media reports of an impending disaster. The 2005 fear of bird flu had reached such alarmist levels that during a question-and-answer session on the safety of Thanksgiving turkeys and bird feeders, one woman suggested killing all domestic birds and poisoning food along bird migration routes!

On the evening of March 13, 2010, a popular Georgian TV station reported that Russian troops and tanks were pouring over the border in an all-out attack that included the bombing of Tbilisi airport and the assassination of the president. Chapter 12 looks at the panic that ensued as residents fled into the streets with fresh memories of the Russian invasion of 2008. The Georgian president later apologized for the hoax broadcast which began with a disclaimer, but anyone tuning in immediately after the start would have been easily fooled. The program included news footage from the conflict and an address by the Russian president, along with U.S. president Barack Obama condemning the invasion. Some believe the broadcast was a deliberate attempt by the president of Georgia to highlight the continuing threat of a Russian invasion.

Chapter 13, by Peter Hassall, looks at the video scare. During the early 1970s, when videocassette players proliferated in the United Kingdom, there was widespread concern that certain uncut home videos would lead to the decline of morality among youth. After a storm of controversy fueled by the tabloid press, the 1984 Obscene Publications Act led to every video in the country being assessed under auspices of the courts which had to determine whether it was likely to "deprave and corrupt" youths of the day. This led to a series of police raids and the confiscation of various "harmful videos" that were thought by authorities to lead to social decay. Nowadays the notion that such videos are harmful is considered laughable in all but the most extreme conservative circles.

Arguably the greatest hoax of the 19th century is the subject of Chapter 14, when, during the summer of 1835, a series of newspaper reports appearing in the *New York Sun* caused a worldwide sensation. The brainchild of journalist Richard Locke, it claimed that astronomer Sir John Herschel had perfected the world's strongest telescope in South Africa and spotted strange creatures with bat-like wings on the moon. He dubbed them *Vespertilio-homo*. As news of the discovery of the bat-men spread, there was great excitement in New York City. Most newspapers fell for the hoax, including *The New York Times*. After the articles appeared, Locke quickly published the accounts in a pamphlet which sold sixty thousand copies within a month. The New York–based *Journal of Commerce* newspaper eventually unmasked the hoax. During the deception, the *Sun* boasted the largest circulation of any paper in the world, selling nearly 20,000 copies a day, 3,000 more than the prestigious *London Times*.

Chapter 15 revisits the events of November 9, 1874, when New York City residents awoke to the news that the city was under a state of emergency after a hoax story in the *New York Herald*. The report said that scores of ferocious animals had escaped from the Central Park Zoo and were roaming the city, killing and maiming bystanders. It was claimed that National Guard troops were patrolling the streets, and that at least forty-nine people were dead and upwards of 200 were injured. The hoax was intended to shock citizens and raise awareness about the flimsy state of the zoo's cages, showing what could happen if improvements were not made. The hoax was unveiled in the last paragraph — but many never read that far. A *New York Times* editorial described the episode as "intensely stupid."

The Great Halley's Comet Scare of 1910 is analyzed in Chapter 16. In early February, the *Washington Post* and the *New York Times* triggered a global fear that poison gas in the tail of Halley's Comet could wipe out all life on earth. The *Post* proclaimed: "Poison in it's [*sic*] Tail ... Prof. Deslandres Says Hypothesis That Gas Is Liable to Affect the Earth's Atmosphere Is Not at All Absurd." On the evening of May 18, as the comet passed by, some people sealed up windows, stuffed rags in keyholes, and barricaded themselves in their cellars with oxygen cylinders. In many parts of the Deep South, there were all-night prayer vigils and many refused to work, opting to be with their families. Similar scares were reported in Russia, Japan, parts of Europe, Mexico, Bermuda and Puerto Rico.

Chapter 17 describes the case of the "Mad Gasser" of Mattoon, Illinois, in 1944, when a single newspaper article sparked a city-wide hunt for a madman supposedly stalking victims in their homes and spraying them with a noxious gas. After nearly two weeks of terror, police announced the results of their investigation: the gasser never existed, but was the product of fear and press sensationalism.

Chapter 18 documents the strange case of Australian journalist Phillip Knightley and his creation of an imaginary criminal. Knightly tells of working for the Sydney tabloid *Truth* in 1954, when, during a slow news stretch, he was pressured by the editor to make up a catchy story. He created a sex pervert called "The Hook," who stalked the rail network, lifting up girl's skirts with a wire coat hanger hidden under his right sleeve. The story ran under the headline: "Hook Sex Pervert Strikes Again." Shortly after the account appeared, he received a phone call from police saying they had just arrested the man! Knightley called the police roundsman and confirmed that the officer was not having a joke at his expense.

Two years later, another imaginary criminal was created by the press. In the spring of 1956, residents near Taipei, Taiwan, were terrorized by a mysterious figure who was reportedly slashing people at random with a razor-like weapon. After interviewing the 21 victims and analyzing their wounds, police concluded that the slasher was imaginary. Chapter 19 looks at alarmist press reports about the existence of a slasher, heightening fears. As people went about their daily business, everyone was on the lookout for the slasher. It was against this backdrop of fear and suspicion that as people boarded crowded buses or walked crammed streets, they received minor bumps, scratches and scrapes from innocent people, which were redefined as slasher-related. In one instance, a man told police in detail how he had been slashed by someone carrying a mysterious black bag. When a doctor determined that the wound was made by a blunt object and not a razor, the patient admitted that he could not recall exactly what had happened, but assumed that he had been slashed "because of all the talk going around."

Phantom clown panics are the subject of Chapter 20. Beginning in the mid–1980s, newspapers across the United States reported on a series of alleged child-abduction attempts by people dressed as clowns. To date, no one has been arrested, leading many police investigators to conclude that the episode is a type of urban legend — a form of living folklore stemming from movies and TV shows about evildoing clowns. A Boston police spokesman summed up their frustration: "No adult or police officer has ever seen a clown. We've had calls saying there was a clown. We've had calls saying that there was a clown at a certain intersection and we happened to have police cars sitting there, and the officers saw nothing. We've had over twenty calls on 911. When the officers get there, no one tells them anything." Throughout the sporadic bad clown reports, no hard evidence was ever found, and no children were actually abducted. The first clown scares occurred in the early 1980s and 1990s, and coincide with books featuring evil clowns such as Stephen King's best-selling horror novel *It* and films such as *Killer Klowns from Outer Space*.

Chapter 21 turns to the Internet and its promotion of the global fears of so-called chemtrails. Since the late 1990s, intense public interest has swirled on the Internet around the belief that jet contrails in the sky are the remnants of secret, systematic experiments by the U.S. military and its allies, for a variety of purposes. Theories range from the relatively benign, such as altering the weather or slowing global warming, to the more sinister, like testing new chemical and biological agents on an unsuspecting public.

The sudden emergence of a new illness — Morgellons — as a result of Internet websites is explored in Chapter 22. These sites have served as magnets for people with a variety of vague ailments — from "brain fog" to fatigue — and giving them the name. This new "disease" may be the first case of mass hysteria to spread via cyberspace.

The Internet reaction to Hurricane Katrina is once again under scrutiny in Chapter 23. Soon after Katrina struck Louisiana and Mississippi in August 2005, Internet rumors began circulating about outrageous behavior by displaced residents who appeared to be ungrateful for the help they were given. The stories ranged from stealing everything in sight to dealing drugs and perpetrating violence on others. As was the case in Chapter 11, the claims were unfounded and based on popular stereotypes of how residents were expected to react.

In Chapter 24, folklorist Bill Ellis examines the "Good Times" e-mail virus hoax which began in December 1994 and continues to spread fear through the cyber community even today. It is claimed that the virus is spread by opening an e-mail with the subject "Good Times," and just opening the message will cause all kinds of bad things to happen to your computer. Frustrated by the persistence of the hoax, some companies have taken to posting websites devoted to dispelling the myth and alleviating needless anxiety. Why has this particular myth been so widespread and persistent throughout the community of Internet users? The hoax is arguably the most successful cyber myth in the Internet's short history.

Today many urban legends commonly appear in the media, presented as real accounts. Chapter 25 introduces the topic to readers and looks at the media's role in inadvertently spreading them.

In Chapter 26, folklorist David Clarke delves into the mystery of "the

Curse of the Crying Boy." In 1985, a British newspaper published a report of fire badly damaging a house in South Yorkshire. Miraculously, a cheap painting of a crying toddler was found amongst the damage, perfectly intact. The story claimed there had been a pattern of fires in homes after hanging prints of the Crying Boy had been hung in them. What's more, in each case the prints were untouched by the fire. Folklorist David Clarke looks into the origins of this urban legend and the role of the media in spreading it.

Have you ever seen a photo that appears to show a miracle? Since the advent of photography, people have claimed to have taken photographs where mysterious ghostly images appear in the background. In recent times, such photos have reached cyberspace. In Chapter 27, "Photos of the Gods," folklorist David Clarke looks at three famous photos supposedly showing Jesus Christ — "the Miracle in the Snow," "the Hidden Christ Picture," and "the picture that took itself" — and asks what's going on. Where do these claims emanate from and why do they stubbornly persist in society?

In the early 1980s, bizarre tales spread across America about a network of satanic cults kidnapping and sacrificing children. Strangely enough, thousands of people eventually stepped forward to claim that they too had been the victim of satanic ritual abuse. Chapter 28 shows how the scare was fueled by over-enthusiastic psychotherapists who suggested to their clients that they may have been ritually abused, even though they had no conscious recall of the abuse. In turn, the clients, often while under the suggestible state of hypnosis, created wild tales of abuse at the hands of imaginary satanists.

Chapter 29 examines Halloween panics. Each year on Halloween, politicians, police, and the news media join forces to scare parents and their children about the dangers posed by evildoers preying on children and poisoning their candy. Surprisingly, over the past 100 years there has not been a single confirmed case of a child dying from eating poisoned Halloween candy as a random act by a stranger. The real threat to children on Halloween isn't poisoned candy or sex offenders; it's being hit by a car crossing a dark street or wearing a flammable costume or taking a relative's medication. Police, parents and teachers would do better to spend less time on imaginary threats and more on basic safety precautions. With regards to sex offenders, contrary to popular belief, most attacks on children occur in their own home by someone they know, and attacks are no more likely during Halloween.

One of the most common panics in America over the past decade is the subject of Chapter 30: sexual predators. The news media feature a barrage of alarmist, misleading, and greatly exaggerated reports of the threat of predators. While such crimes certainly occur, they are far less common than the media portray them to be. TV shows such as the *CBS Evening News*, *Dateline NBC*'s

"To Catch a Predator," *The New York Times* and *Oprah* have only served to inflate these fears.

Additionally, school shootings are extremely rare events that receive heavy media coverage, leading to the widespread perception that they are far more common than they are. Chapter 31 calculates the odds of being murdered at school. Students are twice as likely to be struck and killed by lightning.

Chapter 32 examines the shark attack scare during the summer of 2001. After two high-profile shark attacks on American beaches, the media reported on countless sightings and encounters, no matter how minor. But when the figures were tallied, it turns out that 2001 was actually a below-average year for attacks, with above-average media interest.

The great Puerto Rican vampire panic is the focus of Chapter 33. In 1995, sensational news reports began to circulate in Puerto Rico about the existence of a mythical vampire monster known as the *chupacabra*. Nearly half of all *chupacabra* stories in the Puerto Rican press were created by the same writer. Concerned citizens in Puerto Rico formed patrols and vigilante mobs, armed with rifles, machetes, pitchforks, and baseball bats, hoping to find and kill the *chupacabra*. In one case "a massive mobilization of searchers was outfitted with infrared lights, shotguns, electrical equipment, helmets, and riot shields." No sign of the creature was found.

Are cell phones hidden killers? In Chapter 34 we look at claims that cell phones are hazardous to your health. In 1999, medical researcher George Carlo appeared on the ABC TV newsmagazine *20/20*, which aired a sensationalized story that cell phones caused cancer, triggering a national panic. It turns out that a fellow researcher involved in the same study concluded just the opposite! Other shows such as *Larry King Live* helped to foster the myth. In 2009, YouTube heightened the scare when a series of videos purported to show several cell phones causing popcorn kernels to pop "simply by pointing ringing phones at them," then suggesting that the same energy waves "fry" your brain. The videos were a hoax.

Chapter 35 examines organ theft panics. According to alarmist news media reports, body-snatchers lurk in the most unlikely places, waiting to lure the innocent into evil traps and steal their organs. In 1993, a British/Canadian television program titled *The Body Parts Business*, and later broadcast on a French TV show titled *Organ Snatchers*, reported that an Argentine boy claimed that his corneas had been forcibly removed. The boy later admitted to a hoax after an eye doctor found that his corneas were diseased and he had in fact lost his sight from natural causes. Similar media reports have also turned out to be hoaxes. The organ-snatching legend reached a peak of popularity in the mid–1990s, when several prominent organizations gave the rumors credibility. In South and Central America, such rumors have had deadly consequences.

In the Guatemalan highlands, an elderly Japanese tourist was killed in 2000 after stroking a baby's head. The baby's mother panicked, believing that the foreigner was a bloodthirsty satanist who might stab her child and rip out its heart for use in a ritual. Like all media scares, the organ-theft panics come and go. They appear now and then, fueled by anti–Western sentiment, political agendas, bad journalism, misunderstandings, and tabloid sensationalism. These horrific stories tell us nothing about the trade in stolen organs, but much about the social and cultural climate in which these panics appear.

In Chapter 36, physician Felicity Goodyear-Smith and immunization center research director Helen Petousis-Harris look at two vaccine scares on the small island nation of New Zealand that have occurred in the early 21st century. Fear surrounding rumored side effects from young girls being immunized against cervical cancer has left a portion of the population at risk for getting the often deadly disease — deaths that are 90 percent preventable. This tragic situation highlights the dangers of media scares and the impact on society.

These case studies of media scares raise many questions. How could so many veteran journalists reporting on Hurricane Katrina get their stories so wrong? How has the recent threat to humans from bird flu been overblown in the media? Why do scores of people around the globe believe the wild theories on web sites and blogs which claim that the U.S. government is secretly lacing our skies with toxic chemtrails? How did the British Broadcasting Corporation fool viewers into believing that one of their news crews was under attack by evil spirits? Could a *War of the Worlds*–type radio scare happen again? The authors ask these and other penetrating questions in documenting classic cases of media false alarms.

Section One

It Came from the Airwaves — Radio

CHAPTER 1

The London Riot Hoax

> The first major radio scare occurred in 1926, when the British Broadcasting Corporation aired a drama about a frenzied mob running riot through London. Many listeners believed that the government was about to topple.

"London is in the grip of a terrible uprising of anarchists and unemployed.... Police and troops are powerless to hold the rioting mobs in check, and they have begun what promises to be a long reign of terror."

Radio listeners across England and Ireland were stunned by the news that their government was under siege and could topple at any moment in a bloody uprising by disgruntled workers. In reality, the streets were calm; listeners had heard a play and had been frightened by the use of realistic news bulletins during what seemed to be a regular program.

When most people think of infamous radio hoaxes, one event springs to mind: the Halloween Eve "Martian invasion" broadcast that frightened over one million Americans in 1938 (see Chapter 2). In reality though, the first major radio hoax took place twelve years earlier in England and Ireland. On January 16, 1926, Father Ronald Knox was conducting his regular Saturday evening radio show of comedy and entertainment. One of the segments was a twelve-minute skit on a fictitious riot in London. The drama broadcast reports of chaos and mob rule in central London resulting from a populist revolt. The idea for the skit hadn't come from thin air; at the time the British government was under great pressure from unions. In fact, one of the biggest strikes in the country's history was just months away — the British general strike of May 3–12. This landmark event rocked the government to its foundations as over one and a half million workers from various occupations took to the streets in an unsuccessful bid to improve wages and working conditions for coal miners. Leading up to this standoff, there was great unease across the country as the Russian Revolution of 1917 was still in people's minds. The stage was set for a mass delusion using the air waves on a subject which seemed plausible: worker rebellion.

Knox was a famous Catholic priest and successful novelist who was respected and trusted by his audience. The episode began when he announced that he was about to present a skit on a London riot. Many listeners either missed the disclaimer or weren't paying attention and thought they were hearing actual reports of their government under siege.

The skit began with a typical discussion of eighteenth-century literature, which was interrupted by reports that an unruly mob of unemployed workers were rampaging through London. Listeners heard that the traffic minister had been lynched from a pole, while trench mortars were used to destroy Big Ben. The announcer stated: "The clock tower, 320 feet in height, has just fallen to the ground, together with the famous clock, Big Ben.... Fresh reports, which have just come to hand, announce that the crowd have secured the person of Mr. Wotherspoon, the minister of traffic, who was attempting to make his escape in disguise. He has now been hanged from a lamp post in Vauxhall Bridge Road."[1]

Reaction was swift: jittery callers flooded newspaper and BBC offices to learn more details and try to ascertain if relatives living in the area were safe. Police and other government agencies were also deluged with calls. Some wanted to know if King George and Queen Mary had been safely evacuated. Several concerned citizens phoned the British Admiralty to inquire when the fleet was going to sail up the Thames to launch a counterattack by landing troops.[2] The BBC broadcast announcements throughout the evening, telling listeners that the show was fiction, but at the time, many people did not have radios and heard the news second-hand from neighbors who did. The countryside was rife with rumors about the rioting in London. Suspicions turned to fear the next morning when newspaper deliveries were delayed owing to snowy weather. Many residents took this delay "as confirmation that the worst had happened."[3]

Parts of the Knox skit were highly realistic, including the sounds of shrieks from the crowd, explosions rumbling in the distance, and buildings crumbling. In fairness to Father Knox, anyone listening closely to the sarcastic content should have realized that the program was a skit, yet the BBC was such an authoritative and respected institution, and the drama's tone so serious, that it managed to fool many listeners. Another factor in creating the scare was the use of what sounded like regular programming interspersed by "live" news reports. The following sequence is typical: "That concludes the news bulletin for the moment; you will now be connected with the band at the Savoy Hotel [gramophone dance music can be heard].... London calling...."[4]

Ironically, a few days after the broadcast, the *New York Times* published an editorial titled "We Are Safe from Such Jesting," arguing that Americans were immune from similar scares. Later that year, in March 1926, a journalist for the *Syracuse Herald* in western New York interviewed the manager of one of America's top radio stations, asking if he thought a similar scare could happen in the United States. The executive, who was not identified, gave an arrogant response. "As for spreading a hoax of any kind, mischievous or otherwise, such a thing would never be thought of. It is beyond the bounds of possibility."[5] Authorities failed to anticipate what happened in 1938, when Orson Welles caused an even greater uproar with his broadcast of a Martian invasion, which was heard across the entire continental United States, and history would repeat itself on a grander scale.

CHAPTER 2

Radio Daze — The Martian Invasion Broadcast

In 1938, a small group of actors and musicians in a tiny New York studio frightened the most powerful, educated society on earth. For a short time, over a million people thought that Earth was under attack by Martians. How was it done? We may be vulnerable to similar scares in the future.

It was arguably the greatest hoax of the twentieth century. Shortly after 8 o'clock on the evening of Sunday, October 30, 1938, many Americans became frightened after listening to a radio drama about a Martian landing in the New Jersey marshlands. The broadcast was heard live across the continental United States on 151 CBS affiliates. The play made references to real people and places, and used convincing sound effects and special bulletins to enhance its credibility. The drama was produced by Orson Welles and aired on CBS's *Mercury Theatre of the Air* from the Manhattan studios of WABC. Remarkably, Welles was just 23 years old at the time. The actual play was written by an obscure scriptwriter named Howard Koch under Welles' direction and was loosely based on the 1898 blockbuster *The War of the Worlds* by British science fiction writer H.G. Wells. (Koch soon became world famous, but not for helping to craft the Martian script. This man, who had a knack for realism and a flair for the dramatic, was a budding literary genius who soon penned the script to one of the greatest films of all time: *Casablanca*.)

Parts of New Jersey and New York City were the most seriously affected, since the drama described Martians attacking both states. The center of fear was tiny Grover's Mill near Princeton, New Jersey, the "Martian landing site."[1] An eerie fog shrouded the region that evening, contributing to the anxiety. Upon hearing radio reports of the towering Martian machines operating nearby, several Grover's Mill residents grabbed their guns and bravely ran out to fend off the invaders, opening fire on a huge outline barely visible through the mist. When dawn broke, it became evident that the would-be heroes had punched several holes into the local water tower.[2] In one Newark, New Jersey, block, over twenty families fled their homes, covering their faces with wet handkerchiefs and draping towels over their heads to protect themselves from the "poison gas."[3] Fifteen people were treated for shock at St. Michael's Hospital.[4] Phone lines jammed as police were swamped with calls from residents desperate for information on the "gas raids."

At the Port Norris station, one New Jersey police officer wrote in the blotter: "Between 8:30 P.M. and 10 P.M. received numerous phone calls as result of WABC broadcast this evening re: Mars attacking this country. Calls included papers, police departments including N.Y.C. and private persons. No record kept of some due to working teletype and all thru extensions ringing at same time. At least 50 calls were answered. Persons calling inquiring as to meteors, number of persons killed, gas attack, militia being called out, and fires. All were advised nothing unusual had occurred and that rumors were due to a radio dramatization of a play."[5] At the *New York Times* offices, 875 phone calls were logged. At Manhattan police headquarters, the thirteen telephone switchboard operators were overwhelmed.[6] Hearing the initial reports of a large meteor impact nearby, two Princeton University geologists rushed to ground zero, only to find others, like themselves, searching for the object.[7]

The effects of the broadcast rippled across the country. In Indiana, a woman burst into a church shouting: "New York destroyed; it's the end of the world. You might as well go home and die. I just heard it on the radio."[8] In the American heartland of Lincoln, Nebraska, hundreds of panicky residents jammed the police switchboard wanting to know if it was true and what they should do.[9] St. Louis residents huddled in the streets of some neighborhoods to discuss a plan of action in the face of the impending war. A Pittsburgh man returned home during the broadcast only to find his wife clutching a bottle of poison, screaming: "I'd rather die this way than like that."[10] North in Toronto, station CFRB was flooded with inquiries from worried Canadians.[11] Anxious Washington State residents jammed the phone lines of police, fire and newspaper offices in Seattle. Most terror-stricken were residents in the tiny town of Concrete, sixty-five miles northeast of Seattle. When electricity failed at a critical point in the broadcast, some loaded their families into cars and headed into the mountains; others fainted.[12] In Mason City, Iowa, there was confusion and fear as a man entered the bus station, shouting: "Tragedy in New York. Turn on your radio." People huddled around a radio to listen to the broadcast until it became evident that it was a drama.[13] In New York, theater actor Caroline Cantlon broke her arm as she rushed downstairs after hearing that smoke was billowing from Times Square.[14] In London, H.G. Wells expressed agitation upon hearing news of the reaction, remarking:

"I gave no permission whatever for alterations which might lead to the belief that it was real news."[15]

The drama appeared in newspaper schedules across the country on the day of the broadcast, clearly identified as a play, but many listeners did not make the association. An opening announcement clearly stated its fictional nature: "The Columbia Broadcasting System and its affiliated stations present Orson Welles and the Mercury Theatre on the Air in *War of the Worlds* by H.G. Wells."[16] The trouble was, many people tuned in late. Radio ratings company C.E. Hooper estimated that at 8 o'clock, 3.6 percent of radio listeners across America had tuned in to hear Welles, compared to the popular *Edgar Bergen and Charlie McCarthy Show* which captured nearly 35 percent of the audience.[17] It was a David and Goliath battle, and each week Welles was being devoured in the ratings. How could he compete with the most popular show on radio? In 1938, listeners commonly tuned back and forth between radio programs, especially during the first few minutes. Known as airplaning, it was the modern equivalent of TV channel-surfing. Each week Welles had a small window of opportunity to hook listeners. The weakest part of the *Edgar Bergen Show* was after his opening comedy routine, when introducing a guest singer. If the performance was not outstanding, listeners would airplane for something better, before switching back.[18] Welles likely planned his script with this in mind, using live dance music interrupted by special bulletins to grab listeners as they were switching stations.[19] Two separate surveys after the broadcast estimated that roughly half of listeners to the Welles drama tuned in late, missing the opening disclaimer, leading many to believe it was a live news report.[20]

After the opening announcement that listeners were hearing a drama, the show began as a typical radio program of the era. "Good evening, ladies and gentlemen. From the Meridian Room in the Park Plaza in New York City, we bring you the music of Ramon Raquello and his orchestra."[21] The music was interrupted at intervals with special bulletins of increasing length and gravity, describing, at first, explosions on Mars followed by a meteor crashing near Grover's Mill. "Live" bulletins from the scene followed. The meteor was later identified as a "metal cylinder" that, before the announcer's eyes, sprouted legs and towered into the air. The cylinder contained hideous Martians who opened fire with "death rays," scorching onlookers.[22] The reporter cried: "A humped shape is rising out of the pit. I can make out a small beam of light against a mirror. What's that? There's a jet of flame springing from that mirror, and it leaps right at the advancing men. It strikes them head on! Good Lord, they're turning into flame!" Shortly after, dead silence and a grave announcement followed: "Ladies and gentlemen, I have just been handed a message.... At least forty people, including six state troopers, lie dead in a field east of the village of Grover's Mill, their bodies burned and distorted beyond all possible recognition."[23] Later the announcer describes a bleak and devastating scene as the Martian machines are marching on New York City: "All communication with Jersey shore closed ... army wiped out...."[24] Soon a voice was heard saying: "I've just been handed a bulletin. Cylinders from Mars are falling all over the country. One outside Buffalo, one in Chicago, St. Louis...."[25]

The Federal Communications Commission immediately investigated the broadcast amid the subsequent public uproar. Just one day after the incident, Iowa senator Clyde Herring delivered a blistering attack on Welles, CBS, and the entire radio industry, which he intimated could not be trusted. He called on his fellow legislators to pass a law that would require the content of all radio programs to be reviewed by a board of censors. "Radio has no more right to present programs like that than someone has in knocking on our door and screaming," Herring said.[26] His censorship drive failed, and five weeks later the FCC announced that it would take no action against either Welles or CBS. Concerned with censorship, Commission members decided not to create more bureaucratic regulations, noting that the actions taken by CBS since the episode "were sufficient to protect the public interest."[27] In its ruling, the Commission cited a letter from CBS saying that they would refrain from using the technique of live news interruptions and bulletins in future dramas.[28]

Was the Reaction Exaggerated?

Of the estimated six million people who heard the drama, as many as 1.7 million believed they were hearing a news bulletin.[29] While there are claims that hundreds of thousands panicked and tried pack belongings, flee in cars or arm themselves with weapons, such claims may be a media exaggeration.[30] Mass fright? Yes. Panic? No. The mass panic claim was promoted in a 1940 study by Princeton University psychologist Hadley Cantril. Much of Cantril's study was based on interviews with just 135 people. Sociologist William Bainbridge believes the extent of the panic has been exaggerated and is critical of Cantril for citing just a few colorful stories from a small number of people who panicked. Bainbridge contends that on any given night, out of a pool of over a million people, at least a thousand would have been driving excessively fast or engaging in rambunctious behavior. From this perspective, the notion of a Martian panic was primarily a news media creation.[31]

Sociologist David Miller notes that while many newspapers published accounts of suicides and heart attacks by frightened citizens, the day after they proved to have been unfounded and have passed into American folklore.[32]

Miller takes Cantril to task for failing to show substantial evidence of mass flight from the "attack," citing just a few examples. Cantril quotes American Telephone Company figures indicating that local media and law enforcement agencies were inundated with up to 40 percent more phone calls than normal in parts of New Jersey during the broadcast, but no one knows what they were talking about. Miller says that some callers probably wanted information like which military units were being called up, where they could donate blood or if casualty lists were obtainable. "Some callers were simply angry that such a realistic show was allowed on the air, while others called CBS to congratulate Mercury Theater for the exciting Halloween program," Miller writes. "It seems ... [likely] many callers just wanted to chat with their families and friends about the exciting show they had just listened to on the radio."[33]

Many newspaper reporters may have had a hidden agenda and were motivated to exaggerate the extent of the reaction. In 1938, the print media and upstart radio were at war with each other as radio was an emerging threat to their advertising coffers. This antagonistic relationship may have prompted journalists to consciously or subconsciously exaggerate the extent of the panic in their press reports.[34] Radio historian Justin Levine is suspicious that with the exception of newspapers, there are no independent historical accounts describing the panic's severity.[35] Immediately after the scare, many newspaper editors took the opportunity to condemn radio. The *Chicago Tribune* took a brutal swipe at both listeners and the radio industry, noting that of those who became frightened, "it would do them a serious injustice to say they were frightened out of their wits; all evidence indicates they never had any wits to lose." It was then noted that "the radio audience isn't very bright ... many a program is prepared for their consumption."[36] The *St. Louis Post-Dispatch* said that radio is inherently flawed as listeners often hear bits and pieces of programs or tune in late—flaws not shared by newspapers.[37]

Whether it was a scare or panic, the impact of the broadcast was undoubtedly serious in parts of ground zero. Trenton city manager Paul Morton was furious after the mass disruption to his city, warning that they were lucky no one was killed: "If there had been a three-alarm fire or other emergency during that interval, we would have been helpless." Morton said the program "completely crippled communication facilities" for the city's police department for three hours as concerned relatives from across the country tried to get through to loved ones. He also found it difficult to believe that the broadcast was not a deliberate attempt to scare the public. "I can conceive of no reason why the name of Trenton, and vicinity should have been used on this broadcast. The State Police were equally handicapped and it is indescribable the seriousness of the situation."[38]

The extent of the panic remains open to debate. The same is true for

Welles' intent. Immediately after the broadcast, Welles vehemently denied having any intention of deceiving listeners; years later he said otherwise.[39] We get a clue as to what Welles may have been up to from reading the draft script. Prior to its airing, CBS censors deemed the script too realistic and made no fewer than twenty-eight changes. The working script had such phrases as "New Jersey National Guard," "Princeton University Observatory," "Langley Field," and "Magill University." While appeasing the censors, Welles and Koch managed to substitute similar, official-sounding names such as "state militia," "Princeton Observatory," "Langham Field," and "Macmillian University." "The United States Weather Bureau in Washington D.C." became "The Government Weather Bureau" and "St. Patrick's Cathedral" was shortened to "the cathedral."[40] It seems clear from this information alone that Welles was out to give listeners a fright in order to boost his sagging ratings — and it worked. The use of real-sounding place names was highly effective in fooling listeners. Typical was the experience of Louis Winkler who lived on Clay Avenue in the Bronx borough of New York City. Winkler said the broadcast was so realistic that he was certain the Martians were coming. "I didn't tune it in until the program was half over, but when I heard the names and titles of federal, state and municipal officials and when the 'Secretary of the Interior' was introduced, I was convinced that it was the [real] McCoy." Winkler then grew frightened and ran outside, where his suspicions were confirmed. "I ran out into the street with scores of others, and found people running in all directions. The whole thing came over as a news broadcast and in my mind it was a pretty crummy thing to do."[41]

While the drama may seem implausible to listeners today, in 1938, Mars was the subject of frequent speculation about intelligent life, and news bulletins on the escalating war in Europe were common. It is the modern equivalent of someone tuning into CNN and being riveted by a catastrophic storyline, and assuming it was on all channels. After the initial uproar, Welles' popularity soared and his radio ratings rose threefold,[42] and the giant Campbell's Soup Company signed on as a sponsor.[43] But Welles paid a high price for his mischief-making and lived out his life lacking something that all journalists cherish: credibility. This is no more evident than in the events of December 6, 1941, when during a live reading on network radio, Welles was interrupted by a news flash: the Japanese had attacked Pearl Harbor. Many listeners refused to believe the report, suspicious of the coincidence.[44]

Was Orson Welles a hero or a villain? Was he a malicious prankster or mischievous boy wonder? Regardless of his motives, Welles' actions sparked a healthy debate on the power of the media and its potential to control the masses. For most people, the scare lasted less than an hour, but that was enough to offer a glimpse of the power of radio. Today, changes in media technology are occurring so fast that we have little time to assess their potential impact. With more syndicated programs, we may be more vulnerable than ever to future Welles-type scares that have the potential to race through our global village at the speed of light. One day soon we may experience a *War of the Worlds*–type scare on a global scare.

CHAPTER 3

The Martians Return

Shortly after the infamous Martian invasion broadcast of 1938, many experts were convinced that the event, whether accidental or intentional, was a fluke produced by the genius of Orson Welles. Surely, they reasoned, something as outlandish as people believing that Earth was being invaded by space aliens could not happen again. They were wrong.

"Radio Drama About a Martian Invasion Triggers Widespread Fear." If you guessed that this was a headline from the United States in 1938 after the infamous Orson Welles broadcast that frightened the nation, you'd be mistaken. Remarkably, similar events have happened twice in South America. It was the same formula that was used in the BBC London riot broadcast in 1926 and the Orson Welles affair twelve years later. Both South American scripts began with what sounded like regular programming, interrupted by news bulletins of increasing gravity. The dramas featured local announcers, impersonations of local and national officials, and realistic sound effects, and were well crafted. Both scripts were based on the book *War of the Worlds* by H.G. Wells.

Just after 9:30 on the night of November 12, 1944, listeners in Chile heard news of the Martian invasion. The chilling reports emanated from a radio station in Santiago and was broadcast on numerous other stations on the Cooperative Vitalicia Network. Thousands of listeners across the country were fooled. There were many reports of people barricading their homes or fleeing in panic.[1]

The scriptwriter was American William Steele, a talented man who was not only familiar with Orson Welles, but wrote for the enormously popular radio show *The Shadow*. Welles had been the voice of "the Shadow." Steele and writer Paul Zenteno placed the invasion point as Puente Alto, fifteen miles south of Santiago.[2] Upon receiving news of the invasion, one provincial governor declared a state of emergency and began mobilizing artillery units.

The drama used an actor to impersonate the interior minister, and referred to well-known organizations that one would expect to be involved in such an event, such as the Red Cross. The broadcast described a desperate scene of vehicles loaded down with people and belongings, clogging the roads leading out of Santiago.[3] More reports followed telling of futile attempts by the Chilean military to stop the invading force, which was said to be nearing Santiago. It was then reported that the air base of Marisal Sucre had been leveled by the invaders.

The program was listed in newspapers as a drama, and the radio station broadcast several disclaimers in the week before it aired, but this was not enough to overcome the power of "live" news bulletins. During the program, there were two more disclaimers but many listeners, in their haste to protect themselves, failed to notice them. Angry protesters later pressured the government to permanently close the station and suspend those involved, but no official action was taken owing to the numerous warnings that went unheeded.[4]

The Phantom Invasion of Ecuador

The power of radio and of simulated news bulletins was again on display five years later, 1,300 miles to the northwest of Chile in the capital city of Quito, Ecuador. It proved to be the worst case of its kind during the twentieth century, even outdoing the infamous Welles broadcast.

On the evening of Saturday, February 12, 1949, a radio play based on the H.G. Wells novel sparked pandemonium in Quito. An Associated Press reporter in the city of 175,000 said the broadcast "drove most of the population of Quito into the streets" as terror-stricken residents sought to escape imminent Martian "gas raids."[5] The bogus news bulletins told of Martians closing in on the city after landing in nearby Latacunga, twenty miles south, which was reportedly quickly turned into a wasteland of smoldering rubble.

The Spanish language program was broadcast on Radio Quito, and included the names of real places, impersonations of popular local politicians and reporters, and offered vivid "on the scene" accounts of the carnage. Once residents realized that the panic had been triggered by a play, many vented their anger by going on a rampage of destruction through the streets. Crowds of people began to chant, "Down with the radio." One mob, many many of the participants still dressed in pajamas, surrounded the three-story building housing the radio station and began hurling stones through windows. While some people escaped through a side door, others ran upstairs to the third floor, which proved to be a poor decision.[6] The crowd soon burst in, lit wads of paper that were in abundance, and began hurling them around before retreating out-side, repelled by the smoke and heat. As the flames reached the third floor, terrified occupants began leaping off the building; others desperately tried to save themselves by forming a human chain down the side of the structure. These chains occasionally broke, sending terrified residents plunging to their deaths.[7] The station program director Leonardo Paez wrapped paper around his body from the giant rolls used for the newspaper presses, then jumped, landing on several bystanders in the street. He survived the fall but was seriously hurt.[8]

Police and soldiers were slow to respond, as most were in the countryside on their way to fight the Martians. By the time authorities dispersed the crowd with tanks and tear gas, twenty people were dead and as many as fifty were hurt.[9] At least four of the injured were security guards who received head wounds when the crowd turned on them.[10] Others included police and firefighters whom the rioters attacked. Ecuador's defense minister Manuel Diaz Granados personally took command of the crisis.[11] The building was destroyed, and along with it the offices of the radio station and the country's oldest and largest newspaper, *El Comercio*, which owned the radio station, and the afternoon daily *Ultimas Noticias*.[12]

The drama began as an ordinary music show that was interrupted by news bulletins, starting with, "Here is an urgent piece of late news."[13] At one point, the announcer appealed to nearby Peru and Colombia to come to the aid of Ecuador. Ground zero was said to be the nearby town of Cotocollao. Announcers impersonated a government minister and the mayor of Quito, who urged citizens to evacuate before the city was attacked. The "mayor" could be heard saying: "People of Quito, let us defend our city. Our women and children must go out into the surrounding heights to leave the men free for action and combat."[14] A *New York Times* reporter on the scene said that it was at this point that residents "began fleeing from their homes and running through the streets. Many were clad only in night clothing."[15] Ironically, shortly after, in response to a deluge of calls to the radio station by worried residents, the station immediately cut into the broadcast to announce that what they were hearing was just a drama. The same announcement was repeated several times at varying intervals but many failed to hear it, having already fled. The terror was nationwide but to a lesser extent outside the capital, since the drama placed the fighting in the vicinity of Quito. In the countryside, hundreds of people headed for the mountains.[16] It wasn't until 4 A.M. that the rioting was under control.

Within days of the panic, Ecuadorian police had arrested sixteen people for their involvement in drama, or for taking part in the riots.[17] The incident was yet another vivid reminder of how vulnerable people can be to media outlets in whom they place their trust. In recounting these tragedies, it is perhaps fitting to recall the words of Walter Lippman who once wrote that "under certain conditions men respond as powerfully to fictions as they do to realities, and ... in many cases they help to create the very fictions to which they respond."[18] History had repeated itself once again.

Chapter 4
Infamous Disc Jockey Hoaxes

> Being a DJ is a demanding job that requires constant vigilance to maintain all-important audience ratings that pay the bills. But sometimes the temptation is too great and they ring false alarm bells in order to receive instant attention.

It has to have been one of the dumbest ideas in the history of radio. It's hard to imagine how grown men and community leaders could have devised such a ridiculous idea. In 1974, Arthur Gropen was hired as the new morning DJ at KIKX-FM in Tucson, Arizona. He and general manager Dennis Forsythe met to think up ways to get Gropen noticed. They settled on a surefire idea to get him into the public spotlight, if not make him into a local household name: Stage his kidnapping.

On January 19, the plot was hatched. The station broadcast news of Gropen's kidnapping, complete with a fake interview with the police, and a description of the vehicle used. Concerned listeners immediately rang the police and radio station. The police, who had already been notified that it was a publicity stunt, complained to the station that the promotion was tying up their phone lines, and urged them to stop the stunt. Meanwhile, a local TV reporter learned what the station was doing and reported that it was a hoax. Incredibly, station officials continued to vehemently deny the report, insisting that the kidnapping was real. Complicating matters, Forsythe wasn't even around when the plot unfolded, but was at a golf tournament in Florida. Later that weekend he heard phone reports as to how the plan was going and issued instructions for the deception to continue but to stop using the word "kidnapping." He was not told of the police complaints.

By the time Forsythe showed up for work on Monday morning, events were spiraling out of control. Yet it wasn't until Wednesday, January 22, that Forsythe finally canceled the hoax and met with Gropen to make repeated on-air apologies to both the police and their listeners. It was too little, too late. The Federal Communication Commission rarely shuts stations down, but in this case it decided to pull the plug on KIKX when its license was up for renewal.[1] Law judge Thomas Fitzpatrick said the station had unduly alarmed the public over several days, and hampered the ability of the police to do their job. "That the public was both shocked and concerned by the purported 'kidnapping' is amply evidenced by the numerous phone calls to the station and to the police. The program format of KIKX was such that it catered to a young and impressionable audience. The announcements of the 'kidnapping' had the ring of authenticity," said Fitzpatrick.[2] KIKX had paid the ultimate price for what can only be described as a massive display of arrogance.

Getting Away with Murder?

On June 13, 1990, KROQ-FM in Los Angeles grabbed national headlines when station personnel staged a fake murder. It happened during the *Kevin and Bean* morning show when hosts Kevin Ryder and Gene "the Bean" Baxter ran a program called "Confess Your Crime." The show began with a series of "true confessions." One caller admitted to stealing bowling balls; another claimed to enjoy running over cats. Then a caller rang to say that he caught his girlfriend in bed with another man and killed her. The DJs sounded shaken by the remark before the anonymous caller hung up. Listeners quickly lit up the phone lines, wanting to know if the call was genuine. The DJs were adamant that it was.

The incident came to the attention of the Los Angeles County sheriff's department who had numerous unsolved murders on the books. The DJs continued to maintain their innocence and even handed over a tape of the show to the sheriffs as part of their investigation. The "mystery murder" was featured on a segment of NBC-TV's popular show *Unsolved Mysteries*. The department spent months investigating. It wasn't until April 1991 that the DJs were forced to admit that the murder call had been made by their friend, Doug "the Slug" Roberts, after the deception was uncovered by a *Los Angeles Times* reporter.[3] Roberts was working in Phoenix at the time of the hoax, but was later hired as the KROQ night DJ.[4] Many listeners were furious upon hearing the news that they had been duped. The sheriff's department sent KROQ a bill for the $12,170 it cost to investigate the incident and to match details in the case with other unsolved murders.[5] The DJs were also unpopular with the relatives of local murder victims who were hoping to find closure.

The Federal Communications Commission decided to let the men off with a slap on the wrist, noting that it was an isolated incident involving just a few people, and that station higher-ups were not involved. In fact, when management learned it was a hoax, they took action: The trio were suspended for five days and ordered to split the Sheriff's tab three ways. On top of this, they had to serve nearly 150 hours of community service.[6] The FCC also took red-faced station officials up on their offer to write a booklet on how to prevent future radio hoaxes and to distribute it to stations across the country.[7]

Here are a few famous cases of DJs creating false alarms:

April 1, 1949: Radio 1ZB in New Zealand — Phil Shone reported that a huge swarm of wasps a mile wide were approaching the city of Auckland, frightening thousands.

April 1, 1989: KSLX-FM in Phoenix, Arizona — announced that the station had been taken hostage by Native Americans, tying up police and 911 lines. The station was let off the hook when the FCC ruled that it was a one-time incident, and the station took steps to prevent a recurrence of similar hoaxes.[8]

July 1991: WALE-AM in Providence, Rhode Island — news director Tom Moriarty reported that personality Steve White was relaxing outside the station during a break when someone shot him in the head. Police and reporters rushed to the scene, only to find White alive and well. Within ten minutes of the "shooting," it was announced that the incident was a hoax, done at White's prompting. White and Moriarty were fired. The FCC let the station off with a warning.[9]

April 1, 1993: KGB-FM in San Diego, California, reported that the space shuttle had been diverted to tiny Montgomery Field in the middle of the city, resulting in over a thousand people rushing to the airport to glimpse the Space Age marvel. Traffic was tied up for hours, as were police trying to unravel the jam. Because the incident did not fall under FCC regulations against crimes, disasters or catastrophes, they took no action.[10]

June 2001: KEGL-FM in Dallas, Texas — DJs Keith Kramer and Tony "Twitch" Logo, reported that pop superstar Britney Spears and friend Justin Timberlake had died in a car crash. They were promptly fired.[11]

Radio analyst Jeff Smulyan has observed, "Whenever you have a creative medium, people are going to do some things on the edge. The question of defining what is merely clever and what goes over the line is sometimes difficult."[12] While often true, some stunts clearly cross the line of what is acceptable. Kidnapping and fake murder confessions are so far over the line that it's hard to imagine rational adults actually going through with such stunts, thinking there would be no repercussions.

CHAPTER 5

Playing with Fire: Nuclear Scares

Since the 1970s, several radio stations have broadcast bogus reports of nuclear accidents, resulting in varying degrees of fear.

The Swedish Barseback Panic

Radio is a local medium that is quicker to respond to breaking local news than television, which is better in providing regional coverage. It takes time for TV crews to get organized and reach the scene of most incidents within their broadcast area, which typically encompasses hundreds or thousands of square miles. Such responses can take hours, and in some non–Western countries, days. On the other hand, radio is often on the scene of a disaster within minutes, as a reporter can simply jump in a mobile unit (a car or truck with a radio or mobile phone) and race off without waiting for a camera crew or loading bulky equipment. Local radio is also more intimate. While we may watch TV personalities on the afternoon and evening news, many people listen to local DJs and news announcers day after day, hour after hour, to the point where they may seem to be part of the family. It's also much easier to pick up the phone and talk to them personally about something they said, whereas TV personalities are notoriously harder to contact.

On the afternoon of November 13, 1973, a small college radio station in the tiny southern Swedish community of Barseback broadcast news of an accident at a local nuclear power plant that was under construction. At 5 o'clock listeners were told that a cooling system had malfunctioned, spewing radioactivity into the atmosphere and it was heading downwind. Based on a survey of over 1,000 listeners who heard the broadcast, about 70 percent thought it was real. Surprisingly, owing to either ignorance or confidence in the government's ability to deal with a leak, 30 percent of those responding said they were not frightened.¹ Despite this, at least several hundred phone calls were placed to local media and police agencies, and the two area telephone systems failed during the program owing to the sudden volume of calls. Some calls were from other parts of Sweden, checking to see if their relatives were safe, while others sought advice. Many called to complain that while they had not been deceived, they were angry that the program managed to fool one of their relatives.² At the nearby Lund police station, before the phones failed, a weeping woman and her father told the police that a terrible accident had occurred. The puzzled officers knew nothing of the hoax and briefly assumed the worst. One officer even rang his family to tell them to stay inside.³ While there was not a single documented case of a listener fleeing the area, Swedish sociologist Karl Rosengren and his colleagues concluded that "the Swedish program must be considered a worthy rival to that of Orson Welles" based on the high percentage of listeners who took the broadcast to be authentic.⁴

While there was potential for widespread panic, it did not erupt for three reasons. First, the broadcast was only 11 minutes long. Second, many of the listeners were aware that the plant in question had not yet been finished and therefore couldn't have expelled radiation. Third, the program was set in 1982, not 1973, though many listeners failed to notice. The show's producers said they aired the program in an effort to stimulate public debate on the issue of nuclear safety. If this was their aim, it worked. The Swedish Radio Council investigated the incident, which was also discussed in parliament and received heavy media coverage. The success of the deception was attributed to its realistic nature, including the use of real locations, popular radio voices and ambulance sirens.

The Springfield "Disaster"

It was over almost before it began, and one cannot help but wonder: What if, on November 9, 1982, local authorities hadn't stopped WSSR-FM in Springfield, Illinois, from broadcasting its fictional radio drama about a local nuclear power plant disaster? The program aired for just two and a half minutes before it was stopped, after worried residents began to phone emergency service agencies to find out if it was true. During that short time span, the drama claimed "that a nuclear cloud was headed for Springfield." Chuck Jones of the Illinois Emergency Services and Disaster Agency said: "I'm still shocked that someone out at that station let that get on the air." The drama was intended to air for half an hour on a public station under the control of Sangamon State University. The nuclear power plant mentioned in the play was just 25 miles northeast of the city, but was not operational at the time of the broadcast.[5]

"Testing ... Hello"—The Reagan Incident

On August 11, 1984, prior to his weekly radio address, President Ronald Reagan was testing his microphone to see if it was working, and warming up his voice, when he quipped: "My fellow Americans, I am pleased to tell you today that I've signed legislation that will outlaw Russia forever. We begin bombing in five minutes." His comments never made it to the air, and his aids and a crowd of reporters laughed at the remark, recognizing it as a joke. Nevertheless, the journalists in attendance reported his comment, sparking an international outcry. Soviet leaders were not amused, placing their military on alert. The Soviet TASS news agency said the remark was a sign of hostility towards Russia, and damaging to peaceful relations.[6] The incident sparks the question: Should the media have reported the off-air comment in the first place? It could be argued that Reagan was a prominent public figure, and given the nature of the remark, there was an obligation to report what he said. On the other hand, Reagan was clearly joking, and if the media hadn't reported it, it wouldn't have prompted Soviet authorities to place their military on a higher state of readiness.

Gulf War Hoax

In mid–January 1991, the Persian Gulf War broke out between the United States and its allies against the Iraqi regime of Saddam Hussein after his invasion of Kuwait. It was a time of great tension across America. There was a sense of unease with reports that Iraqi infiltrators might try to attack the United States with chemical or biological weapons. It was within this context that a disc jockey in the Midwest exercised what can only be described as poor judgment. While doing his morning show on KSHE-FM in Crestwood, Missouri, Don Ulett, unhappy over the U.S. involvement in the war, decided to stage a protest. Ulett interrupted music with this announcement: "Ladies and gentlemen, we are experiencing technical difficulties, please stand b —." Suddenly the sound of an air raid siren could be heard in the background as a second voice said: "Attention, attention. This is an official civil defense warning. This is not a test. The United States is under nuclear attack." Startled listeners then heard screams and explosions. Ulett soon came on to say that regular broadcasting would resume shortly. It did. The phone lines at KSHE quickly lit up from concerned listeners. Two hours after it began, Ulett admitted that the announcement had been a hoax and that he was sorry. The station then aired recorded apologies throughout the day and on their local news the next day, but it was too late.

The Federal Communications Commission immediately investigated. Station management, who had no prior knowledge of the stunt, promptly suspended Ulett from his job for one week without pay, and drew up a plan to prevent a similar incident in the future. While a major panic didn't occur, the FCC was not satisfied given the potential gravity of the situation as it happened during wartime when people were in a heightened state of anxiety and alert, and thus, the hoax "had the potential to create widespread panic." Remarkably, the FCC allowed Ulett to keep his job after the suspension, but he did get fired as the public address announcer for the St. Louis Cardinals baseball team. As for KSHE-FM, it was fined $25,000.[7]

Nuclear hoaxes on radio illustrate the power of placing "live" bulletins in what appear to be regular broadcast programs. When we are dealing with local events, no other medium is as responsive as radio. Some critics might view listeners as being ignorant for not checking other radio or TV stations to see if the event was being reported. But in the first few minutes or hours, one cannot realistically expect other stations or channels to have the story. Therein lies the potential for radio to wreak havoc in the future.

Section Two

It Came from the Small Screen — Television

CHAPTER 6

"This Just In…" NBC Frightens Viewers

> In 1983, NBC broadcast the TV movie *Special Bulletin* about terrorists threatening to set off a nuclear bomb in the United States. Some viewers thought the show was a live news event and became frightened that a nuclear attack was imminent.

It was everyone's nightmare, a worst-case scenario if there ever was one: news reports of a group of terrorists with a nuclear bomb, threatening to set it off, potentially killing millions. This fictitious event was the subject of the NBC Sunday night movie on March 20, 1983. The trouble was that some viewers thought it was real.

The movie *Special Bulletin* was highly realistic and featured superb acting that was so good it won several Emmy Awards. Soon after the show aired, phone calls from worried viewers started pouring in to network affiliates around the country and to police agencies. After a brief opening text denoting its fictional nature, the movie begins "cold," without opening credits. Instead, viewers see what appear to be previews of different shows followed by a jingle for a fictitious network: "RBS — we're moving up." Next, what appears to be a typical game show starts and is interrupted by a special bulletin, followed by a "live" report from the scene of a hostage drama. The movie was intended to show how a TV network would handle a breaking story of a nuclear bomb in the hands of terrorists, who were said to be holed up on the tugboat *Liberty May* in South Carolina's Charleston Harbor. Conveniently, among the hostages are a reporter and a cameraman, who become the mouthpiece for the group, who call themselves anti-nuclear activists. The terrorists demand the detonators for 968 nuclear warheads so as to take them out to sea and dump them overboard, rendering them useless. Their stated goal is to deactivate the missiles as the first step towards global disarmament. It was reported that their bomb was as powerful as the ones dropped on Japan at the end of World War II; the government had 24 hours to give in to their demands or else. In the end, a team of elite government troops try to forcibly end the siege but the weapon explodes, wiping Charleston off the map.

In order to simulate how a real network might react to such a scenario, the show kept switching back and forth from news anchors in New York City to journalists at the White House, the Pentagon, Congress, and in Charleston. Throughout the movie, these special bulletins are interrupted by so-called "live feeds" from the terrorists on the tugboat. A series of disclaimers appear during the show, starting at the very beginning of the movie when these words appear: "The following program is a realistic depiction of fictional events. None of what you are about to see is actually happening." This brief, silent disclaimer could have been easily overlooked by viewers. During commercial breaks, viewers were again reminded of the show's fictional nature. Also, at key moments, the word "dramatization" appears on the screen. Occasionally, reporters would stumble over words, adding to the sense that it was a live broadcast. The movie also used WPIV as the call letters for the fictional NBC affiliate in Charleston — very close to the real affiliate, which is WCIV.

In Charleston, WCIV-TV was swamped with 250 calls; others rang the police, though most of those were reporters seeing if anyone had called. Only a handful of worried residents had done so. This occurred despite the local affiliate taking the extraordinary step of permanently superimposing the word "fiction" on the screen.

At KING-TV in Seattle, Washington, it was a similar story as worried viewers bombarded the switchboard with calls, most within the first twenty minutes. One caller told the operator that he was concerned for the welfare of his son who lived in nearby Virginia. At San Francisco's KRON-TV, 50 calls were recorded in the first half hour. One woman was convinced what she was watching was real, and complained that the station was giving too much air time to the terrorists! In Chicago, once callers realized it was a fictional story, many became irate. One angry viewer rang WMAQ-TV to demand that the show be taken off the air in five minutes or he would blow up the TV station. A blind woman called KGW-TV in Portland, Oregon, to ask if the program was real as she couldn't see if there were any disclaimers on the screen. At WCMH in Columbus, Ohio, out of 38 calls, switchboard operator Gene Ostle said, "Three or four people were hysterical, crying." One woman told him she had to take tranquilizers in order to calm down.[1]

A spokesman for St. Louis TV station KSDK said about 60 calls were received. "Most of the callers thought the events they were watching on their television screens were really happening."[2] At WDAF in Kansas City, the operator said that of the 37 calls recorded, "One-half complained that we shouldn't put something like this on television, and one half had just tuned in and thought it was for real." One man who called WDAF claimed that his mother became distraught during the show and suffered a heart seizure.[3] However, just one man rang the Kansas City Police to inquire if the show was real. In St. Louis, not a single inquiry was logged by police.[4] Based on these reactions, while some callers were clearly concerned or frightened, few were panicky; otherwise, it's likely that more would have called police instead of ringing the TV stations.

Curiously, NBC officials worried that some viewers might mistake the broadcast for the real thing. The day before the movie aired, Associated Press writer Tom Jory published a story titled: "NBC Hopes Warnings Will Avert Panic during *Special Bulletin*." Jory quoted the president of WTMJ-TV in Milwaukee, who decided not to air the movie because he was worried "that people will be deceived into believing it's an actual broadcast." He was especially concerned for viewers tuning in late. "They tune in for a moment and say, 'My God, what's happening?'"[5]

The historical context of the broadcast was also instrumental in its believability. In 1983, the fear of a nuclear war with the Soviet Union was still a worry, and American schools were routinely conducting nuclear attack drills along with regular fire evacuations. The radiation leak at the Three Mile Island nuclear plant near Harrisburg, Pennsylvania, in March 1979 was also fresh in the popular mind, helping to set the stage for the reaction to *Special Bulletin*.

Even before *Special Bulletin* aired, NBC executives received complaints from their news division, concerned that the show was too similar to a real broadcast. The movie was recorded on tape instead of film, to give it a live flavor. The president of WCIV-TV in Charleston, William Lucas, said he didn't think people would become worried while watching the movie — though he clearly had some misgivings. "I wish they had chosen a hypothetical city," he said.

CHAPTER 7

"Look! Up in the Sky!" Asteroid Panic

>When CBS aired *Without Warning* in 1994, it prompted thousands of worried viewers to think that earth was about to be pummeled by asteroids. There is evidence to suggest that some CBS executives expected and even hoped for such reactions. How the real media handles asteroid scares continues to be a subject of ongoing debate.

At 9 o'clock on the night of October 30, 1994, CBS television broadcast its Sunday night movie *Without Warning*, triggering fears that asteroids were about to crash into earth. The program, written by former ABC reporter Peter Lance, was highly realistic and featured "live" reports from fictional disaster sites in Asia, Europe and the United States. The "Evening World News" was presented like a real news program, fooling many. It was reported that asteroids had already struck in Wyoming, France and China, and more were on the way. At the end of the program, more asteroids struck earth and TV screens went blank. Adding to the realism, veteran television journalist Sander Vanocur played himself, anchoring the news desk as he switched to apparent live footage of the aftermath of the impacts. The word "live" also appeared on the screen as actors and real reporters continued their deception. Other real-life TV journalists played correspondents, including Sandy Hill, Warren Olney, Ernie Anastos and Bree Walker. One segment even featured an interview with space scientist Arthur C. Clarke.[1]

During the broadcast, telephone calls poured into stations that were airing the movie. After the program began, the network advised audiences that what they were about to see was a "realistic depiction of fictional events. None of what you are seeing is actually happening."[2] The problem was, after the initial warning, there was no advisory for the next 15 minutes, a critical time in establishing the tone and mood. The program began like an ordinary Sunday night movie but was interrupted by news bulletins from such respected organizations as the Associated Press and Reuters, showing scenes of death and destruction. The movie even recreated a White House press conference during which it was announced that F-16 fighter jets equipped with nuclear weapons had been scrambled to blow up the asteroids before reaching earth.[3]

It may have been no coincidence that the program aired on October 30 and was likely inspired by the infamous 1938 Martian invasion scare which aired on the same date (see Chapter 2). During the TV broadcast, the switchboard at CBS headquarters in New York was jammed with anxious callers, wanting to know if what they were watching was real.

When the movie was over, one New York affiliate led their local news with viewer complaints. After covering the incident as a news story, the show's anchorman then said: "Now, here's the real news."[4] In Minneapolis, Minnesota, CBS affiliate WCCO anchorwoman Amy Marsalis apologized to viewers: "CBS broadcast disclaimers at every commercial break but in spite of that we got almost a hundred calls from people alarmed, upset, some in tears.... For those of you who called here, we're sorry for any bad moments."[5]

Media columnist Ted Cox believes that the movie was a setup by CBS in order to create another Orson Welles–like scare that would boost ratings and the network's profile. Cox notes that at the time the movie aired, CBS ranked third among the three major networks and relished the publicity of viewer reaction. Clearly network executives knew that the movie would deceive some viewers into thinking they were watching a real news event; the only question was to what extent. As Cox observes, the use of high-profile news veteran Sandy Vanocur seemed designed to intentionally fool the audience. There were other clear signs of the intent of CBS executives. For instance, WBBM TV 2 in Syracuse, New York ended its *Sunday Evening News* with a caution to viewers that some may be fooled by the movie it was about to air. The station also placed a recording on its phone line, advising callers that *Without Warning* was fictitious, seemingly anticipating the reaction.[6]

Low-key disclaimers about the realistic nature of the movie and the Halloween Eve air date led many reporters to connect the dots and anticipate a *War of the Worlds*–type reaction. Indeed, CBS communications vice president Tom Goodman admitted that early Sunday evening, "The news desk received more calls from reporters seeing if we'd received any calls [other] than calls [from] themselves."[7]

This incident underscores just how easily the public can be fooled by dramas involving what appears to be a regularly scheduled event seemingly interrupted by live news bulletins. This is especially so when the bulletins are given by real TV journalists.

Rolling the Cosmic Dice

Just what are the odds of a large asteroid slamming into earth and causing global destruction? Very, very slim. Astronomer Rachel Webster says the odds are "remote and not worth losing sleep over."[8] They are measured in millions of years. She says the greater threat is from smaller asteroids and comets, which pose a regional danger as they occur roughly once every 100 years. But with today's sophisticated tracking equipment, in most cases we should have ample warning to be able to do something about it. Surprisingly, blowing up the object — as was the plan in *Without Warning*, could make matters worse, sending hundreds of projectiles raining down on earth. The preferred method is to place a small rocket on the object in order to nudge it slightly off the course.[9] The United States military already has contingency plans to do just that.

The media has a spotty track record when it comes to reporting on asteroid scares. On July 3, 2006, an asteroid as big as a football stadium passed near Earth. Despite Internet rumors of possible doom, including giant dust clouds and tidal waves, as predicted, Earth survived unscathed. The giant space rock, dubbed XP14, caused concern when it was first identified on December 10, 2004, by astronomers at the Cambridge Observatory in Massachusetts. It was immediately classified as a PHA — that's space talk for Potentially Hazardous Asteroid. There was a lot of Internet chatter about XP14, including suggestions that NASA calculations could be wrong, or that it could crash into the moon. Despite Internet speculation, newspapers, television and radio didn't play up the flyby, and it quickly became a non-event. By the time July 3 arrived, it was reported as an innocent sideshow, posing no threat to Earth. This is not always the case.

In August 2003, the British government's Near Earth Object Information Centre issued an alarming press release, warning of a possible collision with asteroid QQ47 in 2014. The statement triggered a brief media frenzy and disgust among astronomers who said there never was a realistic threat. The media warning was issued even though the collision odds at the time were set at roughly one in a million. Shortly thereafter, the odds went down to zero once more information was gathered and more precise calculations could be made.

In March 1998, the media was briefly abuzz with reports of an asteroid scare when astronomer Brian Marsden circulated a notice among his colleagues that asteroid 1997 XS11 looked to be on a collision course with Earth in 2028. Within hours, the story hit the media. Upon reading the notice, two NASA scientists specializing in tracking Near Earth Objects, Paul Chodas and Donald Yeomans, quickly determined that a collision was impossible. In announcing their results, the pair were critical of Marsden for circulating his collision notice. Yeomans has said that when someone locates a large object that appears to be on a collision course with Earth, he or she should not run to the media and make the information public right away. He advocates circulating the data privately among astronomers. This way, asteroid experts can analyze the information and reach a consensus before going to the media and creating undue alarm.[10] Marsden defended his announcement and said he would do it again.

On December 23, 2004, a worrying statement released by NASA made headlines around the globe: Scientists had detected a giant asteroid 400 meters across that, based on calculations, had a one-in-sixty chance of clobbering Earth on April 13, 2029. A short time later it was announced that based on more precise calculations, there was no threat. Science writer Terence Dickinson notes a concerning pattern in recent years. In each instance, "the first news release would give the odds as such-and-so that the killer asteroid would collide with Earth on a specified date. Then, days or weeks later, astronomers would find images of the asteroid in the photo archives that allow more accurate orbital calculations and — poof!— the sky isn't falling after all."[11] Why not just wait a few days or weeks when astronomers can gather sufficient data to say with more clarity that Earth will be struck? Part of the reason may be the news media's competitive urges to break a potentially hot story over its rivals — even if it's not in the best interests of the public. It would appear that when journalists get wind of a potentially huge story, it's hard to sit on it until more accurate data comes in and the threat is confirmed.

CHAPTER 8

Pokémon Panics and Creepy Crawley Scares

> It's one of the greatest cases of mass suggestion in history. In 1997, Japanese TV reported that watching a cartoon could make children sick. The reports triggered a wave of mass hysteria across the country.

In Japan during mid–December 1997, thousands of Japanese schoolchildren and their parents heard terrifying accounts of children going into frightening seizures after watching an episode of the popular cartoon Pokémon. In hindsight, we now know that the initial report was true: Several hundred children who watched the program had a rare, pre-existing condition and were susceptible to what doctors call "photosensitive epilepsy" or PSE. Intense flashes of light during one part of the show triggered the relatively harmless and short-lived seizures in a small number of children. But TV reports of the first batch of children falling ill triggered a wave of mass hysteria across the country. Within days, over 12,000 more schoolchildren — fearing that they too might fall ill as they had watched the episode — reported feeling unwell.

The Pokémon panic began on the evening of December 16, with the airing of episode 38, "Computer Warrior Polygon." The broadcast began at the usual time of 6:30. Fifteen percent of the nation's TV sets were tuned in to the popular show. During the show, Pikachu, a yellow mouse-like creature with super speed and agility, enters cyberspace with several companions. About twenty minutes into the program, Pikachu battles the forces of evil by using his special ability to throw bolts of electricity. It was at this point that viewers saw a sequence of light flashes. Doctors later determined that a tiny fraction of children out of the millions of viewers reacted with seizures. These children had sensitive nervous systems, and as the nerves that send messages to the brain became excited, their muscles began to twitch and spasm.[1] While the

8. Pokémon Panics and Creepy Crawley Scares 45

A display at the Guinness World Records museum in Niagara Falls, Canada, describes the Pokemon Panic (photograph by Benjamin Radford).

condition is not serious, it can be frightening to watch. The 12,000 other children who watched the show and became ill were suffering from a variety of anxiety-related symptoms: headaches, breathing problems, nausea, vomiting, blurred vision, and fatigue.

The cartoon was so popular with children that in Toyohashi, researchers estimated that 70 percent of the city's 24,000 elementary students were watching.[1] Twenty-one minutes into the program Pikachu's attack began to send flashes across television screens. Japan's Fire Defense agency reported that within 40 minutes of the flashing sequence airing, 618 children had been taken for hospital evaluation with a variety of complaints. The illnesses were headline news across the country that evening. But, in a lapse of judgment, several TV stations aired replays of the flash sequence, sparking a second wave of child seizures.[2]

In their investigation of 80 elementary schools on Kyushu Island, researchers led by Dr. Yushiro Yamashita had teachers ask their students who had watched the show, and if they could recall feeling unwell. Questionnaires were also mailed to area health clinics. Just one of 32,083 enrolled students had had a seizure; 1,002 others reported "minor symptoms"— about 6 percent of the children.[3] A separate survey of a dozen hospitals in the same prefecture found that 17 children were treated for convulsions. Of course, this doesn't mean that they had convulsions but were treated for them. Dr. S. Tobimatsu, who headed the study, examined four children who had been affected by Pokémon and diagnosed with photosensitive epilepsy.[4] He and fellow researchers suggested that "the rapid color changes in the cartoon thus provoked the seizures." The researchers believe that the children's sensitivity to color — in particular, rapid changes between red and blue — may have played a role in triggering the seizures. As for the vast majority of other children who fell ill, mass hysteria was the culprit.

Strawberries "Virus"

In May 2006, a TV show in Portugal was blamed for causing mass hysteria. At least 300 Portuguese children from various schools developed a mysterious ailment characterized by breathing problems, dizziness and rashes. Doctors concluded that the outbreak was a case of mass suggestion and dubbed it the "Strawberries with Sugar Virus"— after the popular teen television soap opera blamed for triggering the malady. The symptoms appeared within days of an episode depicting characters coming down with similar symptoms, caused by an imaginary virus which swept through a school. "What we concretely have is a few children with allergies and apparently a phenomenon of many other children imitating," said one doctor.[5] Another physician, Mario Almeida, said: "I know of no disease which is so selective that it only attacks school children."[6] Anxiety levels may also have been high, as the illness coincided with final exams.

The Incy Wincy Spider Scare

The media was also implicated in triggering other scares. In late July and early August 2006, in Austria, when several people were bitten by the yellow sac spider — an event that happens each year — the media ran a series of reports about the spider's habits and bites. Classic symptoms include headache and nausea — symptoms that are also common in the general population and triggered by stress. Soon, scores of people who were exhibiting these vague symptoms and suspected that they too had been bitten rushed to local emergency rooms. In reality, the bite of the yellow sac is painful but not lethal. Over a two-week period starting in late July, 190 people had visited the main hospital in Linz, fearing that they too had been bitten by the dreaded creature. Of these, no more than eight were diagnosed as having been bitten by the yellow sac. Medical centers across the country were also inundated with calls from worried residents. At the main hospital in Vienna, spokesman Dieter Gruber described the episode as a "wave of hysteria," with hundreds of callers inquiring as to the dangers posed by the spider.[7]

The New Zealand White-Tail Panic

The Austrian episode is reminiscent of other media-generated insect panics, but instead of television, newspapers have been the main culprit. In recent decades, sensational press reports in New Zealand about the potential dangers of Australian white-tailed spiders have triggered a spate of imaginary spider bites. Between 1900 and 1979, not a single case of a white-tailed spider bite was recorded. But in recent years, stories such as "Spider Suspect in Death Mystery" and "Fears of Biting Spider Plague" conditioned the public to immediately suspect the white-tail in cases of swelling, localized discomfort and rash. After examining the records of "white-tailed spider bites" recorded at the Christchurch Hospital between January 2001 and 2003, a team of doctors noted several curiosities. In no instance did the "victim" see the spider actually bite them. Bacteria from the patient's skin cultures were re-examined and there was no indication of a reaction to spider venom. The investigators found that it was unlikely that any of the patients had been bitten by the white-tail.[8] The spider scare can be traced back to 1991, when popular newspaper columnist Denis Welch was reported to have become ill after being bitten by a white-tail, resulting in a surge in queries to spider experts about dangers posed by the spider.[9]

How could the diagnosing physicians and the media been so wrong? Money and politics. New Zealand's Accident Compensation Corporation or ACC requires a specific diagnosis before it will pay out. The researchers noted that the ACC stipulates that an external force "be identified before sudsidising medical care and paying benefits to people unable to work. If an external force is not identified, the ACC will not cover the costs."[10] Most journalists are not experts on the subjects they write on; many write several stories a day on different topics. In this instance, they simply reported what the doctors and patients were telling them. Few journalists were equipped with enough background knowledge on white-tailed spiders and medicine to understand what was really going on.

The American Kissing Bug Terror

"Kissing bug" is a generic term for numerous insect species that suck blood from mammals, so called for their tendency to pierce the exposed skin of sleeping victims, most often on the face and especially the lips. Other common names include "assassin bug," "cone-nose" and "big bed bug." Its romantic nickname became popular during the summer of 1899, when scores of Americans claimed to have been bitten on the lips while sleeping.

After biting its victim, the kissing bug ungraciously defecates on the host, a practice which can transmit potentially fatal Chagas disease. In the fecal matter is a parasite which can severely damage the heart, nervous system, brain, colon and esophagus. The bug is rampant in parts of Central and South America where 25 percent of the population is at risk, an estimated 17 million are infected, and 50,000 deaths occur annually.[11] However, the species of kissing bug on the mainland United States rarely bites humans, and when they do the chance of contracting Chagas is extremely low, as these more polite American cousins do not defecate while feeding, greatly reducing the transmission risk.[12] The bug's notorious reputation outside the United States may have sparked the great kissing bug scare of 1899.

The scare can be traced to *Washington Post* police reporter James F. McElhone, who, in the course of making his journalistic rounds in mid–June, began to note an influx of patients seeking treatment for bug bites at the Washington City Emergency Hospital. Upon interviewing Hospital physicians on June 19, he learned that several people had indeed been treated for redness and swelling, typically on the lips, "apparently the result of an insect bite."[13] Curiously, no one ever caught their attackers in the act. On June 20, McElhone published a speculative, sensational account of the bug bites, describing victims as having been "badly poisoned" and warning that it "threatens to become something like a plague."[14] Other Washington papers quickly reported the story, followed by papers along the east coast and then nationwide.[15]

Soon, any insect bite or swelling or pain of any kind on or near the face was attributed to the evil "kissing bug." Leland Howard, Chief of Entomology for the U.S. Department of Agriculture in Washington, D.C., described the ensuing scare as a "*newspaper* epidemic, for every insect bite ... [not] recognized was attributed to the popular and somewhat mysterious creature."[16] At the Philadelphia Academy of Natural Sciences, entomologists analyzed the remains of "kissing bugs" collected by purported victims. Among the insects identified: houseflies, beetles, bees and a butterfly.[17] Newspaper accounts of kissing bug attacks grew increasingly sensational.[18] One report from a Chicago woman more closely resembled a vampire attack than a bug bite.[19] At the height of the scare, beggars in Washington, D.C., bandaged themselves and went about soliciting donations, claiming to have been out of work and requiring donations to subsist until their full recovery from kissing bug bites.[20]

CHAPTER 9

The "Documentary" That Fooled England

> On Halloween night in 1992, the BBC decided it would have some fun by presenting a spoof documentary on a haunted house. The program frightened the nation and triggered a wave of protests. It was also blamed for cases of post-traumatic stress syndrome and at least one suicide.

Michael Parkinson is one of the best known and respected figures in British media circles. He is the English equivalent of Jay Leno or Oprah Winfrey. That's why many citizens were surprised to learn that Parkinson had taken part in a hoax broadcast that remains the subject of bitter debate. On October 31, 1992, the much revered British Broadcasting Corporation aired a 90-minute television special that promised to be a TV first: a live investigation of a "real" haunted house in England. A forerunner of today's reality television, promotions for the program billed it as a documentary. The show discussed the supposed plight of Pam Early, who, viewers were told, lived in a haunted house in Northolt, Middlesex, with her two daughters. The Earlys told of having suffered through countless incidents of paranormal harassment at the hands of a restless spirit.

After seeing that the beloved Mr. Parkinson was the host, and following the gripping storyline, an estimated 11 million viewers tuned in to watch. While the show was meant to make fun of sensational docu-dramas, many were fooled and thought what they were watching was really happening. As the "documentary" opened, a stone-faced Parkinson set a serious tone: "The program you are about to watch is a unique investigation of the supernatural. It contains materials which some viewers may find disturbing." Parkinson had a satellite link-up with reporters who were supposedly at the haunted house.

The program gradually built in intensity. At first, the incidents were tame: The on-the-scene reporters heard a series of strange noises in the house. Then viewers were taken on an emotional roller-coaster ride. Just when it seemed that something supernatural was taking place, one of the girls, Suzanne, appeared to be caught in the act of making the spooky sounds. But a short time later, it became evident that there really was a ghost and scratch marks suddenly appeared on Suzanne's face. The situation quickly deteriorated as both girls began speaking a strange language, the lives of the two reporters appeared to be in peril, and, back at the studio, Parkinson was possessed by an evil spirit.

Viewer reaction was swift: 20,000 phone calls lit up the lines, protesting the show. Some were upset that a trusted media figure like Parkinson would take part in such a hoax. Many parents were angry over the effect the show had on their children as the two reporters at the "haunted house" were popular presenters of children's TV programs — Sarah Greene and Craig Charles. Many children were unable to separate fantasy from reality and grew distraught. *The British Medical Journal* published two cases of post-traumatic stress syndrome resulting from the program, both in ten-year-old boys. Symptoms included trouble sleeping, nightmares, anxiety attacks, depression, separation anxiety, memory problems, and intrusive thoughts and flashbacks about the show.[1]

One of the boys became obsessed with the notion of ghosts and witches, and talked about the subject constantly in order to receive reassurance. He was also afraid of being in dark places for fear that something bad would happen. He began sleeping with the light on, would not be left alone upstairs, and experienced panic attacks. The psychiatrists who treated him said he suffered nightmares and flashbacks, and would bang his head in hopes of getting rid of any unwanted ghostly thoughts. Prior to watching the show, his mother said he was a normal child, though he was "sensitive" and "a worrier." The boy was hospitalized for eight weeks before the symptoms subsided.

In the second case, as with the first, the boy was also described as a nervous type, and was frightened during the show. He felt ill and weepy, and refused to enter his bedroom, believing that someone or something was watching him. His parents allowed him to sleep with them, and had to repeatedly offer reassurance about the fictional nature of the show. They finally sought professional help, and life soon returned to normal.

The participation of Michael Parkinson in the deception was pivotal. Parkinson appeared doing what he was renowned for: discussing major news events in a credible fashion. He was so convincing that he even fooled those who tuned in expecting to see a play about ghosts. *Ghostwatch* scriptwriter Stephen Volk told a friend to tune into the program and clearly described it as a drama. Yet, upon seeing Parkinson, she quickly assumed that what she was seeing was real. "One friend of mine, whom I'd told the week before that I had a drama on TV at 9:30 the following Saturday, phoned to tell me that she totally believed it was happening for real. I said, 'But I told you I'd written it!' 'Yes, I know,' she said, 'but as soon as I saw Michael Parkinson I thought you must have got it wrong!'"[2]

Volk was surprised that so many people took the program seriously. While admitting that the show was intended to trick the audience into thinking they were watching a "live" show, the deception lasted much longer than he anticipated. "We thought that people might be puzzled for two, perhaps five minutes, but then they would surely get it, and enjoy it for what it was — a drama. The curious thing about *Ghostwatch* is that while one part of the audience didn't buy it for a second, another part believed it was real from beginning to end."[3]

One suicide was blamed the show. Five days after airing, 18-year-old Martin Denham hung himself. Denham was intellectually impaired and had the mental abilities of a 13-year-old. After watching *Ghostwatch*, Denham became obsessed with ghosts. He was found hanging from a tree near his family's Nottingham home. The suicide note read: "Mother do not be upset. If there is ghosts I will now be one and I will always be with you as one. Love Martin."[4]

British primary schoolteacher Robert Kensit reflected the sentiments of many viewers. In a letter to the *Radio Times*, he said: "I describe myself as a pretty hard-bitten sceptic, but by the time it had finished I was feeling very frightened indeed." Kensit said "all that was needed was to have a message flash on screen every few minutes which would have informed people that this was a fictional account."[5] Volk disagrees. He thinks that writers have to have a degree of artistic license, otherwise TV would become too boring. "If we had a screaming banner across the screen reading 'This is not true,' what is the point of that? You might as well have a comedian give you the punchline before he tells you the gag.... What do you do? Destroy the fun of the programme for the people who might enjoy it, for the sake of pleasing those who might be offended?"[6] On the other hand, Martin Denham might still be alive today if it hadn't been for the show. And what of the responsibility to the many child listeners who recognized Sarah Green and Craig Charles from their popular kids' show roles? At best, it seems to have been poor judgment to have cast them in roles where they would be attacked. How many other children suffered varying degrees of PTSD or emotional upset? Not every child watches TV with their parents, and certainly, not every parent thought the show was fictional.

Are these isolated cases involving mentally imbalanced people? How much of an impact do scary television shows and movies have on audience members? University of Michigan researcher Kristen Harrison has found a worrisome long-term effect. She asked a group of American university students if they had ever been frightened for a long time after watching a scary film or program. Surprisingly, 9 percent said yes, with many remaining scared for a year or more. Of this group, one in four said their fear persisted beyond a year. Eating and sleep disturbances were common in about half the subjects. Remarkably, some students didn't even realize that they had been affected until being in a similar situation. One woman noted how she seemingly enjoyed watching the movie *Jaws*, yet when she went swimming, she was seriously affected by the film. "I was surprised at the effect it had on me when I went swimming in Wisconsin lakes.... If someone yelled 'Jaws!' and I was in the water my heart would start racing and I would fly out of the water. It lasted a good year."[7]

There is a famous cartoon where Bugs Bunny and Daffy Duck are in front of a live audience, and each tries to outdo the other in a series of more dangerous stunts. Finally, an exasperated Daffy takes a stick of dynamite, lights it and swallows. An explosion follows. Bugs gives Daffy his due, complimenting him on such a spectacular trick. Daffy responds, as his ghostly spirit floats skyward, by saying there was only one problem in performing it — he could only do it once. *Ghostwatch* was a great "trick," but the BBC paid a hefty price for airing it. After the firestorm of controversy that it created, *Ghostwatch* wasn't released to the public for a full decade after it first aired. The lesson is clear: Anyone who hoaxes the public will forever be looked upon with suspicion — even media icons such as Michael Parkinson and the BBC.

CHAPTER 10

Hurricane Katrina Mythmaking

Reports of bodies stacked in the Superdome and mass murder and mayhem across New Orleans in the aftermath of Katrina will be forever etched in our minds. But was it true?

Matthew Arnold once described journalism as "literature in a hurry." In today's information age, reporters have the unenviable task of being instant experts who are constantly battling deadlines to either break a big story or keep up with the competition. As a result, the truth is often distorted, as complex stories are condensed into 30-second sound bites or a few paragraphs. How the American media reported on the aftermath of Hurricane Katrina is a classic example.

Make no mistake: When Katrina swept through the eastern Gulf states as a Category 4 storm on August 29, 2005, she crippled coastal Louisiana, Mississippi, and Alabama. New Orleans, 10 feet below sea level, was hit hard by flooding when the city's outdated levee system failed. Katrina resulted in at least 1,300 deaths, 100 billion dollars in damages, and the displacement of over a million residents. Yes, Katrina was a major storm that packed a wallop, but if you believed the media reports immediately after she hit, the worst was yet to come.

Shortly after Katrina struck, there were sensational accounts of mayhem and mob rule in New Orleans: of children with their throats slit, gangs roaming the Superdome raping and murdering terrified evacuees, rescue personnel being shot at, and a surge in murders. Attempts to confirm these early TV reports by interviewing eyewitnesses and checking police records portray a radically different picture. The *St. Petersburg Times* from September 2 perhaps best summed up the public perception, proclaiming: "At the Edge of Anarchy."[1]

On September 1, CNN reported that the Superdome evacuations had been suspended after a ferrying helicopter was fired on. The ugly story was flashed around the globe in an instant. The Associated Press headline read: "Katrina Evacuation Halted Amid Gunfire ... Shots Fired at Military Helicopter." But the sniping never happened. Officials from the Louisiana National Guard, the Air Force, Coast Guard, and Civil Air Patrol — all of whom had choppers in the air over New Orleans — made inquires and found that none of their pilots reported being fired on.[2] That same day, during a live, nationally televised news briefing, Louisiana Democratic Senator Mary Landrieu announced that she had heard unconfirmed reports that some deputies and sheriffs had been killed or injured. These also proved unfounded. As of September 1, just one law officer, out of thousands in the region, had been reported shot — a self-inflicted leg wound that occurred during a struggle.[3]

The impression of chaos at the Superdome was widely broadcast in the media and promoted by city officials, who in turn, were relying largely on media reports. On September 6, New Orleans police superintendent Eddie Compass told TV talk queen Oprah Winfrey chilling accounts of babies being raped there. Mayor Ray Nagin contributed to the hype when he said on the same broadcast that the Superdome was a major crime scene: "They have people standing out there, have been in that frickin' Superdome for five days watching dead bodies ... watching hooligans killing people, raping people."[4]

Incredibly, none of it was true. Louisiana National Guard Major Edward Bush said the Superdome "morphed into this mythical place where the most unthinkable deeds were being done."[5] The little panic there was at the "Dome" was being stirred by the news media. The public address system wasn't working and cell phones were useless, so National Guard troops communicated to the masses by walking the stadium and using bullhorns. With the difficulty in communicating, many evacuees became distraught after listening to their portable AM radios. It was within this backdrop that Major Bush said, "They would listen to news reports that talked about the dead bodies at the Superdome, and the murders in the bathrooms of the Superdome, and the babies being raped at the Superdome, and it would create terrible panic." Indeed, Bush spent much of his time as a salesman trying to convince evacuees that what they were hearing wasn't true.[6] Bush said, "People would hear something on the radio and come and say that people were getting raped in the bathroom or someone had been murdered. I would say, 'Ma'am, where?' I would tell them if there were bodies, my guys would find it. Everybody heard, nobody saw."[7]

But how could the media get it so wrong? Apparently, with widespread power outages and reporters unable to move about easily, they reported not what they saw, but what others said they saw — which often turned out to be rumor, gossip and hearsay.

Contributing to these dark images was journalist Brian Thevenot of the New Orleans *Times-Picayune,* who published an article on September 6 about the Superdome horrors, including quotes from National Guardsmen who told him that a Superdome freezer contained 30 to 40 bodies, including a "7-year-old with her throat cut." The Arkansas National Guard conducted a review of the claims when the existence of the bodies couldn't be verified. Lt. Colonel John Edwards headed the probe, which came to a startling conclusion: There were no bodies. Had the troops lied to the media? Not quite. It turns out, the excited Guardsmen had heard the freezer story while waiting in line for food at Harrah's Casino next to the Superdome. At the time it was being used as a military and law enforcement staging area.[8] Essentially, they had repeated hearsay as fact. Thevenot had taken the reports at face value — something that reporters at every newspaper in the country do every day — they interview authorities or supposed eyewitnesses and assume they're being truthful.

On September 26, Thevenot and fellow journalist Gordon Russell corrected their earlier misinformation about the Superdome freezer and other Katrina myths. Shortly thereafter, the floodgates opened, with *The New York Times, Los Angeles Times* and *Washington Post* publishing similar exposés. Cable TV and radio talk shows were soon running hot with similar myths. As for the supposed spate of murders after Katrina, New Orleans District Attorney Eddie Jordan said that as of September 27, there had been four confirmed homicides, and not a single official report of rape.[9] Not bad figures for a one-month period in a major U.S. city.

A major reason for the flurry of rumors was the disruption of communication in Katrina's aftermath. Denise Bottcher, press secretary to Louisiana governor Kathleen Blanco, said: "The television stations were reporting that people were literally stepping over bodies and violence was out of control [in the Superdome].... But the National Guardsmen were saying that what we were seeing on CNN was contradictory to what they were seeing. It didn't match up."[10]

Sociologist Robert Granfield says the flurry of false reports of criminal mayhem in New Orleans in the wake of Katrina reflect popular stereotypes of minorities and the poor. In several cases, Granfield said that rumors were reported as reality. "Reporters had neither the time nor the ability to investigate these claims, and so repeated them as facts. One gunshot or drowning or stolen television became 10, and 10 became 100. Hungry people taking bread off shelves were generalized into 'massive looting' and then typified as the rule, not the exception."[11] Granfield contends that the accounts of widespread murder and mayhem were believed because for years the media has been hyper-inflating the news in order to sell their product to the public and keep them watching. In reality, he says that in the United States, person and property crimes were the lowest they had been in more than thirty years. "The public, constantly exposed to lurid news stories of child murder, bombings, rapes and other kinds of violence, is not aware of the declining crime rate. Many apparently believe that we're just one police department or one National Guard unit away from anarchy."[12] The result was a media-fueled delusion where journalists reported what they thought was happening, based on what they expected to happen. The irony was not lost on Granfield, who observes that the behavior of many journalists turned out to be "as shocking and shameful as the behavior we assumed to be true."[13]

Thevenot is more forgiving. He expresses what happened as the meeting of space-age technology with stone-age storytelling. "A person might have seen a man passed out from dehydration in the Superdome ... and assumed he was dead, then assumed there must be more dead. In the retelling, it becomes, 'There's bodies in the Dome.' Retold a few more times by stressed and frightened people — all the way up to the mayor — and it became, 'There's so many bodies in the Dome you can't count them.'" Then the media showed up and broadcast these claims around the world in the blink of an eye, not realizing that ordinary rules of sourcing did not ensure accuracy because people were repeating exaggerated, distorted stories through word of mouth without firsthand confirmation. The result was fish stories that got bigger and bigger — with the "bodies in the Dome" story being a whopper. Ultimately, once the facts were scrutinized, it turned out to be the proverbial one that got away.

Then there was the rope story. On September 5, several media outlets broadcast shocking news of police finding 22 bodies of people who had drowned in the storm — all tied to a single rope. The bodies were found near Violet, Louisiana, east of New Orleans. The report quoted St. Barnard Parish Sheriff Jack Stephens who said the bodies were wrapped around a pole. The problem was, the area was under water and transport was difficult. By early November after water levels had receded and the reports were checked, no bodies were found. In the words of St. Barnard Fire Chief Tom Stone: "It's a hurricane urban myth. It's fictitious. It never happened. Thank God." How did the story of the roped drowning victims get started in the first place? Stone thinks he knows. At the peak of the storm surge, a resident living near where the incident had supposedly taken place said he spotted a bunch of people roped together. According to reporter George Pawlaczyk, "The story quickly spread among harried Sheriff's deputies and firefighters in dozens of commandeered pleasure boats, but they had to concentrate on saving the living. Somewhere along the way, the number 22 became attached to the story." Stone said that in Katrina's aftermath, all sorts of wild rumors were flying.

"It was getting to the point that if I didn't actually see it, I didn't believe it," he said.[14]

Bad Water or Bad Journalism?

There were other media-generated myths about Katrina, most notably about the quality of drinking water and reports that it was a storm of unparalleled strength.

News agencies commonly described the New Orleans floodwaters as a "witch's brew" and "toxic soup" of pollutants that could easily prove fatal if swallowed, and would pose a long-term health threat to those inhabiting the area. Yet water tests during the first week of September, indicated otherwise. Most of the pollution was from feces, pesticides and petroleum-based chemicals, and slightly elevated amounts of metals. Chris Piehler of the Louisiana Department of Environmental Quality, said that tests taken shortly after the storm hit, found no "specific toxic pollutants at any levels of concern." When asked if water pollutants could pose a hazard for returning residents, he said bluntly: "No. The limiting factor is going to be what structures are going to be salvageable and which ones are not."[15] Jerry Fenner from the Centers for Disease Control echoed Pichler's sentiments: "[A]ll the test results show there shouldn't be any long-term problems of health and habitability."[16] Based on the results of daily water samples taken by the Environmental Protection Agency, New Orleans floodwaters yielded levels of hexavalent chromium, arsenic and lead above agency drinking water standards. Yet, EPA officials were not worried, issuing a statement that read in part: "These compounds would pose a risk to children only if a child were to drink a liter of flood water a day. Long-term exposure [a year or longer] to arsenic would be required before health effects would be a concern."

A prime ingredient in the floodwater — fecal matter — came from the city's underground sewage system after the city's sewage treatment plant shut down. As disgusting and unhealthful as this sounds, by September 7, fecal bacteria was already declining and health officials said they would have no lasting effect on the water quality. Fenner said: "The stuff will desiccate and you can clean it up. You fertilize your lawn? It's the same thing."[17] Further, and contrary to popular belief, the city's drinking water does not come from Lake Pontchartrain (pronounced ponch-a-train), where officials were pumping the floodwater, but the Mississippi River.[18]

Unfortunately, in the days after Katrina, many journalists on the scene based their reports on fragmentary accounts from unverifiable sources. Media critic Matthew Felling compares what happened to "the fog of war," and feels that journalists needed to show "more patience and less feigned certainty."[19]

Was Katrina a Super Storm?

As for widespread media claims that Katrina was a super storm created by global warming, scientists from the National Oceanic and Atmospheric Administration (NOAA) attribute the record number of hurricanes in the United States during 2005 to natural cycles in the tropics. Based on detailed weather records, there is a consensus among weather scientists that roughly every 20 to 30 years, there is an upsurge in hurricane activity, followed by a lull for a similar period. According to a statement issued by NOAA, natural weather cycles were responsible for "the increased Atlantic hurricane activity since 1995, and is not related to greenhouse warming."[20]

How does Katrina compare to other major hurricanes in the region? It was weaker. Katrina made landfall as a Category 4 with gusts in excess of 140 mph (225 kph). In 1969, Hurricane Camille roared onto the Mississippi coast as a Category 5, while in 1980, Hurricane Allen, another Category 5, came ashore near Brownsville, Texas. Both storms had sustained winds of 190 mph (306 kph).[21]

Never before have so many people been living so near to vulnerable coastal areas, resulting in ever-increasing damage amounts in the aftermath of storms. Much of the damage caused by Katrina was the result of human incompetence, apathy and neglect. How else can one explain why New Orleans, a coastal city below sea level and surrounded by a crumbling levee system, wasn't better prepared? It was a manmade disaster waiting to happen. Geographer Brian Handwerk concurs with this view: "Populations are concentrating along the world's coastlines — particularly in large urban areas. Improved forecasting and emergency response have lowered hurricane casualty rates, but as more people and infrastructure move into harm's way, storms are likely to become more destructive."[22]

As poorly as the media performed in the difficult days after Katrina, we should remember two key things. First, after reviewing what went wrong, no one was trying to deliberately deceive the public. Journalists were in a race to report what was happening, and in their haste, had to cut corners because they couldn't move about as easily as they ordinarily would, due to the breakdown in communications and difficulty in getting through floodwaters. Second and most important: The media eventually got the story right. Journalism instructor Poynter's Woods said it best: "Don't forget, the journalists kept reporting — the reason you know that things were reported badly is because the journalists told you."[23]

CHAPTER 11

Chicken Little and the Bird Flu Panic

> Many experts now believe that the global fear over an impending outbreak of avian influenza, which began in 2005, was mostly a media creation.

Starting in 2005, TV screens and newspapers around the world carried terrifying headlines of an imminent global catastrophe from a bird flu pandemic. Month after month, there were stories of some new outbreak and images of people in white "space suits" culling birds and spraying potentially infected areas. When the spread between humans didn't materialize, we were shown sensational TV movies like *Fatal Contact: Bird Flu in America*, first broadcast in May 2006. When ABC aired the movie, some states issued press releases cautioning residents about the alarmist nature of the movie. Epidemiologist Dr. Tracy Murphy called the movie "a work of fiction designed to entertain in a very dramatic fashion."[1] How dramatic? One man coughs so hard that his rib cartilage shreds! Another scene shows a landfill full of corpses.

Avian or bird flu occurs naturally in birds and, to a lesser extent, in other animals. Each year there are seasonal epidemics of influenza caused by substrains of flu viruses that are already circulating among the population. Pandemics are rare occurrences that take place when a new flu subtype emerges — one that has never circulated among humans or has not circulated for a long period, resulting in illness and death rates much higher than seasonal influenza.[2] In 1918–19, the world experienced a global pandemic of "Spanish flu" which killed an estimated 50 million people after spreading from birds to humans. Despite the media hype, an outbreak of bird flu is not necessarily just around the corner.

Since December 2003, there have been hundreds of cases of bird flu reported in humans, most after having contact with infected birds, usually chicken. While the transmission from birds to humans is rare, all flu viruses have the capacity to mutate into a new virus that spreads from person to person. Humans are susceptible to strains of bird flu as we have little immunity from them.[3] There were three flu pandemics during the 20th century: the "Spanish flu" after World War I, the "Asian flu" of 1957–58, and the "Hong Kong flu" of 1968–69, the latter two outbreaks being mild. The global death toll from the Asian flu was about a million, while the Hong Kong flu killed between one and four million.

Much Ado About Bird Flu

Several prominent scientists are critical of the sudden fear of a bird flu pandemic, which began in 2005. They believe that the likelihood of an outbreak was no greater than in previous years. Historian Paul Mickle cautions that there have been many past flu "epidemics" which failed to materialize such as the 1976 swine flu panic. At the time, leading health officials in the United States warned of an impending pandemic that could kill one million Americans. On February 6, 1976, 19-year-old Army private David Lewis died at Fort Dix, New Jersey, of what health officials later identified as a highly communicable variation of swine flu, triggering a global scare. Studies later revealed that 500 other recruits at Fort Dix had contracted the same flu strain, but none died or were even seriously ill. Private Lewis was the only official American death from swine flu that year, but ironically, dozens died from side effects during the vaccination program. The inoculations began on March 1 with the goal of injecting all 220 million Americans. The program was suspended by the government on December 16 after 40 million Americans had received shots. At that point, Americans feared the vaccine more than contracting the swine flu.[4]

Science writer Michael Fumento says that while no one can accurately predict when the next flu pandemic will occur, "there is never such a thing as helpful hysteria. And the line between informing the public and starting a panic is being crossed every day now by politicians, public health officials, and journalists."[5] The 2005 fear of bird flu had reached such alarmist levels that during a question-and-answer session on the safety of Thanksgiving turkeys and bird feeders, one American woman suggested killing all domestic birds and poisoning food along bird migration routes.[6]

A classic example of media hype surrounding the fear of bird flu is a *Reuters* headline proclaiming: "Flu Pandemic Could Kill 150 Million, U.N. Warns." The health authority cited in the story had stated that the death toll from a bird flu pandemic was between 5 and 150 million. Just how these figures were reached is unclear. Fumento says that such wildly disparate figures are tantamount to wild guesses. He blames his media colleagues for focusing on the more alarmist "experts."[7]

Fumento lists several "experts" who have helped to exaggerate the bird flu threat. Topping his list of "Chicken Littles" is Dr. Irwin Redlener, who heads the National Center for Disaster Preparedness at Columbia University. During a nationally televised interview on September 15, 2005, Redlener made the dramatic assertion that "we could have a billion people dying worldwide." When questioned later by Fumento, he qualified this claim by saying: "[O]ne billion ill." The same TV program introduced the topic with chilling words: "It could kill a billion people worldwide, make ghost towns out of parts of major cities, and there is not enough medicine to fight it.... It is called the avian flu."[8]

No one can predict the statistical probability of a bird flu outbreak in any given year. Contrary to popular belief, pandemics do not strike in predictable cycles. In fact, humans and sick birds have been mixing for years without a pandemic. Fumento observes that the bird flu virus (H5N1) was first identified in 1959 when it was found in a group of chickens in Scotland. Hence, "H5N1 has been flying around the globe for over four decades and hasn't done a number on us yet. That doesn't mean it won't ever; but there's absolutely no reason to think it will pick this year or next," he says.[9]

In October 2005, Pittsburgh microbiologist Dr. Henry Niman issued the following warning about the 2005 bird flu strain: "We've known about the seriousness of H5N1 mutations and different forms of the virus for some time. We've had avian flu before, but this year the situation is extremely critical for a variety of reasons, including the many different strains detected and the unusually high mortality rate for some of those strains." Dr. Niman's recommendation sounds like a script from a Hollywood film: "I would stock up on antiviral medication. Besides that, devise a plan to isolate yourself with enough food and water for an extended period of time."[10]

Dr. Niman and others have expressed concern over reports that thus far, avian flu in humans kills just over half of those they infect. This scary figure is in stark contrast to the Spanish flu which is estimated to have had a mortality rate of between 2.5 and 5 percent. Seasonal flu kills under one percent. These chilling figures are misleading. The small number of avian flu deaths thus far have occurred in poor countries with poor medical systems. Michael Fumento says the 50 percent mortality rate "comes from those ill enough to require medical attention — the sickest of the sick. Our experience with normal influenza is that many who become infected have no symptoms at all, nary a sniffle."[11] Wendy Orent, author of *Plague*, concurs: "We have no idea how many people in Asia contracted H5N1, came down with a mild infection, and became immune. Research from 1992 has shown that Asian chicken farmers have antibodies to many different forms of the H protein, including H5, in their blood."[12] University of Ottawa molecular virologist Earl Brown says that it is common for chicken farmers around the world to have antibodies to various bird flu strains.[13]

Orent says that from the standpoint of evolutionary biology, "the worst-case scenario — a lethal, transmissible, world-destroying flu — cannot happen, any more than Ebola or Marburg can steal out of the jungle and destroy the human race. If we have an H5N1 flu pandemic, which is certainly possible, we have no logical reason to believe it will be deadlier than the pandemics of 1957 and 1968." Orent believes the largest effects of the flu are fear and hysteria.[14]

British sociologist Frank Furedi says politicians are partly responsible for spreading the bird flu fear as a way to hedge their political bets so that in the unlikely event an outbreak were to occur, they cannot be accused of having not warned us. He cites statements by Great Britain's Chief Medical Officer, Sir Liam Donaldson, as illustrating his point about creating needless fear. Donaldson warned British citizens that a Bird Flu pandemic that will kill at least 50,000 citizens is inevitable, though he doesn't know exactly when. According to Furedi, "Donaldson knows that when he says that a flu pandemic is inevitable he will never be proved wrong. Such an unspecific warning about the risk of an avian flu that can mutate so it can spread easily between humans could have been made by chief medical officers in 1919 or 1920 or at any time since the 1918 influenza pandemic."[15]

Furedi says that even if 50,000 Britons were to die of bird flu, about 12,500 citizens die from the flu during a typical year, according to estimates by the British Department of Health. "It is estimated that during the 1989–90 epidemic around 30,000 people died from the flu. Not quite 50,000 — but near enough. Every single death is a personal tragedy. Which is why we can do without additional doom mongering," Furedi says.[16]

Dr. Marc Siegel of the New York University School of Medicine says that while the fear of bird flu is real, the likelihood of an outbreak in 2005 was exaggerated. "If anything is contagious right now, it's judgment clouded by fear."[17] Dr. Gary Butcher of the University of Florida's College of Veterinary Medicine concurs with Siegel's assessment of the threat. Butcher holds a doctorate in poultry virology and specializes in avian diseases. He calls the chances for an avian flu pandemic a long shot. "For it to become dangerous to humans, it has to go through a pretty significant genetic change. If you put this in perspective, it's not going to happen. For a person to be infected now, it appears that the exposure level has to be astronomical."[18]

The Internet has played a major role in accelerating the bird flu scare through the actions of bloggers — which one group of public health experts describe as "techno-agitators and armchair epidemiologists who see each new flu report or update as a call to arms, and use their blogs as a medium to inform and scare the daylights out of each other."[19] Bird flu bloggers typically contend that the mainstream media is doing an inadequate job of communicating the serious threat from the illness and vow to get the message out.

Even in the unlikely event that a bird flu outbreak were to occur in any given year, physician Marc Siegel points out that medicine is far more advanced than in 1918. "There were no vaccines for flu or antiviral drugs, no antibiotics or steroids to treat flu patients with pneumonia or asthma, no world-spanning public-health network."[20] Another difference from 1918: media tentacles which now reach to every corner of the world with alarmist images of impending bird flu Armageddon.

Chapter 12
The Russians Are Coming!

> In 2010, residents in former Soviet Georgia were sent fleeing into the streets after a state-run TV news show reported that Russian troops were pouring over the border.

On the evening of Saturday, March 13, 2010, residents in the former Soviet Republic of Georgia panicked, believing that their country was under attack by its Russian neighbors after state-run TV reported that Russian troops had crossed the border. The scare came at a time when tensions between Georgia and Russia were high; in August 2008 Russian troops launched an invasion of Georgia. The broadcast was successful in scaring many residents. The TV program was highly realistic and showed actual archival footage from the 2008 conflict, including comments by Russian President Medvedev and Prime Minister Vladimir Putin. There was also 2008 footage of Georgians fleeing for their lives. After showing pictures of Russian troops and tanks pouring across the border and planes dropping bombs in the capital, there was a shot of U.S. President Barack Obama calling on the Russians to cease hostilities — footage from the 2008 conflict.

The half-hour broadcast was aired on a Saturday night and later claimed to have been a "simulation" of what would likely happen if the Russians were to invade again. However, the program failed to include on-screen messages alerting viewers that the events were not happening. A disclaimer only appeared at the very start — which many viewers either missed or failed to notice — and at the end of the broadcast. Further heightening tensions, the announcer also claimed that the Georgian political landscape was in tatters after the president had been assassinated and the country's opposition had formed a provisional government that was pro–Russian and welcomed the invaders. The show included a news anchor providing "updates" on the latest position of Russian forces, who were said to have bombed the airport in the capital city of Tbilisi.

The head of the Georgian Orthodox Church, Patriarch Ilia II, was scathing in his criticism of the bogus attack. "This kind of experiment is a crime to our people and to humanity," he said. Meanwhile, a refugee of the 2008 war, Tamuna Okhadze, said: "People were in panic. Some people started getting dressed to flee to Tbilisi. People wondered where they should hide their children."

A spokesman for Georgian President Mikheil Saakashvili said that he was "very concerned and alarmed of what he saw on TV.... I understand the position of the journalists.... I understand that it is possible to make such projects, but it mustn't impact the population of the country. No one must pour oil on the fire and cause alarm among the people. This is a very sensitive topic." The president tried to defuse the situation by going to the studio after the broadcast to apologize to the nation in person. However, given the tightly controlled nature of state TV, some critics claimed that the president would have to have known of the program.[1] The Reuters news agency concurred, describing it as "a barely disguised swipe at opponents of Saakashvili who recently met Russian Prime Minister Vladimir Putin in Moscow and called for the countries to restore ties."[2] Indeed, the day after the broadcast, President Saakashvili seemed to back away from any apology, noting that the real enemy was the Russian government: "But the major unpleasant thing about the yesterday's report — and I want everyone to realize it well — was that this report is maximally close to reality and maximally close to what may really happen, or to what Georgia's enemy keeps in mind."

Sarah Marcus, a journalist based in Georgia, was in the heart of the scare, noting that news of the "invasion" spread quickly. "I heard when my neighbour, in a state of distress, knocked on my door to tell me about it, someone else saw people on street begin to run in panic, the mobile phone networks crashed as everyone tried to contact friends and family. The emergency services reported a peak in calls from people who'd suffered heart attacks." One of her friends have parents in Gori, hit hard during the 2008 war. The friend "and her brother frantically tried to work out how to gather enough money to get their parents out of the city by taxi — presuming taxis would already be charging rack rates to go in and out of Gori, as they did during the real war."[3]

The program began as follows: "Good evening. This is a breaking-news edition of *The Chronicle*. In a few minutes, President Saakashvili is expected to make a special statement on the situation in the country. We don't know if it's going to be a recorded or a written message. It's being reported that the Russian troops deployed at Leningor have been put on combat alert." A journalist in the capital during the broadcast, Matthew Collin, said that pandemonium followed: "People rushed out of cinemas. They rushed out of theaters. The mobile phone networks briefly crashed. Some people in the region where the war actually happened actually got ready to flee their homes yet again, and there were several reports of people having a heart attack."[4]

Chapter 13

The Video Nasties Scare

by Peter Hassall

> Violent, sadistic and perverted video films are as great a danger to a child's mind as any infectious disease is to the body. Yet, children are being exposed to them every day. High street retailers, so obsessed with profit that they have these films on their shelves, plumb the depths of greed ... these obscenities can be bought or hired in any town.
> —Daily Mirror *(London), November 25, 1983*

Decades before the appearance of violent TV shows featuring psychopaths like *Criminal Minds* and *Dexter*, England and New Zealand were in the grips of a media-generated fear about the effect of violent horror videos on youth. This chapter looks at how the video witch hunt started in the United Kingdom and spread to New Zealand, creating outrage and panic in conservative quarters.

Video players started to appear in homes in Western countries during the late 1970s. Before this time they were so expensive that only universities, TV stations and a few companies owned them. But by 1983, price wars and consumer demand created a boom in the number of machines appearing in homes. Video shops began popping up like mushrooms. They rented not only videos but also players to people who wanted to watch movies on video but did not have their own machine. For the first time, the average person could walk into a video shop and rent a range of movies — from classics to recent releases. Some films that had never been released in New Zealand were also available on video. Many were low-budget comedy, action and horror movies.

Peter Hassall *is a professional stunt performer and fight choreographer for television and films. He has appeared on such shows as* Crimewatch, The Tribe *and* Man's Work; *his film credits include* Brain Dead, The Warrior's Way, Separation City *and* The Water Horse. *Peter is the author of the UFO book,* The NZ Files *(Bateman, 1998).*

There was another benefit to the video revolution: If viewed in a private home, movies were not subject to New Zealand's strict film censorship laws. For example, the video release of Bruce Lee's 1973 classic *Enter the Dragon* was uncensored, yet the cinema version had almost five full minutes of bone-breaking fight scenes cut. New Zealand's chief film censor instructed to Warner Brothers to "delete all views where chain stick [nunchuk] is used ... reduce views of use of spiked claw hand by Han and also subsequent use of 4 bladed knife hand."[1] Ironically, you can now buy the uncut two-disc DVD edition for $10 in New Zealand.

The scare began in the early 1980s where was claimed that children were watching uncut horror movies containing scenes of extreme sadistic violence. These were given the nickname "video nasties." The British media frenzy about them reached a peak between 1983 and 1984. During this time, British sociologist Clifford Hill, an ordained minister concerned with protecting family and child values, claimed that more than 10 percent of children aged nine and ten had seen *Driller Killer* while over 3 percent had seen *Cannibal Holocaust*. He added that a "significant number of children of all ages reported that they had suffered nightmares which they attributed to watching video nasties."[2]

One writer observed that "it could be argued that it is less destructive for them [boys] to prove their emergent manhood by watching torture, than by crashing motorbikes or mugging or killing their first man by the age of 13, like Alexander the Great. Only I doubt it works like that. There is the desensitising process for a start. On a diet merely of cop thrillers from the United States, our family heard someone shot to death in the street and hardly reacted — we had heard too many shots on the telly before."[3]

Unverified claims became more extreme. One English survey given to parliament reported that 40 percent of six-year-olds had seen one or more horror films on video.[4] There are obvious flaws with this claim. Would children that young be telling the truth? Would they be able to accurately match a movie title with a memory of scenes they saw in a video? These are not frivolous questions. Some children may have ticked or circled as many titles as possible in an effort to please. There were five cannibal movies on the official British video nasties list — all with remarkably similar and likely confusing titles: *Cannibal Apocalypse*, *Cannibal Ferox*, *Cannibal Holocaust*, *Cannibal Man* and *Cannibal Terror*. One way to test the accuracy of such surveys would be to add in a few fictitious movie titles and see if any children claimed to have watched them. Guy Cumberbatch and Paul Bates did just that. They tested five classes of 11-year-olds with the same basic survey but with a few fake titles added such as *Vampire Holocaust* and *Zombies from Beyond Space*. Their finding: 68 percent of the children said they had seen one or more of the fictional titles.[5]

Gradually, the anti-video nasties movement in New Zealand gathered momentum. In January 1984, MP Paul East successfully persuaded four video stores in Rotorua to return their copies of *The Texas Chainsaw Massacre* to the distributor. Remarkably, East admitted he had not even seen the film.[6] A few months later delegates at the Women's Division of Federated Farmers waded into the controversy at their 69th jubilee conference in Rotorua. Spokeswoman Teresa Donaldson said: "I think it would be fair to say that our members would like to see stricter control of videos. Violence between men and women, and sadistic violence involving rock groups can be hired and viewed in any New Zealand living room without restriction."[7]

Trevor Morley, a Wellington security consultant and private investigator, showed a compilation of violent scenes from video nasties. About 50 of the 1,000 delegates left the screening in tears. Teresa Donaldson was typical, reacting with disgust: "I was shocked and still am. I just did not realise you could get that sort of thing."[8] The plan was to show the same compilation video to members of parliament, but the chief film censor, Arthur Everard, disagreed. Videos shown in private were one matter, but videos shown publicly had to be examined by the censor first. Everard said the video probably broke copyright laws. He also noted that "material that might be acceptable — but not desirable — in context would be repulsive with the sheer cumulative effect."[9] Morley voluntarily destroyed his copy of the video compilation, but the anti-video nasties steamroller ploughed on.

The Minister of Women's Affairs, Mrs. Hercus, believed all videos should be censored and some should be banned totally: "There are certainly two or three videos that I have seen — and I have not seen many — that I regard as totally degrading, particularly to women. I do not believe they should be available to anyone. While I understand the argument that says you cannot interfere in the privacy of what happens in a person's home, I believe there is another set of values that is as important — a community interest that says in a modern democratic society we should not portray women in filthy, degrading circumstances."[10]

The August issue of *Grapevine*, a monthly Christian family magazine distributed free to over a quarter of a million Auckland homes, had an emotive cover. Two young girls and a boy stare in shock at an unseen video. The accompanying article title is "Video Nasties: Loose in Your Living Room?" The content of the article was alarmist, noting that in some video shops "on the same shelves as Mickey Mouse and *The Sound of Music*, there are others that are sick and even downright savage.... On any given evening, adults who normally WOULDN'T— and kids who certainly SHOULDN'T— are treating their eyeballs and their memory-banks to movies that in many cases have never been permitted on a cinema screen (at least in their uncut version). These are the VIDEO NASTIES...." The magazine went on to assert just how easily children were seduced into watching these videos. "It's not hard to see how it happens. Your 10-year-old boy stays overnight with a friend and ends up watching *The Texas Chainsaw Massacre* while the adults are out at the pub. Your 13-year-old girl joins an end-of-term party at a nice home down the road only to be exposed to *Deep Throat* [a controversial pornographic film starring Linda Lovelace] as a late-night unscheduled 'treat' organized by some enterprising youngster."[11] The bulk of the article repeated rhetoric from Women Against Pornography, a group formed in January 1983 after a "Reclaim the Night" march. While their focus was banning pornography, WAP also opposed any depictions of violence against women — whether in sex, horror or crime movies.

Three months after their first failed attempt, opponents of video nasties made another effort to sway political opinion in parliament with another film of video violence highlights. This time it was created by an overseas expert, Chief Superintendent Peter Kruger, former head of Scotland Yard's obscene publications branch. He was flown to New Zealand by the Society for the Promotion of Community Standards to help them lobby against video nasties. SPCS was founded in 1970 by a former nun named Patricia Bartlett. Although mainly concerned with sexual content in magazines, in movies and on TV, SPCS has also tried to ban violent movies. Fundraising to fly in overseas "experts" on pornography and violence was a favorite tactic of SPCS. Local newspapers, radio stations and TV channels lapped it up every time. Drumming up a moral panic always proved to be a circulation and viewer booster for the media. Whether people agreed with the moralists or not, they were drawn to the articles and programs covering the controversy.

Kruger's compilation video had violent scenes collected from dozens of video nasties — titles such as *The Boogie Man, The Burning, Cannibal Holocaust, Don't Go in the Woods Alone, Don't Go Near the Park, The Evil Dead* (an early film made by the Spider-man trilogy director Sam Raimi), *The Exterminator, I Spit on Your Grave, Last House on the Left, Night of the Bloody Apes, The Texas Chainsaw Massacre, Tool Box Murders, Nightmares in a Damaged Brain, Snuff,* and *Zombie Flesh Eaters.* A similar compilation tape in England had been instrumental in swaying political opinion in favor of strict censorship controls on videos. Only a few people questioned the validity of doing this. Nigel Andrews, a film critic, commented: "It is extraordinary that MPs, who complain more vociferously than any other group in the community when they are quoted 'out of context,' can allow context to be thrown to the winds so thoroughly as this. If you gave me a pair of scissors, I could readily go through Alfred Hitchcock's oeuvre and blacken his name by compiling 20 minutes of highly gruesome Grand Guignol — and 20 minutes of gory foul play from Shakespeare's work, encompassing blindings and limb-loppings, would be even easier."[12] The highlights video had been sent in advance to the customs department and they passed it on to the film censor. Ironically, Everard refused to allow it to be shown in parliament due to the extreme violence and anti-social activities in it.[13]

Undeterred, SPCS and Kruger tried to arrange a screening of the movie *Driller Killer* in the Beehive theater but that would have cost more than they could afford in copyright fees. They then invited 28 MPs to a private screening in Kruger's hotel room. It would have been a very crowded screening if they had all turned up. Luckily, on the night only one MP, John Banks, watched the film. He later observed that "we can live without this sort of thing. I just feel that we have enough violence in our society."[14] *Driller Killer* was banned in England but in New Zealand it had been passed by the censor with an R18 rating including a warning about graphic violence. The low-budget film is about a man called Reno who lives in a squalid New York apartment. Driven crazy by the pressures of daily life, including the loud music of a punk band who are his neighbors, he vents his frustrations by using a power drill to kill drunks, the homeless and prostitutes on the streets at night. The real mystery is why he didn't kill the band members!

Was the film really as nasty and violent as Bartlett, Kruger, and Banks said? Two journalists, Colin Hogg and Marianne Norgaard, put the claim to the test and watched it. Colin Hogg found it boring: "I saw an ad for a truly terrific cordless (rechargeable) drill only the other week. So did the bloke in this video. Only he wanted to do something a bit different with his new discovery. He obviously hadn't read the instructions properly. Instead of boring handy holes for hanging curtain rails on, this odd-looking character bored holes into people's sensitive parts, convinced that he was part of some totally horrifying horror film. He wasn't. He was part of a very, very boring exploitation pic. A film so inept, so badly acted, so utterly boring, that it's no wonder when I rang my local video shop and asked to book it, they said they'd withdrawn it."[15] Norgaard found it similarly dull, noting that "it's a bit difficult to tell just what Reno's scene is because the screen has a habit of going blank every time Reno fires up his power drill. Or the director sets the scene in a dark, wet alley complete with flickering shadows and pseudo-artistic close-ups of Reno's face.... Reno's an adept killer, though, I'll give him that. He simultaneously manages to bore his victims into the pavement while he's boring us to death on the couch." She said that "the film is so cliché-ridden and badly produced, it's impossible to view it as anything other than pathetically ridiculous twaddle. It's even too absurd to rate as a cult movie."[16] Dan Cross, an Auckland video shop owner, agreed that it was badly made and far less graphic than some other video titles available. "All that publicity is the best thing that ever happened to *Driller Killer*. It used to be in the back of the shop, and it hardly went out at all. Now we have moved it out to the new release section and it goes out about three times a week."[17]

Finally, the video shops hit back at the horror video detractors. Dennis Amiss, the Video Retailers Association secretary, challenged claims that video nasties were available in *all* video rental shops. "Worse, that staff are permitting them to be hired out indiscriminately by minors. It is not our place to dictate what the public should have access to but to ensure that what is available is identified clearly and hired only to suitable age groups." He also pointed out that most of the video-nasty titles mentioned by Kruger had already been rejected by the Video Retailers Association on their own initiative. "That, together with the added protections of stringent indecency laws and a diligent Customs Department have kept this market virtually free of the really undesirable material."[18]

Countering the Video Retailers Association view, the Committee for Children called upon the government to classify and ban videos. According to Committee chair Areta Koopu: "The child's right to protection from harmful material far outweighs the individual adult's right to a completely free choice of entertainment. Classification will make it easier for responsible adults to protect children from unsuitable material. But video watching is a family activity and some children will see whatever is shown. We believe that, to provide a measure of protection for these children, tapes containing obscene material or wholly gratuitous violence should be banned."[19] Using the same line of reasoning, it could also be argued that the use of cigarettes, alcohol and adult books in the home should be banned outright as children may use or see them.

Kruger continued scare-mongering, claiming that in 1975 only 125 videos had been seized by police on obscenity grounds, but by 1983 the number had increased to 25,210, an impressive figure if true. He failed to mention that due to the increase in the number of titles available on video and the much larger number of copies needed to supply all the new video rental shops popping up, it was unlikely that the percentage of total videos that could be termed video nasties had increased. Here is a sample of Kruger's alarmist rhetoric: "The spread of video nasties in the United Kingdom was so quick and so alarming. We are now concerned about the copy cat syndrome — we're having the most brutal and violent incidents that we have ever known. At least once a month lawyers stand up in our courts and offer pleas of mitigation for clients charged with rapes, murder or sexual assaults on the grounds that the accused had been influenced by a video nasty.... Ordinary members of the public [were] coming to us, saying their children had seen these videos. They were concerned about it. Their children were getting them from any retail outlet. There were no restrictions."[20]

It is an easy option for a lawyer to suggest that an accused criminal was influenced by a violent film or TV show. It also allows viewers to give up all personal responsibility for their actions. In addition, there are no known instances of children running amuck with power drills after watching *Driller Killer* and killing pets, other children or adults. Many factors can influence people to act violently, from brain tumors to one's family and community environment, genetics, chemical imbalances in the brain, the use of drugs and alcohol, and so on. Logically, any of these factors acting on an individual over a period of many years would have a far greater effect than a few videos. For what Kruger said to be true about young children getting hold of and watching video nasties would have required a long chain of circumstances to work. The children would need enough money to rent the video. They would have to be away from home in the shopping area unsupervised by their parents. The video rental shop staff would have to knowingly and willingly rent the violent video to the unsupervised child. The parents would have to have failed to monitor what videos their children were watching and only discovered later what had been seen. Even if it actually did happen, a normal parent would be expected to take steps to ensure no repetition of the event occurred.

In England, videos were only banned or censored if they were seized by the police and prosecuted under the Obscene Publications Act. Kruger said it was a slow, frustrating process as "you can seize one video today but the retailers can get as many copies as they like by the next day."[21] Untrue. Police often used their powers under the Obscene Publications Act to seize (and later destroy) all copies of a book, magazine or video. This had serious economic consequences for wholesale distributors. If they chose to fight a seizure they then had to follow an expensive process to take the case to court. Very few of the smaller distributors — typically the ones who imported the low-budget horror movie titles — could afford to do that. Any retail outlet would write off the loss rather than spend hundreds of times the value of the lost stock to go to court. "The media started to get complaints and the public became more and more concerned. Parliament started to get more and more concerned, too. I had prepared a video tape of snippets of video nasties and I showed it to MPs who were absolutely horrified at what they saw. And, of course, they called for legislation. Finally, in June 1984 the Video Recordings Act was created," recalled Kruger.[22] In other words, the British equivalent of the SPCS (Mary Whitehouse and her National Viewers' and Listeners' Association — still going after her death in 2001) complained to the media, the media sensationalized the situation, and the public became alarmed and called for a tightening of the law. What was happening in New Zealand was an exact parallel. Kruger stated, "It is not for me to tell you what to do. I'm not going to encourage anybody. I'm going to state what our law was and describe the new law. The police do not want to be drawn into an argument about censorship. We do not want to be seen as the guardians of public morals. The new law was promoted by public opinion. The police only responded to that opinion. They highlighted the problem and helped with publicity. The police are not here to say you can't smoke cannabis, drink beer or whatever. The police do not decide public morals. It is not a role we would want to be identified with. We would sooner have the public or someone like your Miss Bartlett involved with that."[23] He was, however, doing exactly the opposite of what he was saying. Kruger had been bought and paid for by a conservative moralistic lobby group to push their agenda. Their efforts soon bore fruit.

By the end of the year parliament was set to rush through a video classification act that would ban the worst titles and censor and classify the rest. As the *New Herald* reported on December 13, 1985: "The labelling will indicate, by a simple rating system, the audience for which the recording is suitable. The label will also give a description of the contents similar to those which the chief censor gives to films available for public exhibition."[24] On July 1, 1987, the Video Recordings Act, still in effect now, became law.

The video nasties scare is not the only media-fueled moral panic of this type. Since 1975, there has been widespread alarm over the amount of sex, violence and bad language that teenagers and younger children have been exposed to in a variety of mediums, including video arcade games, handheld console games, PC games, the Internet, music (both records and CDs), comics and graphic novels, cell phones with cameras, and even bubblegum cards!

Media-driven moral panics are nothing new. The following quote could easily have come from the mid–1980s video nasties scare: "Before these children's eyes with heartless indiscriminate horrors unimaginable are ... presented night after night.... Terrific massacres, horrible catastrophes, motor-car smashes, public hangings, lynchings.... All who care for the moral well-being and education of the child will set their faces like flint against this new form of excitement." In fact, it is from an article about the latest form of public entertainment — movies at cinemas. The quote is now almost a century old — from *The Times* on April 12, 1913.

British sociologist Geoffrey Pearson traces the origins of moral panics about popular culture back many centuries.[25] In the 1960s and 1970s the concern was about TV shows and superhero comics. In the 1950s it was rock 'n' roll music, jukebox joints, and comic books about horror and true crime. During the 1930s there were widespread fears about copycat crimes caused by watching cinema movies. In 1938 one psychiatrist confidently stated that "seventy percent of all the crimes were first conceived in the cinema." A 70-year-old magistrate who boasted he had never been to see a film believed "these lads go to the pictures and see daredevil things, and they are imitating them."

In the 1890s and early 1900s, Pearson found that popular music hall entertainments were blamed for encouraging crime and immorality. During the 1840s and '50s "penny gaff" theaters and "two-penny hop" dancing saloons were claimed to have done the same. Even in the 1770s, there was concern about debasing amusements, deficiencies in parental authority, and luxury and idleness among the commoners resulting in "the host of thieves which has of late years invaded us." Newspapers were also viewed in some quarters as leading to moral decline by describing "scenes of villainy" which were considered harmful.

The year 1751 was characterized by "too frequent and expensive Diversions among the lower kind of People" had "almost totally changed the Manners, Customs and Habits of the people, more especially of the lowest Sort." In the 1500s and 1600s Pearson found that "popular songs too often presented criminals as heroes." Watch out, Robin Hood. To the above listing should be added the infamous Grand Guignol theater of Paris. Nightly, from 1897 until 1962, people from across Paris gathered to watch as "screaming heroines were lowered into acid vats, as eyeballs were slowly and horribly bisected by long silver blades, as bodies were torn limb from limb, spraying scarlet freshets of blood in all directions. The victims of these indignities were not really hurt, of course, but night after night they tried very hard, with the help of ingenious special effects and gallons of fake blood, to make the audience believe that the shocking torture taking place on the stage was really happening. The killers and victims were actors."[26] The theater was opened in the Pigalle section of Paris and was named after a traditional French puppet character called Guignol. Founder Oscar Méténier hoped to make it the premier venue for naturalist plays. This type of play strove for absolute realism; they usually dealt with prostitutes and criminals. Each night audiences witnessed half a dozen short plays that ran the gamut from crime dramas to sex farces. Horror plays were only a small portion of the total but they quickly became the biggest draw. According to Jenny Ashford: "Equally important to the horror plays' popularity was the dedication of the actors — Paula Maxa in particular was a big draw, as she suffered rape, torture and bloody murder thousands of times beginning in 1917. But probably the biggest attraction for Paris audiences — much like horror fans of today — was the gore. Technicians at the Grand Guignol used every trick at their disposal — fake blood, collapsing knife blades, tubes, dummies and trapdoors — to make the audience believe they were seeing real death and dismemberment occurring before their eyes.[27] Attendances at the Grand Guignol theater declined during the World War II era (1939–1945) as the real-life horrors of war took precedence. By 1962 their doors had shut. Today there are several groups that have revived the tradition of bloody theater, among them the Queens Players, Thrillpeddlars, Molotov Theatre group, and Circus of Horrors.

If the "moral police" are to be believed, even the great man himself—William Shakespeare (1564–1616)—must shoulder some of the blame for bawdy and violent entertainment that incited the so-called lower classes. His most infamous play, *Titus Andronicus*, was written in the early 1590s. The most accessible version of it is *Titus*, a 1999 film adaptation starring Anthony Hopkins. Director Julie Taymor stayed true to the gore and violence of the original play. A 1955 newspaper article about a London stage production of *Titus Andronicus* makes for interesting reading. A combination of gore and realistic sound effects (e.g., when Titus saws through his own hand) had audience members fainting in droves. Two ambulance staff attended each session to handle up to a dozen fainting audience members every night. Many of the 1,400 patrons at each performance calmed their shattered nerves in the theater bar afterwards. Said one theater official: "There certainly is a realistic noise, and Sir Lawrence Olivier gives a terrifying impression of a man in agony. But the play is a smash hit all the same. Tone it down? Nonsense. In 1923, when it was shown at the Old Vic, they never considered it a good night unless at least 10 fainted."[28]

As the old saying goes, there is nothing new under the sun, and inevitably every new form of popular public entertainment causes a new media scare. My prediction is that within ten years 3D movies and TV shows will get the blame for an increase in violence and perceived lowering of public moral standards. In the words of anthropologist Philip Bock: "Man: maker of tools, rules, and moral judgements."[29]

Section Three

It Came from Ink — Newspapers

Chapter 14

The Batmen on the Moon Hoax

In 1835, a New York newspaper succeeded in convincing many people that that the moon was inhabited by an array of strange creatures. Tabloid journalism was born.

Anyone taking Propaganda 101 has heard of the Big Lie theory. Adolf Hitler popularized the term in his 1925 autobiography, *Mein Kampf* or *My Battle*. Hitler wrote that the Germans were deceived into believing they had lost World War I because the country's press, which was disproportionately comprised of Jews, distorted the truth to mislead the public with a colossal lie. In short, Hitler believed that the bigger the lie, the more likely people are to believe it. Of course, the Big Lie theory is a bit more complicated than this. People won't believe just anything. It must be plausible.

In the summer of 1835, a prominent New York newspaper editor and his star journalist may not have had a name for it, but they practiced the Big Lie to perfection. The editor of the *New York Sun*, Benjamin Day, and reporter Richard Adams Locke hatched a plot intended to boost the paper's sales. Locke was a brilliant writer with a remarkable imagination. He also had impeccable credentials, being a Cambridge graduate and an amateur scientist. He was a knowledgeable astronomer, a fact that plays prominently in this story. Day was an exceptional editor. Together, they concocted a series of stories about the discovery of strange creatures on the moon.

The idea that the moon could be inhabited was well established at the time. However unlikely, the seeds of such a possibility had been sown in the popular imagination. Four years after the death of astronomer and mathematician Johannes Kepler in 1630, *Somnium* (*The Dream*) was published. It tells the story of traveling to the moon on a shadow bridge and discovering inhabitants.[1] In 1638, Francis Goodwin's influential *The Man in the Moone* appeared, about a man, Domingo Gonzales, who is carried to the moon by domesticated geese and meets a race of giants.² In 1827, George Tucker's book *A Voyage to the Moon* told of a trip in a small, cube-shaped copper vessel, where he finds a bustling civilization of Lunarians.³ Among the most notable writers on this topic was seventeenth-century French writer Cyrano de Bergerac, who, in the well-known story, floated to the moon while holding flasks with dew heated by the sun.⁴

Like most good hoaxers, Locke and Day slowly strung along their unsuspecting prey. The deception began on Friday, August 21, when *The Sun* published a brief account under the bland heading "Celestial Discovery," which they reportedly reprinted from *The Edinburg Courant*. Quoting excerpts from other papers was a common practice at the time and would have seemed perfectly normal. "We have just learnt from an eminent publisher in this city that Sir John Herschel at the Cape of Good Hope, has made some astronomical discoveries of the most wonderful description, by means of an immense telescope of an entirely new principle.'" The article was short, credible, and left the reader wanting more. Dry and unsensational, the account was unlike the *Sun*, which made its reputation on printing stories on murder, crime, corruption and scandal intended for working-class readers, and all for just a penny. As someone wrote: "If it bled, it led at the *Sun*."⁵ The sly Day placed the article on page two so as not to arouse too much suspicion. As for what these wonderful new discoveries were, it did not say. The article coincided with Herschel's well-publicized expedition to South Africa which he undertook the previous year in order to use his powerful new telescope that was being set up at a Cape Town observatory. The bait had been laid and the stage was set for one of the greatest press hoaxes of the nineteenth century.

For three days, the paper kept silent. Then on Tuesday, August 25, a lengthy article appeared describing Herschel's telescope in great technical detail. Clearly, Locke and Day were trying to establish credibility. They did so superbly by including minute details. For instance, the telescope was said to weigh 14,826 pounds and have the capacity to magnify objects 42,000 times.⁶ The article included scientific jargon, as well as what were purportedly excerpts from the snobbish-sounding *Edinburgh Journal of Science*— the name of a real journal that had ceased publication years earlier. Few readers would have known this, and, even if they had, they couldn't be certain the journal was not back in publication. Such was life in 1835, before the advent of the transatlantic cable, Morse Code or the telephone. Unlike today, one could not simply pick up a phone or search the Internet to confirm these claims. Verification was much slower.

The second installment announced to the world that Herschel had discovered life on the moon. Continuing to use dry, scientific language, there are descriptions of lush vegetation and rocks of great beauty, followed by an even more fantastic claim — the discovery of various animals including a bluish-gray creature the size of a goat, a powerful looking bison-like mammal, and an array of colorful birds. "In the shade of the woods on the south-eastern side, we beheld continuous herds of brown quadrupeds, having all the external characteristics of the bison, but more diminutive than any species of the *bos genus* in our natural history. Its tail is like that of our *bos grunniens*; but in its semi-circular horns, the hump on its shoulders, and the depth of its dewlap, and the length of its shaggy hair."[7] It all sounded so scientific and plausible.

On August 27, Herschel classified nine separate types of mammals, including a creature that looked like a two-legged beaver. "The last resembles the beaver of the earth in every other respect than in its destitution of a tail, and its invariable habit of walking upon only two feet. It carries its young in its arms like a human being, and moves with an easy gliding motion. Its huts are constructed better and higher than those of many tribes of human savages, and from the appearance of smoke in nearly all of them, there is no doubt of its being acquainted with the use of fire. Still its head and body differ only in the points stated from that of the beaver, and it was never seen except on the borders of lakes and rivers ... [where it] has been seen to immerse for a period of several seconds."[8]

His most astonishing observation came on the fourth day when flocks of human forms could be seen flapping about with bat-like wings. The creatures were given the scientific name of *Vespertilio-homo* meaning bat-man. These angelic beings were peacefully coexisting with their fellow creatures in an environment apparently absent of carnivores. The pretentious yet plausible scientific description of these strange creatures continued: "We could then perceive that they possessed wings of great expansion, and were similar in structure to this of the bat, being a semi-transparent membrane expanded in curvilineal divisions by means of straight radii, united at the back by the dorsal integuments."[9] What a remarkable imagination. Locke went on to describe great oceans and vast land masses,[10] providing his final installment on Monday, August 31.[11] In this article readers were told that the reflection chamber was damaged and further observations were not possible. By the time the series ended, the *Sun*'s circulation had soared to 19,360, making it the highest circulation of any paper in the world.[12]

During the affair, rival newspaper editors who were frantically trying to confirm the claims were faced with a dilemma: missing out on one of the greatest stories in recorded history — or being part of a monumental embarrassment if it proved untrue. They could not wait the several weeks it would have taken to contact Herschel who was incommunicado in South Africa, so many editors and publishers took a gamble and reprinted the story on their front pages.[13] Even the mighty *New York Times* was hoodwinked, remarking that the writer "displays the most extensive and accurate knowledge of astronomy, and the description of Sir John's recently improved instruments ... [and] the account of the wonderful discoveries on the moon, &c., are all probable and plausible, and have an air of intense verisimilitude."[14] Locke soon published the articles in a pamphlet that sold sixty thousand copies within a month to meet the public's insatiable appetite for the story.[15]

The bubble burst when the New York–based *Journal of Commerce* newspaper revealed that Locke had admitted to fabricating the series while drinking with a friend who worked for the *Journal*.[16] The paper's editor would have relished this role of deflating the hoax as they had a fierce, ongoing rivalry.

A bat-like creature resembling those reported on the moon — according to the editors of the *New York Sun* in 1835.

Ever stubborn, Day steadfastly refused to acknowledge the deception. On September 16, 1835, Day published the following editorial in *The Sun*: "Certain correspondents have been urging us to come out and confess the whole to be a hoax; but this we can by no means do, until we have testimony of the Scottish or English papers to corroborate such a declaration. In the meantime, let every reader of the account examine it, and enjoy his own opinion." When word of the episode finally reached Herschel, he erupted with laughter.[17]

The episode is noteworthy in that it may mark the beginning of modern tabloid journalism.[18] True, earlier papers had printed fabricated articles, but none on such a grand scale; this was a series of stories, no less — one designed to boost circulation. But was it sustainable? A year after the moon hoax, the *Sun*'s readership was at a record 27,000 copies per day, nearly 6,000 more than at the height of the hoax.[19]

The hoax was successful because it offered its prime readership — struggling, working-class New Yorkers living in squalor — hope that there was a better life out there by giving them a glimpse of a utopian world on the moon.[20] In short, they wanted to believe so much that they placed hope over reason. In the words of newspaper historian Paul Maliszewski: "They trusted that science made such discoveries possible. They hoped that these wild fancies might one day be matched by reality. And they had faith that ahead lay progress.... All told, they were easy marks."[21]

CHAPTER 15

The Central Park Zoo Panic

> Well over a century later, the *New York Herald* hoax of 1874 — far from a malicious prank — still ranks among the greatest newspaper hoaxes of all time. The debate continues as to whether the *Herald* was justified in publishing its story of mayhem in the streets.

As New Yorkers rubbed sleep from their eyes and began to read their home-delivered edition of the *New York Herald* on the chilly Monday morning of November 9, 1874, there were gasps and raised eyebrows across the city. The *Herald* told of a city under siege after dozens of wild animals had escaped from the Central Park Zoo. New York City was said to be under a state of emergency with National Guard Troops patrolling the streets — or so readers were led to believe. In reality, the streets were calm and the only animals in sight were horses pulling carriages; the article with its scare headline, "Awful Calamity: The Wild Animals Broken Loose from Central Park," was a hoax. Among the many startled residents was the paper's editor, Gordon Bennett, who had no forewarning that the story was to appear.[1]

The account described a scene of chaos and confusion. As of press time, the death toll stood at 49, with another 200 or more injured — many in grave condition. The report said that many ferocious animals had escaped from the zoo owing to its flimsy cages.[2]

The story had a powerful effect on readers. It seemed plausible as safety concerns over the zoo had been widely discussed for years. An editorial in a rival of the *Herald*, the *New York Times*, noted that such a catastrophe "was not altogether unlikely to happen," as the zoo had "the flimsiest cages ever seen."[3]

The *Herald* article was written for maximum shock value. It described a number of attacks in vivid, gruesome detail. One eyewitness told of watching in horror as four small children were ripped to pieces by a lion. Another witness gave an on-the-scene account of a lion "tugging and crunching at the arms and legs of a corpse, now letting go with his teeth to plant his paws upon the bleeding remains, and snap with his dripping jaws at another beast." No one who read the story and believed it was genuine could fail to be moved by it. Other descriptions were equally sickening.

The scene near the zoo was nothing short of carnage as an onlooker told how several animals fought over the lifeless body of zookeeper Hyland Anderson, who was being tossed about like a rag doll. The witness said the breakout happened when Anderson prodded a rhinoceros which then turned on him. "But I could see nothing more than a mingling, gleaming mass, whence arose the most awful cries. Near to me, where Hyland lay, the lioness, the panther, the puma, and presently the Bengal tiger, were rolling over and over, striking at each other with their mighty paws.... I could not help look at Lincoln, the lion.... 'By God, he's looking at me!' I said to myself. I saw him crouch. I turned and ran.... I saw a young man fall from a blow of the awful paw, another crushed to earth beneath the beast's weight."[4]

In their shock and disgust, many people failed to read the entire story. If they had, they would have discovered that the story was a hoax intended to jolt New Yorkers out of their apathy to do something about the poor state of the Central Park Zoo before a real disaster occurred, or so readers were told in the last paragraph: "Of course the entire story given above is a pure fabrication. Not one word of it is true. Not a single act or incident described has taken place. It is a huge hoax, a wild romance, or whatever other epithet of utter untrustworthiness our readers may choose to apply to it."[5] The editor of the *New York Times* attacked the *Herald*, labeling the incident "intensely stupid and unfeeling."[6] Newspapers across the country gave similar opinions. *The Morning Oregonian* branded the stunt as among the most "outrageous practical jokes ever perpetrated."[7] In Texas, *The Galveston Daily News* said the incident was "all a huge sell" in order to boost circulation.[8]

The hoax was the idea of the paper's managing editor, T.B. Connery, who later discussed the incident in considerable detail. Connery said he thought of the scheme while at the zoo one day, and through the carelessness of the handlers, an animal nearly escaped. Connery said he felt obligated to do something to publicize his concerns and was initially going to write an editorial scolding the handlers but soon thought better of it. "What would be the use of a little scolding and a few warnings? The menagerie men would only be a little more careful for a while and then relapse into their old habits.... The public would soon forget all about it." Connery sketched out the idea of the hoax article, then gave the draft to a talented fellow writer by the name of J.I.C. Clarke, who later became a prominent New York editor.[9]

Was the *Herald* justified in creating a fictional story in an effort to get the public to take notice of what was widely deemed to be a public danger? Is a newspaper ever justified in creating hoaxes? Whether intended to be in the public's interest or not, planting hoax stories can pose risks. In neighboring New Jersey, *The Plainfield Times* reported that one of its best-known residents, Henry Martin, grew distraught while reading the article, was stricken with a heart seizure and died. There is always the danger of unintended consequences and danger in trying to anticipate the reaction to alarmist hoaxes. Perhaps the greatest risk is to the newspaper itself, in losing the trust of its readers. Once a business or institution loses its credibility, it is difficult to get it back. The *Herald* survived the zoo scare relatively unscathed. The editor had rolled the dice and won — this time.

Three months later the *Chicago Times* perpetrated a similar hoax, claiming that they too did it to heighten public awareness of fire traps. The imaginary inferno was blamed on a greedy owner who had placed profit ahead of people by allowing too many patrons to crowd in a building that was inadequately designed, and was a disaster waiting to happen. The article was highly realistic and even printed over 100 names of supposed victims — a practice that would be deemed immoral by any modern-day standards of journalistic decency.

The hoax was widely viewed as outrageous at the time and, in terms of sheer scale, outdid even the zoo scare. The editor of the *Fort Wayne Sentinel* called the hoax "brutal," while the *Decatur Daily Republican* labeled the affair "silly and heartless," noting that the paper had not only damaged its reputation, but lost revenue from angry readers canceling their subscriptions.[10] The story eroded the credibility of the paper. On the surface it would appear to have been a clear-cut case of media exploitation — drumming up interest in the paper by creating an alarming hoax.

Regardless of the real motives of the *Chicago Times* editor, history is on his side. On December 30, 1903, a total of 571 people perished after being packed into the overcrowded Chicago Iroquois Theater with several blocked exits; thirty-one others later died from their injuries. Ironically, most people did not die from the flames or even the smoke, but from being trampled to death in the stampede to get out. The panic began when patrons were unable to open the exit doors that had frozen shut from sub-zero temperatures outside. The theater owner had neglected to ensure that they were able to be opened in an emergency. One writer described the horror, noting that in some stairways, "particularly where a turn caused a jam, bodies were piled ever or eight feet deep.... An occasional living person was found in the heap, but most of these were terribly injured. The heel prints on the dead faces mutely testified to the cruel fact that human animals stricken by terror are as mad and ruthless as stampeding cattle."[11] When architect Benjamin Marshall toured the remains of the theater, he remarked: "I cannot understand it at all," noting that "the theater was fireproof."[12] But no building is fireproof when it comes to human error. The *Chicago Times* article had proved to be prophetic.

Chapter 16
The Halley's Comet Scare of 1910

> In 1881, astronomers discovered the presence of deadly cyanogen gas in the tails of comets. When it was later determined that Earth would pass through the tail of Halley's Comet on its next fly-by, newspapers fueled fears of doom and gloom.

The return of Halley's Comet on May 18, 1910, had been eagerly awaited for decades. Since its last appearance in 1835, astronomers had determined that the comet's trajectory would take its tail through Earth's atmosphere. No one had taken much notice of this finding until early February when the *Washington Post* and the *New York Times* published alarmist articles on the likelihood of Earth being poisoned by the comet's tail.

On February 6, the *Post* reported that French astronomer and popular writer Camille Flammarion was fearful that cyanogen gas in the comet's tail could poison the atmosphere. And while the views of skeptical colleagues were given, the article said: "On the other hand ... there is a large quantity of cyanogen gas in the atmosphere surrounding Halley's Comet.... A mixture of this gas with air would lead to certain poisoning."[1] The article ends with a warning from French astronomer M. Armand Gautier, who worried about a possible explosion, noting that, "in the presence of fire or a small electric spark, a mixture of cyanogen gas and air will explode."[2] Despite the presentation of opposing views, one could not read the article without some trepidation.

The next day a more chilling account appeared on the front page of *The New York Times*, reporting that astronomers at the University of Chicago's Yerkes Observatory had identified poison gas in the comet.[3] The anonymous writer noted that cyanogen was so potent that if "a grain of its potassium salt touched to the tongue ... [it was] sufficient to cause instant death." The article conveyed an image of growing alarm by astronomers. "The fact that cyanogen is present in the comet ... is causing much discussion as to the probable effect on the earth. Prof. Flammarion is of the opinion that the cyanogen gas would impregnate the atmosphere and possibly snuff out all life on the planet."[4] The article was misleading in that it gave the impression that Flammarion and other colleagues at Yerkes took the threat seriously. In reality, it was only Flammarion. While it was pointed out that his was a minority view, it must have been unsettling.[5] Flammarion soon recanted his position, though it received less press fanfare. Realizing its mistake, the *Times* quickly published an editorial aimed at reducing anxiety generated by the original story. It confidently proclaimed that the earth could pass through a dozen comet tails without any effect. But it was too late. The damage was done.[6]

Other newspapers and magazines soon followed with their own discussions of possible comet doomsday, seemingly providing balanced coverage of the case both for and against. The trouble was that the case for cometary Armageddon was not based on good science, and presenting this possibility as realistic was both misleading and irresponsible.

Less than a week before the comet was to pass closest to earth, the *Washington Post* was still generating anxiety by referring to the inexact nature of astronomy when it comes to understanding comets: "Comet Quits Its Path. Wanders from Predicted Orbit; Surprises May Follow." The sub-heading was even more alarming: "Poison in Its Tail Again. Cyanogen, Which Disappeared in March, Is Now Revealed by Spectroscope. Prof. Deslandres Says Hypothesis That Gas Is Liable to Affect the Earth's Atmosphere Is Not at All Absurd." The article cites French astronomer Maurice Hamy of the Paris Observatory, who noted that the comet's tail had "increased from five to ten degrees in three days." The implication was clear: With a bigger tail, the earth could expect to be exposed to more poison gas. As if this wasn't enough, Dr. Deslandres of the University of Dijon said he could not assure the public that cyanogen would not impact life on Earth, while his colleague, B.M. Marchand warned: "[T]he comet shows important variations from its predicted orbit, which presage unexpected surprises."[7]

On May 14, *Harper's Weekly* offered readers radically different views on the projected impact of earth's rendezvous with Halley's Comet. Astronomer D.J. McAdam of Washington and Jefferson College discussed possible disaster scenarios, including comet gases penetrating the atmosphere and making people sick. "When we pass through its tail in May we will be in a stream of hydrogen, probably mixed with marsh gas and other cometary gases. Disease and death have frequently been ascribed to the admixture of cometary gases with the air. Enough of such gases as are in the comet's tail would be deleterious." This assertion, without a shred of scientific merit, was a rosy scenario compared to a second possibility discussed by McAdam: the explosion theory. English astronomer Richard Proctor once speculated that if a comet with a hydrogen-dense tail were to pass through Earth's oxygen-rich atmosphere, it could spark a cataclysmic explosion "leaving the burnt and drenched Earth no other atmosphere than the nitrogen now present in the air, together with a relatively small quantity of deleterious vapors."[8] In discussing Proctor's theory, McAdam failed to tell readers that this hypothesis had long been discredited. While the *Harper's* editor was no expert in astronomy, he could have, but chose *not* to, tone down the claims. As the old journalistic saying goes: "Why let the facts get in the way of a good story?" Especially when it helps to boost magazine sales.

Reaction in the United States

On the evening of Wednesday, May 18, Eastern Standard Time, Earth was projected to pass through the comet's tail, though most scientists agreed that any poisonous substances would be so rarefied that the atmosphere would not be affected.[9] In fairness, most people did not panic or become terrified, and many attended comet parties, drinking champagne into the early morning hours. Yet, a relatively small portion of the population were clearly frightened by the alarmist stories. If just one percent of the population were affected, this would translate into roughly 900,000 people as the population of the United States in 1910 was 92 million. Some fearful citizens went so far as to stuff rags in doorways and keyholes.

In Lexington, Kentucky, it was reported that "excited people are tonight holding all-night services, praying and singing to prepare ... [to] meet their doom."[10] In North Carolina, there were similar scenes among African American farm laborers.[11] In numerous communities in western Georgia, the reaction was similar.[12] Meanwhile, thousands of mostly foreign miners in Wilkes-Barre, Pennsylvania, refused to go underground, instead demanding to spend what they thought may be their last hours alive in prayer. Miners near Denver, Colorado, took the opposite strategy, going back into the mines in hopes of avoiding or limiting their exposure to the comet's tail.[13]

Many people took advantage of the scare to sell "comet pills" that were said to protect against cyanogen. In Texas, two salesmen recruited agents to go door to door selling the pills and leather inhalers. The men were arrested, but the sheriff soon let them go when no one would testify against them. Their release may have had something to do with the angry mob that formed outside the courthouse — intent on releasing the men so they could buy their pills and breathing apparatuses.[14] In parts of New York City, "comet pills" were selling briskly at a dollar apiece. Arguably the worst case of exploitation occurred in the rural Towaco, New Jersey, where two gentlemen convinced the local populace that they were scientists intent on studying the comet. They asked residents to write descriptions of the event and said they could get the best view at 3 A.M. on May 19 on Walkman Mountain. They offered prizes ($10, $5 and $2.50) for the top three descriptions. The night proved disastrous. First, heavy fog rolled in, making viewing impossible. Then, by the time the weary residents had reached their homes in the early morning, they found empty chicken coops and hundreds of missing birds.[15] While residents cried foul, the perpetrators were nowhere to be seen.

The Global Reaction

A similar drama was unfolding in other parts of the globe, including major panics in Russia and Japan. In Bermuda, a former British colony, upon the report of the death of King Edward VII, some citizens said the comet's head flared and the tail turned red. Dock workers promptly "fell on their knees and began to pray. They thought that the end of the world was surely coming" and refused to work.[16] The workers were adamant that the observation was a portent that war would occur during the reign of the new king, George. They were also convinced that a great disaster would strike Earth. "They were speechless with fear and worked themselves up in their paroxysms of religious zeal to a ... frenzy."[17] The men only returned to work after the comet had faded from view in the morning sunlight. There were even several reported suicides in different countries due to the comet's appearance.[18] In San Juan, Puerto Rico, hundreds marched in a candlelight parade through the streets and sang religious songs.[19]

In Italy, Pope Pius X called on people to stop hoarding oxygen cylinders.[20] It was reported that not a single Rome pharmacy had an oxygen tank on hand as they "had all been taken by persons in splendid health who had been frightened lest the fumes of the gasses from the comet should choke them."[21] France also saw the hoarding of oxygen as private residents placed them in the cellars which were then sealed off in hopes of keeping the poisonous cyanogen at bay.[22] Those living in the rural areas seemed to be more anxious, though much of the country celebrated with "comet suppers" and "comet balls." The mood in Madrid, Spain, was festive, though the skies were cloudy.[23] While oxygen cylinders were on hand in some London homes, most residents were in a mood to celebrate. The party atmosphere was true in many British cities. Festive comet gatherings were the order of the day in Germany where people sported everything from comet hats to comet umbrellas and even brands of alcohol.[24] In Switzerland, parties were held through the night.[25]

In parts of South Africa, the comet fostered "an extraordinary amount of nervousness," as one man placed a newspaper ad reading: "Gentleman having secured several cylinders of oxygen and having bricked up a capacious room wishes to meet others who would share the expense for Wednesday night. Numbers strictly limited."[26] In Russia, many St. Petersburg residents spent the night of May 18 praying somberly in churches.[27] Crucifixes could be seen on the hilltops around Mexico City as prayer vigils were held, in some cases, ten days prior in an effort "to avert the impending disaster with music, incantations, and weird ceremonies." When the morning sun broke over the horizon the next day, the masses celebrated with feasts and dancing, believing their actions had saved earth from the comet's harm.[28]

The newspaper medium is a business. The ultimate goal is to sell papers and turn of profit. Too often, this is achieved by hyperinflating the news, especially threats. The history of newspapers is the history of hyperinflation. This is no more evident than in the 1910 saga of Halley's Comet. One is reminded of the words of Frank McKinney Hubbard: "Tain't what a man don't know that hurts him; it's what knows that just ain't so!" Yes, and don't believe everything you read.

CHAPTER 17

How the Press Created an Imaginary Terrorist

> In 1944, a single newspaper article about the dubious existence of a "mad gasser" spraying people with a noxious chemical spawned dozens of imaginary attacks — underscoring the power of the press.

The saga of the "mad gasser" of Mattoon began in the fall of 1944. On Friday night, September 1, a housewife named Aline Kearney retired to her bedroom with her three-year-old daughter Dorothy around 11:00 P.M., in Mattoon, a small city in eastern Illinois. Aline's husband Bert was driving a taxi. Her sister Martha was awake in a front room while Aline's other daughter and Martha's son slept in a back room. Suddenly Aline noticed a sickeningly sweet smell. She thought it might be coming from a gardenia flowerbed near her open bedroom window, but couldn't be sure. She summoned Martha. "Can you smell that?" "What is it?" Martha couldn't smell a thing and soon bid Aline pleasant dreams.

As Aline lay in bed trying to sleep, the scent grew stronger and stronger. Her throat and lips began to feel dry and burning, and there was a paralyzing sensation in her legs. "Martha! Martha! Come here." Martha rushed to the bedroom. "I feel strange. Something's wrong with me. It must be that odor! Can you smell it now?" "Yes, I can," Martha replied. When Aline told Martha that her legs felt numb, Martha ran next door for help, where Mrs. Earl Robertson phoned police about the "gassing," while her husband searched the neighborhood but found no signs of an intruder. Before long, police showed up, but they too found nothing.[1] Once Mr. Kearney heard of the "attack," he raced home. Pulling his car into the yard at 12:30 A.M., he caught a fleeting glimpse of a tall, shadowy figure wearing a skullcap,[2] standing near the bedroom window. Police again rushed to the house and searched the area but found no trace of an intruder.[3]

At this point, the gasser's very existence was dubious: All that police had to go on were vague odors, a shadowy figure, and a jittery mother who quickly recovered from symptoms which sounded suspiciously like stress. Aline's daughter Dorothy was also in the bedroom with her that night and felt nausea, but like her mother, she quickly felt better. If Aline had really thought she had been exposed to a toxic gas, one would think that she would at least have had her child checked out by a doctor. She never did.

The next morning, Mattoon's only major newspaper, the *Daily Journal-Gazette*, which had a readership of 97 percent,[4] reported on the story with banner headlines: "Anesthetic Prowler on Loose. Mrs. Kearney and Daughter First Victims... Robber Fails to Get into Home."[5] By the next day, everyone in Mattoon was on the lookout for the "mad gasser."

Ringing Alarm Bells

Mattoon residents were now in a panic and began to think back in recent days if they too had seen or smelled anything unusual. Not surprisingly, people began to recall all sorts of suspicious incidents which at the time they had thought little of. But after reading the *Gazette*'s sensational story, at least four "new gassings" came to light.

The Chicago Herald-American reported that at about the same time as the Kearney "attack," Mrs. George Rider said she had been gassed while staying home with her two sleeping children, awaiting her husband's return from work. Having an upset stomach she began drinking large amounts of coffee. She later told a doctor that she had consumed "several pots" and then took stomach medication before vomiting.[6] Until this point, there was no sign of the gasser. She next lay in bed near her children with the window shut, then heard a "plop"—followed by a odd smell accompanied by a feeling of lightheadedness and finger and leg numbness.[7] Just then her baby began coughing. She assumed that the gasser had forced the fumes through a bedroom window.[8] A more likely scenario: Her caffeine-ridden body was reacting to the combination of coffee, medication, paranoia and nerves. Once again, as with the "first gassing" of Aline Kearney, Mrs. Rider neither went to the doctor nor did she bother to report the incident to police.

Mr. and Mrs. Orban Raef soon claimed that they were gassed in their home the night before Aline Kearney's report. In recalling the encounter, Mr. Raef said he was asleep with his wife at 3 A.M. when fumes came seeping through the bedroom window. He said that both experienced "the same feeling of paralysis" and felt ill for an hour and a half. Again, incredibly, no one bothered to ring the police or see a doctor. Friends sleeping in another room were not affected.⁹ Then there is the case of Mrs. Olive Brown who told police that months earlier, she had been "gassed" but didn't report it, fearing ridicule. She said that near midnight, "she had an experience similar to that related by persons during the past few days."[10]

To their credit, the police weren't buying these stories, which they attributed to imagination. This was noted in a September 8 *Gazette* editorial criticizing authorities for neither believing Aline Kearney nor the four reports that quickly followed by residents claiming "gassings" only after learning of Mrs. Kearney's claim.[11] Despite police skepticism, with the exception of this editorial, readers would have thought the gasser was real.

The four additional gassing claims are dubious as no one reported them to police, fled their home, told friends or relatives, or even bothered to consult a doctor. After believing they were sprayed with poison gas, resulting in burning eyes, dizziness, vomiting, partial paralysis of the limbs, what do these early "victims" do? Go back to bed without calling the police or seeing a doctor. The only way this behavior makes sense is if those involved began to imagine that these "attacks" had happened after the sensational press coverage.[12]

Robert Ladendorf observes that in re-examining Mrs. Kearney's report in the *Gazette* on September 2, no one reported seeing an "anesthetic prowler." A headline writer created the phrase which quickly became a self-fulfilling prophecy as evidenced in the next four prowler reports.

Fear Spreads

By September 6, amid fresh claims of gassings, stories were appearing in most Illinois newspapers as the Mattoon police commissioner, mayor and army experts began describing the gasser as real. On September 5, Mrs. Beulah Cordes claimed she was overcome by fumes after finding a cloth on her porch and sniffing it. It was taken to a police crime lab for analysis. When the results came back, there was no trace of toxic gas. A chemical expert said the substance must have evaporated.[13] With absolutely no physical evidence to support the claim, experts from the Chicago-based Chemical Warfare Service suggested that chloropicrin was the mystery gas.[14] Meanwhile, Richard Piper, superintendent of the Illinois Bureau of Criminal Identification and Investigation proclaimed: "The existence of the anesthetic, or whatever it is, is genuine."[15]

By September 6, readers of such newspapers as the *Chicago Daily Tribune*, *Chicago Daily News* and *Chicago Herald-American* could be forgiven for thinking that Mattoon was under siege. The gasser or gassers seemed to be everywhere, as the city's police force of two officers and eight patrolmen struggled to keep up.¹⁶ On the 8th, about seventy people poured onto Dewitt Avenue upon hearing rumors that the gasser had been spotted nearby. When a crowd member smelled an odor and raised the alarm, many in the group became convinced that they had been gassed.¹⁷

On September 9 and 10, hundreds of citizens were milling around City Hall to be the first to hear the latest news. As a patrol car responded to a call, a procession of vehicles would follow. Police Commissioner Wright soon issued orders to arrest "chasers."¹⁸ By now, vigilante gangs were roaming the streets on foot and in vehicles touting clubs, rifles and shotguns. The commissioner was fearful that some trigger-happy resident might get a case of the jitters and shoot someone by mistake.¹⁹ One woman who was living alone had a loaded gun at the ready and accidentally blew a hole in her kitchen wall.²⁰

By September 9, a new flurry of gassings swept through the city. The *Gazette* continued to describe the story with sensational headlines: "'Mad Gasser' Adds Six Victims! 5 Women and Boy Latest Overcome." That night there was an equally alarming report when sisters Frances and Maxine Smith claimed to have been attacked in their home. Frances, a local grade school principal, said on Wednesday night the pair became terrified after hearing noises by their bedroom windows, thinking it may have been the gasser. The next night, the sisters, spooked and paranoid, claimed no less than three separate attacks. The *Gazette* described the claims with its usual sensational fashion: "The first infiltration of gas caught them in their beds. Gasping and choking, they awoke and soon felt partial paralysis grip their legs and arms. Later, while awake, the other attacks came and they saw a thin, blue smoke-like vapor spreading throughout the room." The paper continued: "Just before the gas with its 'flower-like' odor came pouring into the room they heard a strange 'buzzing' sound outside the house and expressed the belief that the sound probably was made by the 'madman's spraying apparatus' in operations."²¹

As the tension mounted, each day brought new, seemingly more sensational reports. On the 10th, the *Chicago Herald-American* described Mattoon as if its residents were at war: "Groggy as Londoners under protracted aerial blitzing, this town's bewildered citizens reeled today under repeated attacks of a mad anesthetist who has sprayed deadly nerve gas into 13 homes and has knocked out 27 known victims."²² On the weekend, two women were rushed to the hospital after fearing they'd been gassed. The diagnosis: "nervous tension."²³

On Monday, September 11, the cavalry arrived in the form of ten reinforcements from the Springfield police department. Each officer rode with a local volunteer to speed up the responses to calls, and each was issued a shotgun.²⁴ Three officers from Urbana were also brought in. FBI agents were already on the scene to figure out the type of gas the "madman" was using "to knock out his victims."[25] That night a woman grew so fearful of an attack that she had to be hospitalized for "extreme mental anguish."[26]

The Case Crumbles

On September 11, after so many dead-end phone calls and obvious false reports, the press began to turn skeptical, as did authorities. With an army of police and volunteers scouring the city, Commissioner Wright joked that authorities were often able to answer a call "before the phone was back on the hook."[27] At 11:30 A.M. Mrs. Eaton Paradise made a frantic call to police, telling them, "I've just been gassed." Police quickly converged on the house and had the culprit surrounded. Within minutes of entering the residence, they had the suspect in custody: a bottle of nail polish remover that had spilled on the floor.[28] This incident, along with numerous other false alarms, prompted Police Chief Cole to announce on the 12th that it was *all* mass hysteria.[29]

By the 13th, reporters were describing the gasser as the "phantom anesthetist" and "Mattoon Will-o'-the-Wisp," and new reports were being treated jokingly.[30] The next day, under a barrage of ridicule by police and the press, gassing reports in Mattoon ceased altogether. That morning the *Gazette* began its account of a prowler claim the previous night by saying: "One call! No paralyzing gas! No madman! No prowler!"[31] On the 15th, the *Gazette* reported that police in Cedar Rapids, Iowa, received a call from a distraught woman claiming that a man holding a spray gun outside her window had gassed her room. Police said "they found no madman and no gas, but did find a billy goat tied in the yard and an odor that seemed to come from the animal."[32]

Other Illinois papers quickly joined in the gasser-bashing. The *Chicago Herald-American*, until this time the gasser's greatest proponent, suddenly turned into its staunchest critic, comparing the affair to the Salem witch hysteria of 1692.[33] An editorial on the 19th in the *Decatur Herald* made fun of imaginative Mattoonites, noting that autumn was a season of odors: flowers, picnic fires, industrial wastes, and rotting Victory garden produce. "Our neighbors in Mattoon sniffed their town into newspaper headlines from coast to coast."[34] A reporter for *Time* joked that gasser symptoms in Mattoonites consisted of temporary paralysis, nausea and "a desire to describe their experiences in minutest detail."[35] Other letters to the *Gazette* ridiculed the affair. On September 26, an army officer said Mattoon residents had more advanced poison gas training than his unit,[36] while on the 29th another writer referred to the incidents as "hysteria."[37]

The Poison Gas Scare

The responsibility for the "mad gasser" scare rests squarely on the shoulders of the *Mattoon Daily-Journal Gazette* and its alarmist reporting which whipped the community into a frenzy. Before long, residents were terrified, and the "gasser" was being spotted everywhere. The timing was critical. The episode broke out at a pivotal point during World War II when newspapers and magazines were discussing the "poison gas peril."[38] As the tide of World War II turned increasingly in favor of the Allies, concern grew that desperate German commanders might resort to gas warfare.[39] So concerned were the Allies over the possible use of poison gas during their June 6, 1944, D-Day invasion of Normandy that they had a plan to retaliate within 48 hours with two bombing raids of 400 planes, each loaded with chemicals to be dumped on selected targets. Gas warfare expert Frederic Brown says that D-Day was the "most dangerous period for German [gas] initiation"—a credible threat that was widely discussed in the press during latter 1944.[40] The mad gasser appeared just two and a half months after D-Day. It is within this context of war paranoia over the potential use of chemical or biological weapons that the *Journal-Gazette* overreaction must be seen.

About the time of the first gassing report by Aline Kearney, newspapers in Champaign, Chicago and Springfield carried wire service articles about gas use. The August 30 *Champaign News-Gazette* included a page one article: "Believe Nazis Prepared to Use Gas." On August 31 the *Chicago Herald-American* had one on page 2 ("Report Nazis Plan Poison Gas Attack") and another report in the September 1 issue on page 2 ("Allies Ready if Nazis Use Gas"); and an Associated Press article in the (Springfield) *Illinois State Journal* on September 1 ("Unlikely Gas to Be Used in War") appeared on the day of Mrs. Kearney's alleged gassing. The AP article said: "If Nazi extremists bent on ruling or ruining should employ gas against civilian populations in a bitter end resistance, the allies would be in a position through air strength to drench German cities.... Recurrent rumors that the Germans are preparing to initiate gas warfare bring no official reaction here."

While certainly unusual, given the war scare context, and the publicity over an escaped Nazi in the vicinity of Mattoon at the time of the affair, the case is not so bizarre after all. Of course, this is no excuse for the alarmist reporting by such papers as the *Daily-Journal Gazette*, and later by the many Chicago papers, as the hysteria grew into full riot.

CHAPTER 18

The Hook Hoax

There is no better example of the power of the media to create myths and generate mass hysteria, than what happened at a tabloid newspaper in Sydney, Australia, in 1954. It has to rank as one of the most humorous and strangest cases in the annals of journalism.

The infamous Salem witch hunts of 1692 resulted in the executions of twenty people; over 200 others languished in jail where some died before being freed by Massachusetts Governor William Phelps in May 1693. If you find it hard to imagine a similar incident happening in today's modern world, you would be wrong. During the second half of the 20th century alone, the United States of America — arguably the most educated and economically prosperous society on earth — experienced a spate of witch hunts — from the communist Red Scare of the 1950s and the Soviet spy paranoia of the '60s to more recent episodes of satanic ritual abuse in the 1980s and '90s and the exaggerated fear of Muslims after September 11, 2001. While witch hunts are founded on rumors and fear, the mass media has been largely responsible for fueling these persecutions. In 1954, Australian-born journalist Philip Knightley showed just how easy it is to create a monster out of thin air. While what happened was relatively innocent and certainly humorous, it shows how easily events can spiral out of control.

In Knightley's memoir, *A Hack's Progress*, he writes candidly about his experiences as a reporter and editor for several major Fleet Street tabloids. But what happened in 1954 while working for the *Truth* in Sydney demonstrates not only the power of the press in shaping opinion, but also in creating myths. Knightley was working as the news editor for the *Truth*, which was published each Sunday, and was excited about breaking a big story about the local milk industry watering down milk in order to reap bigger profits. He was certain that he was going to nail the industry and expose a massive fraud. He had milk bottles gathered from throughout Sydney, and analyzed the buttermilk fat content. It would make headlines. Late Friday the bubble of excitement burst when the tests came back normal. There was no scandal. He had guessed wrong. Knightley would have to scramble to find a last-minute replacement of equal shock value.[1]

With his deadline approaching, Knightley recalls that his boss, Jack Finch, told him to use his imagination if he couldn't find a story worthy of the front page.[2] He thumbed through several different newspapers for inspiration until he saw a story in *The Sydney Morning Herald* about a man convicted of assaulting a girl on a packed commuter train by pressing his groin against her. "To my everlasting professional shame — I can only plead that I was just twenty-four and very ambitious — I obeyed Finch and used my imagination. I invented a story about a pervert known only to his victims and the police as 'The Hook.'" Knightley wrote that the culprit traveled the Sydney rail network, armed only with a wire hook shaped from a coat hanger that ran from his right shoulder to his sleeve, stopping just under the cuff. The Hook would wait for the train to fill up, then push his way over to a pretty female and pretend he was reading the newspaper. With his prey in range, he would lower his shoulder, extending the wire out, slipping it under her skirt, then lift it back in order to see the tops of her stockings. Just as quickly, he was able to retract the device, all the while appearing to be innocently reading the paper.

As if this wasn't enough, Knightly then created quotations from supposed victims. One anonymous woman vowed never again to ride the train until the fiend was caught. Another unnamed source, a police officer, said he had been overwhelmed by complaints. Knightley even had a staff artist draw a sketch. Knightley said, "The more I worked on my fairy story, the more I enjoyed it. There were no inconvenient facts to get in the way of a perfect narrative. Like Lionel Hogg said — it was how it should have happened."[3] Knightley said that when Finch read the story, he was delighted, making just one change, he had him striking the night before the story appeared, harassing women on their way to center Sydney. Finch then came up with the headline: "HOOK SEX PERV STRIKES AGAIN."[4]

Knightley later learned that rival newspaper reporters had spent hours phoning Sydney police stations in a desperate attempt to confirm the story but couldn't. The duty officers denied that it happened in their section, but couldn't vouch for other districts. On Monday morning Knightley was confident that he had gotten away with the fabrication when the phone rang. Detective Sergeant Ray Iggleden of the Bankstown police was on the other end, asking to speak to Knightley about the story. Having been caught out, he decided to come clean, so he admitted that he had written the story. Sergeant Iggleden's response: "Just wanted to let you know that we got the bastard this morning."⁵ Stunned but relieved, Knightley quickly rang the police roundsman and confirmed what the Sergeant had said. Over the next several weeks, Knightley anxiously awaited the Hook's appearance in court, but it never came. He was hesitant to ring the police to inquire further, fearful of the consequences.⁶

After giving the matter considerable thought over five decades, when it came time to write his memoirs, Knightley came up with several possible explanations. Theory one was that there really had been a sex pervert riding the rail system, who used a coat hanger to ply his trade. Theory two held that a copycat had read the story the day before and decided to become part of the Hook legend. But a third possibility seems most likely. Knightly believes that Sydney police, who were known at the time for fudging crime statistics in order to polish their public relations image, "got rid of a case which promised to be a PR disaster by arresting some pathetic minor sex offender and nominating him as The Hook."⁷

Regardless of which explanation is true, if any, the story of the Hook is a colorful reminder of the power of the media.

CHAPTER 19

The Ghost Slasher of Taiwan

> In 1956, the Taiwanese press reported that a razor-wielding maniac was stalking women and children on the streets of Taipei, slashing them before vanishing into the crowd. Police later determined that the slasher was a creation of the press who had reported rumors as fact, touching off a massive search for an imaginary assailant.

Fear hung in the air during the spring of 1956 in the once-bustling capital city of Taipei on the island of Taiwan. Most people walked in pairs. Children were escorted to and from school by nervous parents. Few ventured out unless in groups. During the first two weeks of May, Taipei was a city under siege, as was the city of Keelung forty miles to the north. Newspapers were reporting that a crazed figure was prowling the streets in broad daylight, boldly slashing people with a razor. Even worse, most of the targets were said to be women, children and babies. It would soon be determined that there never was a slasher; amid rumors, the press had fueled the scare by reporting hearsay as facts.

Journalists printed reams of speculation as to the identity of the slasher. Some thought it was a clever ruse to divert attention from stealing jewelry which was said to have been the real intent; others were certain the driving force was sexual sadism. One theory held that a blood ritual was involved, based on local folklore that drawing blood from children brings luck.[1] Some said the slasher was a woman, others a man; still others said it was a "teenager with a sad smile."[2] Curiously, no one ever saw an actual slashing — not even the victims themselves. While this was a huge red flag that something was amiss, in the heat of the moment, journalists ignored the basic facts in the case and printed speculation. By treating the slasher as a fact, citizens began to look for the slasher because they knew he or she was out there lying in wait for the next victim. Within this cauldron of fear and suspicion, it wasn't long before people grew fearful of their own shadows, and a variety of mundane events and circumstances that would have ordinarily received little attention were being viewed as the work of the slasher.

Here's how the scare unfolded. In early February, rumors began to circulate throughout Taipei that a serial slasher was preying on young children. There was even a story that a six-month-old baby had been slashed. Newspapers kept quiet about the claims because that's all they were — unverified stories with no substance to back them up. Then, on May 3, police began a formal investigation of the stories. When newspaper reporters got wind of the news that the slasher stories were the subject of a formal investigation, it triggered a frenzy of sensational stories starting on May 4, where rumors and hearsay were being reported as facts. Both the *China Post* and *Hong Kong Standard* were typical in their reporting, claiming that one of the slashed children had died after its genitals had been cut off.[3]

When Taipei residents woke up on May 4 they read the morning headlines that two children had been slashed. One eleven-year-old boy was said to have sustained a cut to his left arm but could not recall the circumstances, while a two-year-old boy in a northern suburb noticed a puzzling cut to his leg while playing. Despite the vagueness of these accounts and no one seeing a thing, rumors swept through Taipei of numerous young girls being slashed at primary schools. Again, the press reported the rumors and engaged in endless speculation. Anxiety levels soon reached new heights when one paper erroneously reported that some victims had died.[4] At a hastily called news conference, the police chief scolded the press for reporting such claims. Yet, the chief's own actions fostered suspicion and paranoia when he refused to officially confirm that no one had died. Small children were now being kept indoors as rumors abounded about young girls being slashed at numerous primary schools.[5]

On May 11, the crisis appeared to abate with reports that the slasher was finally caught. Police announced the arrest of a "woman in red" and charged her with the razor slashing of a nine-month-old baby. But after conducting basic interviews with eyewitnesses and examining the evidence, it was soon clear that she was innocent. A mother holding a baby in her arms was walking on the street when the baby was hit by an object from behind and began bleeding and crying. The mother turned and screamed as she noticed a girl walking behind in a red jacket and started chasing after "the slasher." Bystanders joined in the chase, during which the "woman in red" was seen tossing a package away. She was soon arrested by police who fended off the angry mob. The parcel was retrieved and found to contain a razor blade. An investigation revealed that the woman was opening her umbrella when it caught on the baby's sleeve and she panicked. The woman feared for her life, knowing she was carrying a razor and might be mistaken for the slasher. She was a seamstress and used the razor in her everyday work. She pointed out that the blade was wrapped in paper and couldn't have been used as a weapon. A doctor summoned to examine the child stated that an umbrella, not a razor, was the likely culprit.[6] Police realized that the woman had been an innocent victim, in the wrong place at the wrong time, and was lucky to be alive. She was released.

Police soon made a startling announcement: The slasher was a figment of the imagination. When newspapers reported rumors and hearsay as fact, people began to act as if there was a slasher. For instance, a minor cut to the leg that would ordinarily not be given a second thought resulted in people going to the police claiming to have been a victim of the slasher. The investigation revealed that the "slashings" had resulted from accidental, everyday contact in public places. One man told police he had been slashed by a man carrying a mysterious black bag. But when a doctor determined that the wound was made by a blunt object and not a razor, the victim admitted that he could not recall exactly what happened, but assumed that he had been slashed.[7] In another incident, an elderly man with a cut on the wrist sought medical treatment. The attending doctor grew suspicious and contacted police when the man casually noted that a stranger had touched him at about the time he first noticed the bleeding. A more thorough examination led to the conclusion that the "slash" was an old injury that had been re-opened after inadvertent scratching.[8]

Some "slashings" were hoaxes. In one case, a 17-year-old boy told police he had been slashed on the elbow. Upon further investigation it was determined that the boy had been shopping when he rested his arm on a broken glass counter. Fearful of being punished by his mother for carelessness, the boy made up the slashing story. Fortunately for police, someone who observed the boy cut his elbow described to police what had really happened. Despite police labeling this case as a hoax and fining the boy, several newspapers not only printed the police version of events, but also reported the boy's side of the story—that he was actually a victim of the slasher. This angered police, who soon took the boy before Taipei District Court, charging him with spreading rumors during a period of martial law.[9] In another fabricated case, police noticed a crowd milling around a note on a fence in front of a house and investigated. On the note were three pairs of knives placed in the shape of crosses, with an address in Keelung. Nearby, police noticed a boy acting suspiciously. Upon questioning him, his family, and his teacher, they soon realized that the handwriting on the note matched his. The boy quickly grew scared and broke down in tears, admitting that he had written the note to get back at a friend after they had an argument. He was hoping that the note would tie the boy to the slashings.[10]

It was on May 11 that police announced the slasher never existed. Their statistics were revealing. Of the 21 slashing claims they examined, "five were innocent false reports, seven were self-inflicted cuts, eight were due to cuts other than razors, and one was a complete fantasy."[11]

CHAPTER 20

The Phantom Clown Panic

> Beginning in the mid–1980s, newspapers across the country reported on rashes of attempted child abductions by mysterious, evil clowns. It may be an example of "living folklore."

For most people, the image of a clown conjures up happy thoughts: circuses and slapstick, maybe seltzer bottles and big floppy shoes. But clowns can also be terrifying—especially if they are reported to roam America's streets looking for innocent children to abduct, yet vanish just before police can apprehend them. These mysterious figures rank as one of the most bizarre media scares on record.

One of the first reports of phantom clowns occurred on May 6, 1981, when police in Brookline, Massachusetts, issued an All Points Bulletin asking officers to watch for a van containing possible child abductors. The vehicle was distinctive: an older model with a broken headlight, no hubcaps, and side ladders. It was also full of clowns! Several children reported that clowns had tried to lure them into the dark van with promises of candy, and the sinister figures were later reported lurking near Brookline's Lawrence Elementary School.[1] This was only the latest in a series of mysterious threats by phantom clowns; the next day, Boston police again searched the city in vain for another van driven by a creepy clown. The man allegedly stalked nearby Franklin Park. No one else saw the clown, and police searches again came up empty.

As reports spread to surrounding areas and parents grew nervous, Boston Public Schools' Investigative Counselor Daniel O'Connell issued a memo to principals in his school district: "It has been brought to the attention of the police department and the district office that adults dressed as clowns have been bothering children to and from school. Please advise all students that they must stay away from strangers, especially those dressed as clowns." The New England reports subsided, but the clowns soon reappeared in Missouri.

A sixth grader at Fairfax Elementary School in Kansas City told police that he saw a bad clown lurking at her school and described the man in vivid detail to the *Kansas City Star*: "He was by the fence and ran down through the big yard when some of the kids ran over there. He ran toward a yellow van. He was dressed in a black shirt with a devil on the front. He had two candy canes down each side of his pants. The pants were black too.... I don't remember much about his face." Yet no evidence of the phantom clown could be found.[2]

Parents were fearful, children were warned, and police were vigilant, but despite searches and police checkpoints stopping cars driven by clowns, the phantom menaces were never captured. Some people began to wonder who the clowns were and what they wanted; others wondered if they existed at all. Researcher Loren Coleman was one of the first to write about the phantom clowns in his book *Mysterious America*. Coleman writes that "something quite unusual was happening in America in the spring of 1981.... The appearance of phantom clowns in the space of one month in at least six major cities spanning over 1,000 miles of America constitutes a genuine mystery."

While some dismissed the clown scare as a silly hoax, many people took it seriously. One poster on the *Unsolved Mysteries* website wrote: "The denizens of the netherworld have apparently dreamed up a new nightmare to shock us. The cosmic joker is alive and well and living in a clown suit! PLEASE, HELP KEEP OUR CHILDREN SAFE!" Another person suggested that the phantom clowns were actually part of a covert government conspiracy operation designed to diminish the credibility of child eyewitnesses: "Perhaps a 'clown op' was run to discredit the testimony of children ... and lead the public toward discounting even more nightmarish mysteries."

Some reporters, such as Lucinda Smith of the *Montclair Times* in New Jersey, poured cold water on the stories: "Someone dressed as Homey the Clown is not in Montclair trying to hurt children.... And none of the following has been seen in a van attempting to kidnap children in Montclair: Homey, Krusty the Clown, the four Teenage Mutant Ninja Turtles, the Smurfs, Bugs Bunny, the Little Mermaid, Barbie, Ken."[3]

Phantom Clowns as Media-Driven Moral Panics

The first clue to solving the mystery is noting that only young children reported seeing the clowns; adults never encountered them. According to a spokesman for the Boston Police Department, "No adult or police officer has ever seen a clown. We've had calls saying there was a clown. We've had calls saying that there was a clown at a certain intersection and we happened to have police cars sitting there, and the officers saw nothing. We've had over twenty calls on 911. When the officers get there, no one tells them anything."[4]

Throughout the sporadic bad clown reports, no hard evidence was ever found, and no children were actually abducted. This strongly suggests that some form of social delusion was at play. If the clowns were real, why were they so incompetent at actually grabbing little children? Surely at least *one* of the bad clowns would have succeeded, instead of always "just missing." Perhaps children made up the stories to fit in, or because they had heard their peers say the same thing (this occurs in many media-fueled scares such as the Pokémon panic; see Chapter 8). Though adults often assume that young children would not make up a false story of an attempted abduction, in fact dozens of such hoaxes occur each year in America.

The social and cultural climate in which the clown reports took place is also crucial. The first clown scares occurred in the early 1980s and 1990s, at a time when the bad clown was entering the public's consciousness through the entertainment media with books such as Stephen King's best-selling horror novel *It* and films such as *Killer Klowns from Outer Space*.

Perhaps more importantly, it was precisely a time when a moral panic gripped America. *A moral panic* is a sociology term meaning a social reaction to a perceived threat to basic values by "outsiders" and moral deviants. The stranger is defined and blamed or scapegoated for real or perceived threats—often to children. At the time, a rash of lurid, sensational (and later disproven) child abuse cases horrified America. Children accused adults of ritual rapes, torture, and abuse, and the news media further sensationalized the stories. These reports closely coincided with the phantom clown scares. Not far from phantom clown–haunted Boston, Gerald Amirault, his mother Violet Amirault, and his sister Cheryl LaFave were accused of torturing children at the Fells Acres Day Care Center in Malden, Massachusetts. Children claimed that they had been subjected to threats and abuse, including one child who said that he or she had been tortured by a "bad clown" in a "secret room."

Several other notorious cases appeared across the country during the 1980s, including the Little Rascals and the McMartin preschool trials.[5] Children's stories included tales of being abused in a secret tunnel underneath a school, being taken to a church where strangers killed a rabbit and forced them to drink its blood, digging up dead bodies at a cemetery, and even more fantastic stories. Like the reports of phantom clowns, often there was little or no corroborating evidence to support the children's stories. The phrase "believe the children" was often heard, especially in the context of defending sometimes outlandish and impossible reports of abuse or attempted abductions.

According to folklorist Jan Brunvand, "The phantom-clowns tradition involving vans seems to be exclusively a part of childlore, perhaps reflecting children's actual distrust and even fear of clowns, who, ironically, are thought by adults to be invariably amusing to youngsters, most of who would undoubtedly prefer a large, friendly, purple dinosaur to a clown any day."[6] According to Brunvand, "Killer clown rumors surfaced briefly again in 1985, then faded until June 1991—exactly ten years after the first cycle of similar stories.... My first report of the return of the phantom clowns came in a letter from West Orange, New Jersey, postmarked June 12: 'My mom teaches school in South Orange, and the kids at school are all terrified by the rumor that there is someone dressed as a clown driving around kidnapping children. The story has grown to the point where the clown has a name, Homey, and now they are saying that there are a whole bunch of clowns riding around in a van.'"[7]

Rumors of the phantom clowns were published in several newspapers, including the *Newark Star-Ledger*, and the *Boston Globe*. While newspapers were the primary source for information about the fearsome clowns, warnings appeared through less formal local and regional outlets as well. For example, one newsletter sent to parents and teachers in 1986 warned that clowns were responsible for innocent children being "spirited away to join the throngs of missing children whose pathetic faces peer at us from milk cartons, shopping bags, and telephone [posts]."[8] Those who circulated the rumors and stories were clearly doing so out of genuine concern for children, though with less concern for the reality of the danger.

Stories of the child-abducting phantom clowns were not merely an invention of the news media; indeed, as happened in years past, several children reported firsthand abduction attempts. One boy told police that he had been confronted by a clown armed with an Uzi machine gun in one hand and machete in the other. The clown fired off five shots, but the boy counterattacked the surprised clown by throwing his bookbag at him. The clown then ran off. Not surprisingly, the boy later admitted that he had made up the whole story, but his reported encounter with the fearsome clown was only one of many similar reports that circulated in the schoolyards. According to Brunvand, "New Jersey police questioned 700 schoolchildren, many 'petrified' by the rumors, but concluded, 'We couldn't substantiate the existence of a clown. We have no sightings, no assaults, no homicides.'" An East Orange police officer described the panic: "It just spread from one kid to another, and continued until there was a kind of hysteria."[9]

Whether real or a mass delusion, phantom clowns surfaced once again in 1995 in the Central American country of Honduras, where reports circulated that "killer clowns" were cruising the streets of large cities like Tegucigalpa and San Pedro Sula in cars or ambulances, abducting children.[10]

The phantom clowns disappeared for over a decade, until sightings plagued Chicago, Illinois, in October 2008. According to Loren Coleman, "a man wearing clown make-up and a wig was using balloons in an attempt to lure children into his vehicle on the South Side of Chicago, Illinois. The man, who wears a clown mask or white face paint with teardrops on the cheek, has approached children walking to and from school, police said. Witnesses told police he was seen driving a white or brown van with the windows broken out."[11] The first two incidents were reported on October 7 and 10; two days after the second incident, police held a press conference stating that there had been multiple sightings of the phantom clowns at various places around Chicago.

Once again the pattern repeated: Police followed up on several sightings, but developed no leads, and as always no arrests were made; it seemed the evil would-be-abductor clowns simply vanished. The phantom clowns once again disappeared, but it seems likely that the world has not seen the last of these bad clowns.

Section Four

It Came from Cyberspace — The Internet

CHAPTER 21

Chemtrails and Conspiracies

> In recent years, websites on the mysterious presence of "chemtrails" in the sky have spawned bizarre theories of secret government plots.

It has all the markings of a master spy novel: international intrigue, secret formulas, and a global plot by world leaders. Since the late 1990s, there has been an explosion of interest in the belief that the United States military is engaging in a series of secret, systematic experiments involving the dispensing of chemical trails from high-altitude jet aircraft. Scores of websites have appeared discussing the phenomena, usually accompanied by myriad conspiracy theories. Popular radio shows such as Art Bell, George Noory and Jeff Rense have helped to fuel the scare. It is also commonly believed that chemtrails are responsible for a variety of ailments experienced by people on the ground, everything from rashes to the flu to cancer.

One of the conspiracy theories is that chemtrails are created by the military as an inexpensive wireless communication system. Common sense suggests that there must be an easier way than spraying thousands of tons of chemicals into the atmosphere in a massive global deception just to communicate better. Another theory holds that the chemicals are used to control the thinking of the masses — the equivalent of placing Prozac in the water supply. The most popular explanation centers on the view that chemtrails are an attempt to modify the weather. Many websites demonize the United States military and political leaders, claiming that chemtrails are secret experiments conducted with its allies, designed to produce a sky shield in order to protect Earth from the ravages of global warming. Some believers point to a 1994 patent taken out by Hughes Aerospace which entails mixing jet fuel with a variety of reflective materials, including tiny aluminum oxide particles, that would provide Earth with a chemical sunscreen.[1]

In 1998, the issue of chemtrails became a prominent concern in Canada, particularly in the tiny town of Espanola in northern Ontario, where United States KC-135 aircraft were said to be making routine passes over the community and dispensing harmful chemicals. The concerns became so great that on November 18, a representative of Canada's New Democratic Party, Gordon Earle, presented a petition to parliament, calling for the "covert spraying program" to stop. At the time, many residents were claiming to be suffering from ill health as a result of the chemtrails, including dizziness, sudden fatigue, headaches, asthma, joint pains, and flu-like symptoms. The petition stated: "Over 500 residents of the Espanola area have signed a petition raising concern over possible government involvement in what appears to be aircraft emitting visible aerosols. They have found high traces of aluminum and quartz in particulate and rainwater samples. These concerns combined with associated respiratory ailments have led these Canadians to ... seek clear answers from this government."[2] The petition went on to ask politicians to repeal any legislation that permits of dispensing substances by Canadian or foreign aircraft "without the informed consent of the citizens of Canada thus affected."[3]

One scientist who has taken the time to examine the chemtrail phenomena is meteorologist Thomas Schlatter of the National Oceanic and Atmospheric Administration. Schlatter says that in understanding the mystery, it is imperative to define "contrail." The word is short for "condensation trails," which form when high-altitude jets disperse water vapor into the lower levels of the stratosphere (or high troposphere), resulting in saturated air. As for chemtrails (plumes of chemicals emitted from aircraft), Schlatter believes that they don't exist as such. He believes that chemtrails are actually contrails.[4]

Schlatter says that normally contrails dissipate quickly, but this depends on the conditions. Where there is a very cold air temperature combined with high humidity, contrails have been known to stretch 100 miles in length. Whenever the temperature is -40F or lower, and the relative humidity is at least 70 to 80 percent, contrails will develop.[5]

On one website titled "The Spotlight," Mike Blair claims that chemtrails are the result of a secret multi-billion dollar plan by the military to impregnate the atmosphere with "various mixtures of barium salts" in an effort to develop a new type of radar system.[6] Other theories are more bizarre, such as the one claiming that chemtrails are a secret plan by U.S. elites who want to cull Earth's population to no more than 500 million.[7] Their goal: a future utopian world engineered by a small group of leaders and scientists intent on living in harmony and bliss. The site claims: "You may have already heard how several national parks have been designated as world biospheres — that's the plan for all of North America, a giant nature park and playground that will be devoid of annoying human beings."

NASA scientist Patrick Minnis conveys his frustration in refuting chemtrail proponents. "If you try to pin these people down and refute things, it's, 'Well, you're just part of the conspiracy.... Logic is not exactly a real selling point for them.'"[8] In 1999, after receiving a flurry of letters from concerned constituents fearful of the health effects of chemtrails, the New Mexico State Attorney General had physicist M. Kim Johnson investigate the claims.

This ordinary jet contrail (or is it a deadly, toxic "chemtrail"?) appeared over Albuquerque, New Mexico, on November 17, 2010 (photograph by Benjamin Radford).

Johnson said that all of the pictures she examined appeared to be contrails. As for stories of people getting sick from "chemtrails," Johnson said they provide "as much credence to chemtrails as does the belief that drinking milk is casually linked to heroin addiction," as most American heroin addicts were milk drinkers as children.[9]

Chapter 22

Morgellons: The First Internet Disease?

> For the first time in history, a "new disease" has developed and spread —
> almost exclusively over the Internet. It is unlikely to be the last.

It sounds like something from a grade–B horror flick. People get the sensation that invisible insects are crawling over their skin; they walk around in a mental fog and have disabling fatigue; colored fibers appear to be sprouting from skin sores. In 2002, a South Carolina mother named Mary Leitao founded an Internet site called the Morgellons Foundation, dedicated to solving the mystery of the ailment by the same name. Leitao became worried after strange symptoms developed in her two-year-old son. She chose the name after stumbling across a 1674 medical report describing similar symptoms to what he was experiencing. The site quickly became a magnet for people around the world with all sorts of vague symptoms. In 2006 over 4,500 sufferers registered with the site as having Morgellons. Not surprisingly, there are all sorts of elaborate Internet theories as to the cause, including what seems to be every conspiracy theorist's favorite: the secret government cover-up following an experiment gone awry.

Many Morgellons patients are clearly suffering from delusional parasitosis — a rare psychological condition whereby people think that tiny bugs have burrowed into their skin and are causing sores. In reality the sores are caused by their own scratching.[1]

A second category of victims likely have cutaneous dysaesthesia, a disease of the nerves which can give the sensation that there are crawling insects on the skin. One prominent skin doctor who refuses to give his name publicly for fear of being targeted by Morgellon proponents, says that over fifty Morgellons patients who he has treated actually had cutaneous dysaesthesia. As for the mysterious fibers growing out the skin sores, he notes: "In every case I've seen it's a textile fiber, and it's on the surface of the skin."[2]

A third group of Morgellons sufferers may have infections associated with Lyme Disease caused by tick bites. If untreated, the illness can progress from rashes and flu-like symptoms to joint pain and problems with the nervous system.[3]

Yet another group appear to have a variety of vague ailments and have found a new label under which to place these symptoms. For some in this group, it's probably exciting to be part of a new medical mystery — complete with an army of sympathetic bloggers.

The symptoms of many Morgellon sufferers are similar to people with Gulf War syndrome and chronic fatigue syndrome: conditions which remain of dubious origin. What is not in doubt is the power of the Internet to incubate these "ailments," typically with bizarre claims.

While many people scoff at suggestions that GWS is a form of mass hysteria, there is compelling evidence to suggest that's exactly what is happening. No credible cause for GWS has been found, and without a doubt, there is a social component. The classic symptoms of Gulf War syndrome — fatigue, memory and concentration problems, rashes, headaches, and aches and pains of the joints — are all typical of the general population! Like Morgellons, the websites making wild claims have been largely responsible for the rapid spread of GWS. In past wars these symptoms were known by such names as "effort syndrome," "soldier's heart," and "shell shock." None of these illnesses were ever found to have a pathological basis and slowly faded away. Almost certainly the cause was anxiety, and a variety of common symptoms.

Chronic fatigue syndrome is another emotional powder keg. During the 1970s and '80s, the Epstein-Barr Virus was blamed for CFS. We now know that everyone has this virus in their bodies. No clear cause of CFS — which is essentially feeling tired all the time — has been identified. All sorts of possible suspects have been theorized over the years, but nothing has been proven — and it's unlikely to be so. Yet, over the past 25 years, a CFS subculture has developed over the Internet as "victims" compare notes and exchange the latest government conspiracy theories.

Morgellons appears to be a case of old wine in new bottles. It is doubtful that doctors will discover some new ailment that has been operating right under their noses for centuries but have somehow missed it. The interesting aspect of Morgellons is that we've discovered a new disease carrier: the Internet, which has also been instrumental in spreading wild claims about such imaginary illnesses as Gulf War syndrome and chronic fatigue. These may sound like strong words, but the science to support GWS and CFS is lacking, yet many people treat these condition as if they were a proven fact. They are not.

Journalist Debbie Gilbert implicates the media in the sudden emergence of Morgellons cases in recent years, comparing the situation to UFO claims between the late 1940s and 1989. "During the Cold War era, when radio, TV, and movies were filled with stories about flying saucers, many people swore that they, too, had had a UFO encounter."[4]

Another skeptic is psychiatrist Bernard Frankel who observes that Morgellons seems to be spread socially and not biologically. "If (Morgellons) is from a particular insect, or organism, that population would tend to be localized. It doesn't seem like you would have cases spread randomly all over the country."[5] Indeed, the pattern of transmission is *not* tied to a mysterious new bacteria or virus. In this instance, the Internet is the carrier — and the disease is an idea, spread by human insecurity and fear. It is a sign of our changing times, a product of the Information Age.

CHAPTER 23

Katrina Evacuee Myths

> Internet-fueled urban legends stereotyping blacks and the poor of New Orleans, spread like wildfire in the days and weeks after Hurricane Katrina struck the city.

As we learned in Chapter 10, after Hurricane Katrina ripped through the Gulf Coast in late August 2005, misinformation abounded. For instance, the initial reports of widespread murder and mayhem proved to be unfounded. As most mass communications systems failed, and reporters were not able to move around freely due to the flooding, they began to report what they expected would happen, and many so-called eyewitnesses were actually repeating urban myths which, in turn, got reported as fact. It took weeks for reporters to check their early claims with police records and find out that the chaos had been hyped. A similar series of myths soon began to circulate about crimes or poor behavior supposedly committed by displaced New Orleans residents. One example is the case of the Utah evacuees. The story goes like this: Upon arriving in Utah, many evacuees immediately tried to sell drugs, reform gangs and commit rapes. The following account was recorded in a mid-September e-mail by Snopes.com, an organization which gathers and analyzes rumors. This account was purportedly from a relief worker on the scene:

> Let me tell you a few things about the wonderful group of evacuees we received here in Utah. The first plane arrived with 152 passengers. Of the 152; 10 were children. 3 of these children had been abandoned by their parents. As these passengers attempted to board the plane, the National Guard removed from their person; 43 handguns ... 20 knives, one man had 100,000 dollars in cash, 20 pounds of Marijuana, 10 pounds of Crack, 15 pounds of Methamphetamines, 10 pounds of various other controlled substances including Heroin.[1]

The badly punctuated e-mail clearly implies that many of the adults were criminals, drug dealers and drug addicts who were focused on saving themselves, leaving behind their own children to fend for themselves.

It was then claimed that upon reaching Salt Lake City, two passengers immediately began smoking marijuana. During their medical exams, several parents were supposedly found to be using their children to conceal looted goods — the price tag still on the items. About a third of the passengers who disembarked there were said to have been angry that they weren't going to San Antonio or Houston, and most of the evacuees processed on the planes had lengthy criminal records.[2]

The e-mail continued, claiming that by the second night, the shelter was in chaos, with the attempted rape of a relief volunteer, drug dealers were having a field day, and gangs were rebuilding. What's more, it was said that as the evacuees arrived, they had the chance to sort through piles of donated clothing from local charity groups, with many complaining they were secondhand. But the most vicious claim was aimed at their work ethic: "This past Saturday, workforce services held a job fair. 85 of the 582 evacuees attended. 44 were hired on the spot. 24 were asked back for a second interview. Guess the others had no desire to work."[3]

A check of the facts in this account proved to be baseless. The first Katrina evacuees to Utah arrived on September 3, and as happened to later arrivals, they were temporarily housed at a Utah National Guard training center, Camp Williams, where they remained until September 27 when they found more permanent housing. Governor Jon Huntsman said the background of each evacuee was checked and that "None of the guests at Camp Williams have criminal records that would justify booking them into jail."[4]

Rumor expert Barbara Mikkelson said that of 582 evacuees sent to Utah, just 42 had criminal records. "Stories about drug sales, gangs re-forming, and an attempted rape are unsupported by the Utah news media. Though we looked and looked, we couldn't find reportage of any such incidents," she said.[5]

Utah Department of Public Safety spokesman Derek Jensen said the wild tales of unruly evacuees "are just not true. The evacuees have been cooperative and behaved themselves pretty well while they were here." In fact, during their three-week stay, police had not issued a single citation. His sentiments were echoed in a statement issued by the Utah governor: "Guests on the base have displayed exemplary behavior and been cooperative with volunteers and law enforcement. No major crimes or incidents have been reported at Camp Williams since the arrival of our guests."[6]

Mikkelson found similar unfounded accounts of outrageous behavior by transplanted evacuees in other parts of the country. In Tennessee, there were rumors of evacuees behaving badly, including murders, rapes and robberies. The stories triggered a stampede by local residents, who rushed out to buy guns to protect themselves. But once again, the stories proved to be unfounded, and area police report there was no jump in the crime rate after the evacuee arrivals. There were similar claims of violence in Oklahoma, where thousands of evacuees were sent. While a few fistfights had broken out at the Camp Gruber refuge, an Oklahoma Highway Patrol spokesman said that otherwise camp life was quiet.[7]

Mikkelson believes that the rumors of Katrina evacuees misbehaving resonate with common fears about outsiders coming in and changing communities. "By presenting the evacuees as rude or ungrateful or as the crime-riddled worst dregs of society, garden variety xenophobia is cloaked in the more respectable mantle of entirely defensible fear for one's safety and/or distaste for objectionable behavior. In such fashion, the internal tug of war between the selfless ('My heart goes out to these people; what can I do to help?') and the self-centered ('I like my town just the way it is; I hope the refugees don't come here') is quelled."[8]

One of the great dilemmas of the Internet revolution is, while more people than ever have access to more and more information, how do they know what's true and what's not — be it on a website or in an e-mail?

CHAPTER 24

The E-mail Virus Panic

by Bill Ellis

> Folklorist Bill Ellis examines the "Good Times" e-mail virus hoax which began in December 1994 and continues to spread fear through the cyber community even today.

Like many things that are now taken for granted as part of daily life, e-mail was once new and unfamiliar. Its technology was worked out at the same time that the basic programs were developed for sharing files and other information among the users of ARPANET, the first linked network of computers that evolved into the Internet. While a number of programs for sharing messages were tested in the 1960s, it is generally accepted that the first modern e-mail was sent in late 1971 by Ray Tomlinson of the Massachusetts research and development contractor Bolt, Beranek and Newman. These historic messages were routine tests transmitted between two computers that were side by side, though they were connected not to each other but to a server in a remote lab.[1]

The communication tool was tested and improved by technicians, then was widely adopted in academic and work settings during the late 1980s. Commercially available systems such as Delphi, Prodigy, and America Online (AOL) simplified its process to the point that even those with no knowledge of computer technology could use it. E-mail enjoyed breakout popularity among the general public in the early 1990s.[2] But the combination of the medium's novelty, widespread ignorance, even among educated users, of how

Bill Ellis *is a professor emeritus of English and American studies at Penn State University, Hazleton campus. He holds a Ph.D. in folklore from Ohio State University (1978) and is the past president of the International Society for Contemporary Legend Research and the American Folklore Society's Folk Narrative Section.*

it actually worked, and the emergence of real risks combined to spark a series of intense media panics during the period when e-mail was introduced to most Americans' lives.

Almost from the beginnings, rogue programmers began creating programs that could infect operating systems, just as viruses infect a living organism. The first computer viruses were practical jokes, such as "Creeper," a self-replicating program that infected the early Internet in 1971. Fortunately its only function was to display a prank message: "I'm the creeper, catch me if you can." The first really destructive virus was named "Jerusalem," after the location of the first computer complex (Hebrew University) where it was located in 1987. "Jerusalem" was programmed to spread inconspicuously, and then delete a number of files on every Friday the 13th.[3] But even while programmers detected it and similar viruses in computer labs worldwide, other experts expressed doubt over whether "wild" computer viruses actually existed. Peter Norton, later developer of one of the most widely used anti-virus services, reportedly told a journalist in 1988, "We're dealing with an urban myth. It's like the story of alligators in the sewers of New York. Everyone knows about them, but no one's ever seen them."[4]

Things changed later that year when the so-called "Morris worm" created a media sensation. The virus was a small but clever program written by a Cornell graduate student to measure how quickly information spread on the Internet. The experiment worked all too well: When released into the wild in November 1988, it began to multiply exponentially within every computer it infected. Each copy of the program used a tiny amount of the computer's memory, but, like the splinters of the broom used in the *Sorcerer's Apprentice*, its numbers doubled and redoubled, and the infection made one computer after another grind to a halt, including the servers that were the keys to Internet access. The program did no damage to the computers it infected, but the network crash caused disruption of business and work routines across the country.[5]

Users realized that being linked to the Internet was risky, but the topic remained poorly understood, even by many computer technicians. The stage was set for a series of panics, as puzzled reporters routinely took half-understood explanations and exaggerated them into potential catastrophes. In March 1989, a virus named "Datacrime" was detected in a Dutch computer. When analyzed, it was found to be set to activate on the next October 13 (a Friday) and reformat the part of the hard drive that contained the directory. While no files would be destroyed, this simple act would temporarily prevent the user from accessing *any* program or document on the computer, giving the impression that its entire memory had been "wiped out." This program turned out to be ineffective in spreading, but it inspired panicky press coverage. An inventive reporter speculated that the program had been written by Scandinavian hackers to activate on Columbus Day, in revenge for neglecting Viking Leif Ericsson's discovery of America.[6]

An even more intense panic occurred in 1992, when a similar virus was found preset for March 6, subsequently identified as Michelangelo's birthday. The "Michelangelo" virus was the basis of a series of increasingly anxious news articles, which emphasized its supposedly more insidious properties. "It's usually been a rule that a virus can't be propagated by just reading from a data disk," one expert told press, adding "but the virus is hidden and executable and it's doing its thing." Reports also claimed (falsely) that the virus could be spread silently by visiting the e-mail bulletin boards that by now were serving as increasingly popular discussion forums for newly initiated Internet users. On March 2, telejournalist Ted Koppel introduced a feature on ABC's news program *Nightline*, saying "Michelangelo" promised to be "devastating, destroying the memories of millions of computers around the world." A guest compared computer viruses to "doing germ warfare in your own neighborhood."[7]

David Perry, then a technician at Norton's anti-virus support, recalled showing curious news reporters how the malware program shut down all the programs on a test computer, leaving a flashing white cursor on a blank screen. "Is that it? No smoke and fire? No melted down computer?" he recalls one reporter after another exclaiming before leaving with a parting cry of "You defrauded us!" It was then that Perry and his fellow technicians realized that "the public had gotten themselves all whipped up into a frenzy about mythological or, if you prefer, fictional viruses.... We aren't just fighting the real viruses; we're fighting the fictional viruses."[8]

The most widespread and influential of these fictitious threats occurred in early December 1994, a panic caused by a virus called "Good Times." The incident began with a simple message that began appearing on bulletin boards in the middle of November. One early version read: "FYI, a file, going under the name 'Good Times' is being sent to some Internet users who subscribe to on-line services (Compuserve, Prodigy and America On Line). If you should receive this file, do not download it! Delete it immediately. I understand that there is a virus included in that file, which if downloaded to your personal computer, will ruin all of your files."[9] This version of the warning was technically plausible, according to technicians, but given the current state of the art, one would have needed to open the file and manually start it to infect one's computer. Some email programs at the time could be set to execute incoming files automatically, but by disabling this option and using anti-virus scanning programs to check downloads, the threat could be minimized.[10]

However, as this message was communicated from one user to another, senders ignorant of the fine points of how e-mail worked tended to simplify its content while making the threat more dramatic. By the end of November, the warning had mutated to a much scarier form: "There is a virus on America Online being sent by E-Mail," an early version read. "If you get anything called 'Good Times,' DON'T read it or download it. It is a virus that will erase your hard drive."[11] The critical change was that the message suggested that the dangerous computer virus was not in an attached file, which had to be downloaded and activated manually, but was in the text of the email message itself. Certainly this was the sense circulating among computer users on the morning of December 1. One message board contributor observed that the "computer-whiz crowd" in the Boston area was claiming that the virus was so virulent that "If you ... *even read it*, it starts to destroy your hard drive."[12]

On the morning of December 2 (a Friday), the warning was delivered to virtually every message board and private e-mail inbox in the world. Par-

Folklorist Bill Ellis feigns shock at receiving the dreaded "Good Times" e-mail virus (photograph by and courtesy of Bill Ellis).

adoxically, no virus was ever located that had ever been transmitted under the name "Good Times." However, in early e-mail technology, when the message was communicated and discussed, the original transmission headers were also passed on with the new message. So, like the Morris worm, when discussion of the warning erupted worldwide, the sheer numbers of messages transmitted from one user or bulletin board to another cut into available bandwidth. Internet access slowed to a crawl and users' mailboxes were clogged with the same warning exponentially multiplied. Angry users accused those who took the warning seriously of being themselves infected with a kind of "mind virus" that was as destructive as any capability of the malware program itself. However, expert reassurances that "Good Times" posed no threat were often written in a dense technobabble, further confusing many users.[13]

The initial panic was eventually brought to an end by the intervention of The U.S. Department of Energy's Computer Incident Advisory Capability, which published a special email-distributed message on December 6, which declared the warning a hoax. Project Leader Karyn Pichnarczyk compared the emails to "yelling 'fire' on a crowded Internet."[14] Nevertheless, the warning continued to circulate on the Internet, though at a slower rate. A more elaborate version adopted some of the hacker jargon used in the official denials to make the virus's existence credible in the eyes of novice Internet users. "The act of loading the file into the mail server's ASCII buffer causes the 'Good Times' mainline program to initialize and execute," this longer warning claimed, locking a computer's hard drive into "an nth-complexity infinite binary loop," and causing it to self-destruct. Technicians immediately recognized this technical description as bogus, but the "Good Times" email virus warning continued to circulate among message boards throughout the next two years.

Finally, in December 1996, Patrick Rothfuss, an undergradu-

New York Times **bestselling author Patrick Rothfuss, author of the *Good Times E-mail Virus* parody (photograph by and courtesy of Patrick Rothfuss).**

ate working in a University of Wisconsin computer lab, grew weary of responding to queries about how dangerous the "Good Times" virus really was. A talented satirist, he wrote a spoof of the warning, cautioning that the program will not only destroy a user's hard drive, but also rewrite floppy disks stored nearby, scratch CDs, scramble the tracking on a TV, demagnetize credit cards, and cause ice cream to melt in one's refrigerator. "It will seduce your grandmother," Rothfuss added. "It does not matter if she is dead, such is the power of Good Times, it reaches out beyond the grave to sully those things we hold most dear." He concluded, "It is insidious and subtle. It is dangerous and terrifying to behold. It is also a rather interesting shade of mauve."[15] Set wild on Internet bulletin boards by Rothfuss's friends, the "anti-legend" parody circulated even more widely than the original virus warning and successfully drove it out of circulation. As e-mail gradually became a familiar way of life, so did awareness of the workings of real viruses, which were recognized as nuisances rather than catastrophes in the making.

Then, on December 30, 1999, a virus was discovered that exploited a security weakness in Microsoft's Outlook Express, by then the most commonly used e-mail browsing program. Named "KakWorm," the program in fact worked exactly like the legendary "Good Times." The virus silently infects the computer even if it is not opened or read, an official description explained, stating, "Simply reading the received email message causes the virus to be placed on the system."[16]

After all, tomorrow (a Friday) was the eve of Y2K.

Section Five

It Came from a Friend of a Friend — Media-Spread Urban Legends

Chapter 25

Urban Legends and the Media

> The passing on of stories from neighbor to neighbor has long been a part of human existence, but beginning with the first printing press, the mass media has rapidly sped up the process of dispensing rumor and gossip to a planet that has been turned into a global village by ever-evolving communication technology.

Chapter 23 on Katrina evacuee myths highlights the overlapping nature of the urban legends and cyberspace. The myth of the evacuees behaving badly was an urban legend, but it was almost exclusively transmitted via the Internet and hence, has been placed in the category of cyberspace.

Urban legends are also known as "friend of a friend" stories because they are nearly impossible to trace to their original source. When the storyteller is pressed to reveal where he or she heard it from, it usually turns of to be a friend of a friend's mother's cousin who, in turn, heard it from a friend of a friend. These stories are nearly impossible to verify, are passed on mostly by word of mouth, are touted as being of recent origin, and are typically said to have happened in an urban environment—hence the term "urban legend." Put another way, they are a form of living folklore. The world's foremost authority on the subject is American folklorist Jan Harold Brunvand who popularized the term in 1981 in his now famous book, *The Vanishing Hitchhiker: American Urban Legends and Their Meanings.*[1]

Until the 1950s, folklorists viewed these tales as being almost exclusively spread by word of mouth, but soon began to realize that many newspaper accounts turned out to be urban legends in disguise.[2] While urban legends are not considered to be a form of mass media per se, since the development and proliferation of newspapers, radio, TV and film, these various mediums greatly amplify the power of stories that were once only spread from person to person. Not only do they quickly spread their message to a large audience, the very appearance of messages in these mediums can lend credibility to the possibility of their reality. To hear someone say that the president of the United States has been shot is one thing, but to hear it over the TV or on the radio is far more powerful and influential in convincing a skeptical public.

An early example of the power of the media to spread urban legends is the "Paul McCartney Is Dead" scare of the late 1960s. McCartney was the lead singer of arguably the greatest rock band ever: The Beatles. In 1969 newspaper accounts began to appear that the famous rock star had died three years earlier in 1966, but the band had secretly replaced him with a look-alike at the insistence of record company bigwigs who were fearful that, if the truth got out, record sales would plummet and they would lose money. It is worth noting that urban legends usually have a grain of truth to them and they appear plausible, however unlikely. In this case, record company executives are notorious for focusing on the bottom line: profits. Hence, while still outrageous, this history creates just a hint of doubt that it just may be true.

Typical of an urban legend, no one knows where the rumor started. The first known published story appeared on the campus of Illinois University. On September 23, 1969, the college newspaper the *Northern Star* reported that "there has been much conjecturing on the present state of the Beatle Paul McCartney."[3] The story continued to circulate on college campuses until October 12, when a man telephoned a radio station in Detroit, Michigan, and pointed out a number of coincidences involving McCartney suggesting that he really was dead. The disc jockey who fielded the call, Russ Gibb of WKNR-FM, unwittingly helped to spread the story to a wider audience.

The caller, who apparently had a lot of free time on his hands, told Gibb claims that the Beatles had left hidden clues about Paul's demise in their albums. One example he gave was the famous song "Strawberry Fields Forever," where at the end, he said, if you listened closely, it sounded like someone is saying, "I buried Paul."[4] Two days later a University of Michigan newspaper published a long article entitled "McCartney Is Dead," adding even more coincidences.[5]

The story exploded on that national scene on October 21, when a major newspaper, the *Chicago Sun-Times*, published the story. Fans began looking at their Beatles records and album covers in a different light, under the assumption that they may contain hidden clues. On the *Sergeant Pepper* album, McCartney is wearing an armband with the letters OPD. Some suggested that it stood for "Officially Pronounced Dead."

On their *Abbey Road* album, there is a car in the background with the license plate "28IF," a reference, some said, to the fact that Paul would have turned 28 if he hadn't died.[6] McCartney (some said his look-alike) eventually appeared and denied the rumors, which he called "bloody stupid." He observed: "I picked up that O.P.D. badge in Canada. It was a police badge. Perhaps it means Ontario Police Department.... The Volkswagen just happened to be parked there."[7] The hoopla quickly died out after McCartney appeared on the cover of *Life* magazine, with the unusual task of denying his own death![8]

CHAPTER 26

The Curse of the Crying Boy

by David Clarke

In 1985, a British newspaper published a report of fire badly damaging a house in South Yorkshire. Miraculously, a cheap painting of a crying toddler was found amongst the remains, perfectly intact. The story claimed there had been a pattern of fires in homes after hanging prints of the *Crying Boy*. What's more, in each case the prints were untouched by the devastation around it. Folklorist David Clarke looks into the origins of this urban legend and the role of the media in spreading it.

This is the story of how a newspaper reported on and spread an urban legend rapidly across Great Britain, and how with the advent of the Internet, it continues to titillate readers around the world. "True stories" about curses inflicted upon tomb raiders who have looted gems from ancient temples and idols were a staple theme of Gothic horror fiction during the Victorian era — the span between 1837 and 1901, during the reign of Queen Victoria. More recently legends of jinxes visited on modern explorers have become a popular subject for Hollywood movies. Fascination with this type of urban legend peaked in the 1920s when Britain was gripped by fear of a "Pharaoh's curse" after the deaths of archaeologists who were present at the opening of King Tutankhamen's tomb.

In urban legend, curses are not confined to Egyptian relics, or to the fictional adventures of Indiana Jones, but are told by real people of real events or are supposedly "based on a true story." In older traditions, coincidences, jinxes, mysterious deaths and runs of bad luck are common. These beliefs

David Clarke *is a senior lecturer in journalism at Sheffield Hallam University (UK). He has a Ph.D. in folklore from the University of Sheffield and ten years' experience working for weekly and evening newspapers. A researcher for a range of television and radio programs, he has published seven books, most recently* The UFO Files *(National Archives, 2009).*

have become so deeply rooted in the human psyche that some people come to believe that certain inanimate objects have become enchanted with supernatural powers. Portraits are frequently the focus of this type of story. The common experience of being in a room with a portrait whose eyes "seem to follow you wherever you go" has become a staple of many horror films. In folklore, the notion that a picture falling from a wall is an omen of impending death — particularly if it is a portrait — remains one of the best known modern superstitions and can be traced back to the 17th century. In some areas of Britain it is still regarded as unlucky to hang portraits over a door or bed. If you believe a portrait can symbolically represent a real person and that sudden and unexplained happenings are always ominous, this type of supernatural cause and effect becomes understandable. These superstitions are always associated with human likenesses rather than paintings of animals or inanimate objects such as landscapes or bowls of sunflowers. Artwork possessed by, or associated with, evil acts have naturally become a popular theme in literature and film. Oscar Wilde drew upon this theme in *The Picture of Dorian Gray* (1890), which did its owner's ageing for him, locked safely away in an attic. The most chilling adaptation of the idea was in M.R. James's ghost story *The Mezzotint* (1904). This tells the story of a collector of topographical pictures who acquires an obscure illustration of an eighteenth-century manor house. As the owner learns about the house's history, his terror rises as the haunted mezzotint evolves to display a story of murder and revenge from beyond the grave.

A Tabloid-Triggered Scare

A modern variation of the "jinxed painting" legend appeared on British breakfast tables on the morning of September 4, 1985. On this day *The Sun*, at that time the most popular tabloid newspaper in the English-speaking world, published a story headlined: "Blazing Curse of the Crying Boy." The story told how a couple, Ron and May Hall, were blaming a cheap painting of a toddler with tears rolling down his face for a fire which gutted their home in Rotherham, a small mining town in South Yorkshire. The blaze broke out as a grease fire in the kitchen and spread rapidly. Although the downstairs rooms were badly damaged, the framed print of the crying boy wasn't touched by smoke. It continued to hang, seemingly untouched even by smoke, surrounded by a scene of devastation.[1]

Normally a story about a grease fire would merit nothing more than a couple of paragraphs in a local newspaper. What transformed this story into headlines in Britain's leading tabloid was the intervention of Ron Hall's brother

Peter, a firefighter based in Rotherham. A colleague of his, Rotherham fire officer Alan Wilkinson, knew of similar cases where prints of the crying boy had turned up, undamaged, in homes destroyed by fires. Prior to the blaze Peter Hall had warned his brother to get rid of the painting, telling them that "he and his mates had seen the print too often in houses where there had been blazes."

Accompanying the story was a photo of a crying boy, with a caption that again underlined the message: "Tears for fears ... the portrait that firemen claim is cursed." In reality, the firemen concerned had not made this claim, but the report gave the story a further boost of credibility. The curse appeared to be vouched for by members of a professional fire and rescue service whose judgment many *Sun* readers would not think to question. The paper further claimed that an estimated 50,000 crying boy prints, signed "G. Bragolin," had been sold in branches of British department stores, particularly in the working-class areas of northern England where copies were offered as prizes at bingo games. Prints could be seen hanging in the front rooms and lounges of family homes across the nation and one story suggested a quarter of a million had been sold.

The mass media, and newspapers in particular, have played a major role in the transmission of rumors and urban legends. Tabloid news and the overriding priority to provide a good story, have often taken priority over journalistic accuracy, particularly in stories that emphasize the uncanny or bizarre. Peter Chippindale and Chris Horrie in their warts-and-all history of Britain's *Sun* tabloid, *Stick It Up Your Punter!* (1990), credit *Sun* editor Kelvin MacKenzie as the father of the crying boy myth.[2] During the mid–1980s the *Sun* was engaged in a nasty battle for readers with its Fleet Street rival, the *Daily Mirror*. It was also responsible for publishing a series of legendary, horrific and bizarre stories with tenuous origins, of which some — such as "Freddie Starr Ate My Hamster"— lived on in the popular imagination in a similar manner to the more enduring urban legends. Constantly hungry for news, MacKenzie was on the lookout for what journalists call "a great splash." The splash for him was an exclusive story that none of his rivals would dream of publishing first. MacKenzie's stroke of genius was in spotting mention of the "curse" in routine copy about the Rotherham blaze in a "filler" sent to the paper by a regional news agency. They wrote that to the surprise and the consternation of the news staff who thought that MacKenzie "flipped his lid," he ran the "Curse of the Crying Boy Picture" on the front page, asking readers to phone the paper with their own mishaps or fires involving the picture. It worked. The next day the paper was flooded with phone calls. "MacKenzie cleared more space to print the strangest and most horrifying tales, and appealed for yet more. 'This one's got legs,' he confidently announced, using his phrase for a story that would 'run and run.'"[3]

What happened next is a testament to the power of the media. On September 5, 1985, *The Sun* ran a follow-up, reporting that "horrified readers claiming to be victims of the 'Curse of the Crying Boy' had flooded [the paper] with calls.... They all feared they were jinxed by having the print of a tot with tears pouring down his face in their homes." Readers were left with an overwhelming impression of a supernatural link. The language used by the newspaper, "curse," "jinx," "feared," and "horrified" was laden with sinister foreboding. Typical of the new stories was that told by Dora Mann from Mitcham, Surrey, who claimed her house was gutted just six months after she bought a print. "All my paintings were destroyed — except the one of the crying boy," she said. Sandra Kaske of Kilburn, North Yorkshire, claimed that she, her sister-in-law, and a friend had suffered disastrous fires since they acquired copies of the mass-produced print. Another family, from Nottingham, blamed the crying boy for a blaze which had left them homeless. Brian Parks, 22, whose wife and three children needed treatment for smoke inhalation, said he had immediately destroyed his copy after returning from hospital to find it hanging undamaged on the blackened wall of his living room.

As the stories accumulated, sinister new details began to emerge, adding to the idea that simple possession of a print put owners at risk of fire or death. One London print owner claimed she had seen it "swing from side to side," while another from Paignton said her 11-year-old son had "caught his private parts on a hook" after she bought the picture. Mrs. Rose Farrington of Preston, in a letter published by *The Sun*, wrote: "Since I bought it in 1959, my three sons and my husband have all died. I've often wondered if it had a curse." Another reader reported an attempt to destroy two of the prints by fire only to find, to her horror, they would not burn. Her claim was tested by security guard Paul Collier who tossed one of two prints he possessed onto a bonfire in his girlfriend's garden. Despite being left in the flames for an hour, Collier claimed it was not even scorched. "It was frightening — the fire wouldn't even touch it," he told *The Sun*. "I really believe it is jinxed. We feel doubly at risk with two of these in the house [and] we are determined to get rid of them."

A Natural Explanation

Collier's story harkened back to comments by the firemen who recalled the aftermath of a number of house fires dating back to 1973, where the print inexplicably appeared to have escaped damage. The real mystery, from their perspective, was *how* the picture had survived fires that were in themselves explainable. In most cases straightforward explanations of carelessly discarded cigarettes, overheated frying pans and faulty electric heaters had been found during the subsequent investigation. Rotherham fire station officer Alan Wilkinson who, it emerged, had personally logged fifty crying boy fires over a twelve-year period, dismissed supernatural explanations. Wilkinson, who had 33 years' experience in the brigade, said he wasn't superstitious and had satisfied himself that most of the fires had been caused by human carelessness. Despite his pragmatism, he could not explain how they had survived the inferno of a house fire which generated heat sufficient to strip plaster from walls. His wife had her own theory: "I always say it's the tears that put the fire out."

The Sun was not particularly interested in a rational explanation and claimed that "fire chiefs have admitted they have no logical explanation for a number of recent incidents." The story, as MacKenzie had predicted, "had got legs" and soon migrated onto TV news, encouraging the paper's Fleet Street rivals to publish their own crying boy stories. This development had two immediate effects. First, many more examples of house fires where crying boy prints had inexplicably survived came to light, all pre-dating the Rotherham incident by months or years. The earliest was from Ripley, Derbyshire, in 1980. At this stage, the fact that firefighters in Rotherham had records of fires as far back as 1973 was not publicly known. This fact established that a rumor linking the prints with uncanny fires pre-dated *The Sun*'s promotion of the curse in 1985.

Then it emerged that the cursed prints were not all copies of the same painting, nor were all the prints by the same artist. The picture that survived the fire in Rotherham which initially triggered the tabloid campaign was apparently signed by the artist, G. Bragolin. *The Sun* claimed the original was "by an Italian artist." In fact, Giovanni Bragolin was a pseudonym adopted by Spanish painter Bruno Amadio, who is also known as "Franchot Seville." Attempts to trace him floundered as art historians said he did not appear to have "a coherent biography" which added to the mystery. To make matters more confusing, other crying boys — part of a series of studies called "Childhood" — were painted by the acclaimed Scots artist Anna Zinkeisen (1901–1976), whose work had been exhibited by the Royal Academy. The only common denominator shared by this motley collection was that they were the first example of cheap, mass-produced prints sold in great numbers by English department stores during the sixties and seventies. The geographical cluster of fires simply reflected the popularity of the prints among working-class communities in the north. Art historians consulted by the media dismissed the stories as "coincidence and superstition." One said he had never heard of a curse connected with the print, which one described as good example of kitsch: "a mawkish continental urchin with globular tears coursing down his podgy cheeks."

Despite accusations of bad taste the crying boy remained an extremely popular print, particularly for working-class families, and existed in at least five different forms. At least two of these had companion studies of "crying girls" and some people owned copies of both. Others in the series included pictures of girls and boys holding flowers, most of them sad in tone. In defiance of the tabloid headlines, some female owners had developed such an emotional bond with the print that they refused to dispose of them. "I've never cared for the picture myself because of its sadness," the partner of one proud owner was quoted as saying. He then went on to pose two questions which many anxious *Sun* readers wanted answered: "Why would you want a picture of a child crying? Why *was* the child crying?" Naturally journalists turned to "experts" in the field of folklore for an explanation. When a tabloid journalist approached Folklore Society member Georgina Boyes who lived in Rotherham, the interview faltered when she refused to provide a suitably Satanic explanation for the crying boy. As a result, the journalist "went off in search of 'a witch' or 'somebody into the occult' who might make a better headline." Roy Vickery, secretary of the Folklore Society, was ironically the first "expert" quoted by the press who supplied a possible reason *why* the crying boy was crying. He suggested that the original artist might have mistreated the child model in some way, adding: "All these fires could be child's curse, his way of getting revenge."[4]

It was a print of Zenkeisen's *Crying Boy* that became the center of the next fire reported by *The Sun*. This destroyed a council house in Rotherham, a town which had emerged not only as the geographical location of many of the reported fires, but also as the source of the whole phenomenon. Kevin Godber, 23, his wife Julie, 19, and their two small children were left homeless in October 1985 when a fire swept through their council house in East Herringthorpe. Firemen traced the source to an electric fire in the couple's bedroom, but not before the family had found the print still hanging, untouched by fire, in the charred ruins of the house. Kevin said the family had only been in the house for a few months. "There were pictures on either side of the *Crying Boy* picture, and these were destroyed — yet the mystery print was intact," he told the press.

The same story quoted a fire brigade spokesman reassuring owners of the print that although there was no "cause for alarm ... these incidents are becoming more frequent." The feeling of anxiety which publication of this article sparked off led a senior official in the South Yorkshire Fire Service to put out a hasty denial, debunking the connection between the fires and the prints. It pointed out that the most recent fire reported from Rotherham was started by an electric fire left too close to a bed. A large number of these pictures had been imported into Britain, it said, and "any connection with the fires is purely coincidental.... Fires are not started by pictures or coincidence, but by careless acts and omissions." The statement revealed another more definitive explanation: "The reason why this picture has not always been destroyed in the fire is because it is printed on high density hardboard, which is very difficult to ignite."

Journalist Stephen McClarence did his bit to pour cold water on the flames when a crying boy turned up in an exhibition titled *The Bad Taste Show* at Sheffield Polytechnic in December that year. Reviewing the show for the *Sheffield Star*, he repeated the fire chief's theory that the print had survived due to its fire retardant qualities. "But there's another reason — apart from the Revenge of Good Taste — why the *Crying Boy* turns up in so many house fires," he explained. "There are so many millions of copies of the picture in living rooms all over the country — almost as many as there are Haywains — that you'd be hard put to find a combustible home without one or other of them."

A skeptical stance was also taken by agony aunts (British journalistic jargon for someone who writes responses to distressed readers) known as the Old Codgers in *The Sun*'s rival *Daily Mirror*. An elderly woman reader wrote to them for advice about what to do after her son presented her with a framed print of the crying boy. "I can't think why such a lovely picture could suddenly be thought to be jinxed," she wrote. "Yet everyone seems to think that wherever the picture is hung there is a fire, so I should get rid of it." The Codgers told her to ignore the advice: "It's one of the those silly irrational rumours which spring up from time to time. We old pair of legend busters would have thought it wiser to hang onto the picture because if there were any truth to the story it would be the one safe object to cling to! As for other tragedies — there is such a thing as coincidence."

These skeptical voices did little to put an end to the legend which *The Sun* was happily working up. Soon after the Godber story was published, news came of a crying boy that had survived a fire which gutted an Italian restaurant in Great Yarmouth. "Enough is enough, folks," announced the editor: "If you are worried about a crying boy picture hanging in YOUR home, send it to us immediately. We will destroy it for you — and that should see the back of any curse." According to Chippindale and Horrie's account: "Worried readers rang in to ask if they should get rid of their copy to stop their houses burning down. 'Sure,' MacKenzie replied. 'Send them in — we'll do the job for you.' Bouverie Street was swamped.... The *Crying Boy*s were soon stacked twelve feet high in the newsroom, spilling out of cupboards, and entirely filling a little-used interview room."[5]

Most amazing of all, the saga revealed how the cynical, worldly wise MacKenzie had come to believe in his own "curse." Up to that point his team couldn't work out how much credence their boss really attached to the story. This question was answered when the paper's assistant editor took down a picture of Winston Churchill, which had been hanging on the newsroom wall since the Falklands War, and replaced it with a *Crying Boy*. According to *Stick It Up Your Punter!*: "MacKenzie, bustling into the newsroom at his normal half-run, stopped dead in his tracks and went white. 'Take that down,' he snapped. 'I don't like it. It's bad luck.'"

Fireman Alan Wilkinson reacted similarly when, as a joke, his colleagues presented him with a framed crying boy on his retirement from the brigade in 1986. Although, like Kelvin MacKenzie, he denied being superstitious, he immediately handed the picture back to his boss, divisional chief officer Mick Riley, with a note saying: "No thanks, you can keep it." Even Riley, who was responsible for the statement debunking the "curse," wouldn't accept it, saying his wife "wouldn't like it, it wouldn't fit in." Interviewed by his local paper, during *The Sun* campaign, Wilkinson admitted that he had been presented with a print by a worried woman who turned up at his home one night. He took it to work and "as a joke" hung it in the office of the fire station. Within days was ordered by his superiors to take it down. Heaping irony upon comedy, the story continued: "The same day an oven in the upstairs kitchen overheated and the firemen's dinners were burned."

Kelvin MacKenzie faced a similar dilemma. At the end of a six-week crying boy campaign, the superstitious editor of *The Sun* had to devise a way of disposing of 2,500 copies of the print that readers had sent in. A plan to burn them on the roof of the paper's Bouverie Street offices was vetoed by both the London and Thames Valley fire brigades. Both refused to co-operate and denounced the whole campaign "as a cheap publicity stunt." The reasons for their reluctance were clear. It emerged that nationally the fire service had been the focus of hundred calls and visits by anxious folk who believed the prints were cursed, or that they were made of a dangerous flammable material. Eventually reporter Paul Hooper, with photographers and "page 3 girls" in tow, left *The Sun* HQ with two vanloads of prints for burning on a makeshift pyre near Reading.

The Sun splashed the story appropriately on Halloween, under the headline: "Sun Nails Curse of the Weeping Boy for Good," bylining Hooper as the tabloid's "fine art correspondent." A photograph depicted a scantily clad "red hot Page Three beauty Sandra Jane Moore" feeding the bonfire as bemused firemen looked on. Fire officer Barry Davis, who reluctantly supervised the stunt, was quoted as saying, with tongue planted firmly in cheek: "We all listened for muffled cries, but all we heard was the crackle of paintings burning. I think there will be many people who can breathe a little easier now."

The Halloween burning was widely believed to have exorcized the curse of the crying boy and the number of tabloid stories began to decrease. But in March the following year a columnist in the Bristol-based *Western Morning News* pointed out that the industrial turmoil faced by News International (owners of *The Sun*), which involved strikes and violent picketing at their new Fort Wapping production plant, began shortly after the paper's bonfire. Poking fun at its Fleet Street rival, the paper implied the jinx so feared by Kelvin MacKenzie had finally been visited upon its creator!

Crying boy fires continued to be reported into the spring of 1986 but they were fewer in number. In the most serious linked to the curse, a pensioner, 76-year-old William Armitage, died when flames swept through his bedsit [one-room apartment] in Weston-super-Mare. According to *The Sun*, firefighters found the print as they fought their way through thick smoke to the rescue Armitage. One of the officers, Bob Hatherley, found the print on the floor near the man's body. He said Armitage had been smoking, but nevertheless it was a "very weird feeling" when his men spotted the picture. At the scene of one them had gasped out loud: "Oh my god, it's that picture!"

The Legend Morphs

As tabloid interest waned, so crying boy curse tales began to morph into a modern legend. New versions of the story appeared, including one which suggested those who were kind to the print were rewarded with good luck. In March, *Sun* reader Bob Cherry revealed how he had "defied the curse" and been rewarded by the crying boy. He recognized one of the prints when he pulled his barely functioning car into a layby (pull-off) near Glasgow, where it was propped up against a dustbin, and decided to take it home. "When I put the picture inside [the car] it started first time and I haven't had any bother since," he said. Within days Cherry won three unexpected cash prizes at a bingo game, on the football pools and on fruit machines. "It might not seem a lot of money, but three wins in a row is more than coincidence — especially when I've not been lucky before," he said. His story echoed ancient and widespread ideas surrounding good and bad luck which are basic to folk beliefs, but take no account of chance or coincidence. Another example was the idea that placing a picture of the crying girl next to that of the crying boy would bring good luck or avert bad luck.

What the story lacked in 1985–86 was a coherent narrative or story that explained how the crying boy came to be a source of fire. After the initial flurry of media interest the story appeared to die a natural death. But, as with many other urban legends, the arrival of the Internet gave it a new lease on life when a narrative appeared to complete the legend. One web-source claims that during the nineties crying boy fires began to be reported outside the British Isles. It also reflects how the basic story was being molded by professional storytellers and paranormal investigators for a new audience: "A medium claims the spirit of the boy is trapped in the painting and it starts fires in an attempt to burn the painting and free itself. Others claim the painting is haunted or attracts poltergeist activity. Stories of the artist's and subject's misfortune had attached themselves to the painting."

The idea that the crying boy had been badly treated by the artist was gaining popularity. It can be traced to a speculative theory offered to *The Sun* by a member of the Folklore Society a decade earlier. Early in the new millennium this idea re-emerged in an account published by Tom Slemen in his series of books called *Haunted Liverpool*. Slemen's books are a mixture of fact and fiction and are presented in an entertaining, narrative style which appeals to a mass readership. In his entry "The Crying Boy Jinx" he summarizes the stories before stating as fact that the "head of the Yorkshire Fire Brigade" had told national newspapers that the uncanny print turned up in the rubble of houses that had "mysteriously burnt to the ground." According to Slemen, when journalists asked him if he believed the picture was evil, "the fire chief refused to comment."[6]

This factually incorrect account nicely introduced the narrative which explained *why* the picture was evil. This was discovered by "a well respected researcher into occult matters, a retired schoolmaster from Devon named George Mallory" in 1995. Mallory traced the artist who had painted the original portrait, "an old Spanish portrait artist named Franchot Seville, who lives in Madrid." Seville, as astute readers will recognize, was one of the pseudonyms used by Bruno Amadio, otherwise known as G. Bragolin, whose signature appeared on some of the prints. So far so good. According to Slemen, Seville/Amadio/Bragolin told Mallory that "the crying boy was a little street urchin he had found wandering around Madrid in 1969. He never spoke, and had a very sorrowful look in his eyes. Seville painted the boy, and a Catholic priest said the boy was Don Bonillo, a child who had run away after seeing his parents die in a blaze. The priest told the artist to have nothing to do with the runaway, because wherever he settled, fires of unknown origin would mysteriously break out; the villagers called him 'Diablo' [devil] because of this."[7]

The painter reportedly ignored the priest's advice and adopted the boy. His portraits sold well and made him rich but one day his studio was destroyed in a mystery blaze and the artist was ruined. He accused the sad little boy of arson and Don Bonillo ran off, naturally in tears, and was never seen again. "Then, from all over Europe came the reports of the unlucky Crying Boy paintings causing blazes. Seville was also regarded as a jinx, and no one commissioned him to paint, or would even look at his paintings. In 1976, a car exploded into a fireball on the outskirts of Barcelona after crashing into a wall. The victim was charred beyond recognition, but part of the victim's driving licence in the glove compartment was only partly burned. The name on the licence was one 19-year-old Don Bonillo."[8]

Could this be the same orphan taken in by the jinxed artist, the one villagers knew as "Diablo"? The original author and date of this ingenious story is unknown and the mysterious George Mallory proves to be as untraceable as Franchot Seville or Giovanni Bragolin. It completes the metamorphosis of the curse of the crying boy from tabloid obscurity to a fully fledged urban legend whose elements are accessible to anyone via the Internet.

The complete lack of any factual basis for the Don Bonillo story has done nothing to erode its popularity, stoked by supernatural discussion boards on the World Wide Web. In 2002, I was invited to comment on the latest crying boy story in my dual roles as a journalist and "expert" on urban legends on a reality TV series known as *Scream Team*. The series, modeled on the more successful ITV series *Most Haunted*, plucked six young people from hundreds of hopefuls, then sent them out in a silver bus to travel around Britain investigating legends, curses and haunted places. The premise was to encourage the skeptics and believers in the group to resolve each puzzle by drawing upon the collective knowledge of assorted "experts." For the curse of the crying boy, the team was dispatched to Wigan in Lancashire where the owners of a transport café, Eddie and Marian Brockley, had recently suffered a disastrous fire which the local media had linked to what they claimed was "one of the last surviving copies" of the print. Eddie believed the link was pure coincidence but his wife was more anxious. She had heard of similar fires associated with the crying boy and refused to allow the offending print — a copy of *Childhood* by Zinkeisen — back into the café. Although the couple were largely ambivalent about the idea of a curse, they played along with the TV show's plan to draft in their teenage investigators. Then along came the skeptical journalist (the author!) who did his best to place the story in its true context as an evolving urban legend. I summarized the various evolving legends surrounding the print, including Tom Slemen's account of the infant fire-starter. There was no factual evidence, I emphasized, that "Don Bonillo" ever existed outside the imagination of Tom Slemen or whoever his source may have been.

Inevitably, the next guest was a trance medium whose task was to "tune in" to the jinxed painting whose history, the program assured viewers, she knew absolutely nothing about. Nevertheless, within minutes she was able to divine the link between the painting and a real artist who lives in Spain, a sensation of burning and a car crash. She was even able to name the little boy as "Din, Don or Dan," which was enough to convince the more superstitious members of the team that there really was something in the curse. The program ended with the team agreeing to destroy the Brockley's copy of the crying boy outside the café and disperse any surviving evil influence it might retain. The print was duly doused with petrol and attempts were made to ignite it. Three attempts were made without success, before the print finally succumbed, no doubt to the great relief of the *Scream Team*.

Is the crying boy still out there, looking for new victims? A Google search suggests that belief in this urban legend, itself just part of a wider genre of haunted/jinxed paintings, is alive and well. Prints occasionally turn up on the Internet auction site eBay, while a Dutch "Crying Boy Fanclub" website briefly appeared, then disappeared in 2006. Meanwhile discussion boards across the world continue to debate the reality of the curse.

CHAPTER 27

Photos of the Gods

by David Clarke

Since the advent of photography, people have claimed to have taken photographs with ghostly images. In recent times, such photos have reached cyberspace. Folklorist David Clarke looks at three famous photos supposedly of Jesus Christ: The Miracle in the Snow, The Hidden Christ Picture, and "the picture that took itself," and asks the question, what's going on?

A psychological phenomenon involving vague and random stimulus (often an image or a sound) being mistakenly conceived as recognizable. Common examples include images of animals or faces in clouds, seeing the man in the moon or faces on Mars, and hearing hidden messages on records played in reverse.

— *Steven Godstein, 1994*

Soon after the invention of photography, stories began to circulate of miraculous or supernatural images captured by accident on camera. During the 19th century these photos became the focus of stories and rumors aimed at explaining how the images appeared — stories that often drew upon folklore about life after death and sometimes contained a religious message. This type of urban legend became a popular subject for newspapers which were, for the first time, reaching a widening readership. At the same time, as access to and understanding of the photographic process increased, so did the use by mediums of photography to produce pictures of "spirits" and deceased persons. The craze for "spirit photography" peaked after World War I as mediums responded to a demand for images of loved ones killed in the conflict.

David Clarke *is a senior lecturer in journalism at Sheffield Hallam University (UK) (see page 134).*

A "miracle photograph" of a statue of Jesus at Holy Love Ministries near Cleveland, Ohio, taken in 2007 by a pilgrim. The photographer, Kim Tran, believes that the mysterious glowing image around the statue reveals the presence of Jesus (collection of Benjamin Radford).

Today "spirit photographs" continue to be published as genuine supernatural images on the Internet, often appearing as orbs or peculiar patches of light. In most cases the photographer claimed to have detected the image only *after* processing. Where they take on a human form they are frequently identified as figures or faces, or as souls of the dead, spirits, angels, demons and other supernatural entities. The perception of supernatural images in photos or other visual representations is a type of psychological phenomenon that has become so common it has generated its own technical term, *pareidolia*, from the Greek word *para* ("amiss, faulty, wrong"), and *eidolon*, meaning "image." The identification of human faces and figures in natural phenomena such as clouds and rock formations (known as *simulacra*) is also well known, as is the motivation to attribute catastrophes to evil forces beyond our control. In 2001, for example, many people claimed they could see the face of Satan, complete with eyes, nose and horns, in a photograph showing smoke billowing from the blazing south tower of the World Trade Center following the 9-11 atrocities. The picture was taken within 40 minutes of the terrorist attacks by photographer Mark Phillips, who sold it to the Associated Press. He later told the AP that he never noticed a face or any images when he looked at the photos, but after it was published he received hundreds of e-mails from people across the country who said they could clearly identify Satanic features in the smoke.

During the twentieth century a wide range of supernatural or divine phenomena, including angels, Marian apparitions, fairy folk and mysterious creatures such as the Loch Ness Monster, have been perceived in photographs and film footage. For some, photography provided a method to substantiate the reality of the supernatural via the use of an image as "proof," drawing on the old adage "the camera can't lie." A more apt quote when dealing with images such as these is that "every picture tells a story."

One important type of supernatural or miraculous photograph that bridges the gap between "spirit photography" and more recent examples of supernatural photography are a perplexing set of images that Bob Rickard calls "Photos of the Gods." In this category there are at least three separate photographs allegedly showing Jesus. All three were widely published and circulated during the twentieth century and have provided the trigger for elaborate stories told by numerous individuals who own copies of the photographs, which seek to explain the origin and meaning of the image. Some of these stories are so widely circulated that newspapers must have played a major role in creating this type of urban legend.[1]

Perhaps the most famous image from this group has been dubbed "Christ in the Snow," "The Miracle in the Snow," "The Hidden Christ Picture," "the picture that took itself," and by doubters, "the fake photo of Jesus." The image is a familiar one to Christians of all denominations. It shows Jesus in the "Sacred Heart" pose with his right hand raised in benediction and his left hand clutching his robe as though about to expose his chest. However, even the "Christ in the Snow" label is a misnomer for the *very idea* of a snow scene is partly a product of perception and partly the result of the constant copying and recopying of the image over a period of half a century or more. The picture has been circulating since the 1920s and some versions trace its origins to World War I.

In 1976 Maurice Barbanell, editor of the London-based spiritualist weekly newspaper *Psychic News*, testified that he had tried without success for 40 years to pin down the origins of what he called "the fake photo of Jesus." In that time he could find no evidence to support any of the stories which claimed to identify the original photographer. For example, when in 1978 he traced one lady who claimed to have the original negative, it turned out to be only a copy of a copy. Barbanell recalled how *Psychic News* published the photograph for the first time in its Easter 1936 edition, under the headline "The Strange Face on the Picture": "This supernormal face appeared on a picture taken by two girls who knew nothing of spiritualism, when out for a ramble. They were using a film bought that afternoon, and the roll was finished before they returned home, so they left it with a local chemist to be developed and printed.... When they found this picture among their snaps, they thought the chemist had mixed up their negatives with those of another customer, but he assured them it was no mistake."

Publication of the picture brought a flood of letters to the London offices of the magazine from correspondents across the world. Most of them told different stories. In one, a writer claimed the photograph was "of a tree near which an old woman used to sit reading the New Testament and on it the mysterious face appeared." Another sent a copy of the same photograph which was circulating in faraway New Zealand. This time the story was that a mother was taking a snap of her two children and, after preparing the camera, turned away for a moment. Just then she heard a clicking sound and reprimanded the children for messing with the camera. But they denied going near it. She rolled up the film and took the photograph using the next frame. The mysterious picture was found on the unexposed film when it was processed at the lady's drugstore. On another occasion a visitor to Barbanell's office claimed his daughter worked in the same telephone exchange as a girl who said that she saw her dead mother in a dream and was told to photograph a tree at the end of the garden. She had the same dream three times before taking the picture on which the figure of Jesus appeared. Barbanell added: "The liftman at the telephone exchange, I was told, was doing a roaring trade by selling postcard copies at 4d. each."

All the versions of the photograph that came to light following the *Psychic News* stories in 1936 were copies of copies. Bob Rickard says that a basic genealogy of the image can be reconstructed by comparing the way the light and dark patches have become blocked in.[2] The clearer the image is, the older the version appears to be. Using such a method of analysis, it is possible to determine that, while the version printed in the U.S.-based *Fate Magazine* in

This "Miracle in the Snow" photograph has circulated for decades. Many of the faithful believe it is a genuine photograph of Jesus.

1955 is one of the earliest and clearest versions, one of the most recent printings, in *Sunday People* (1977), is a heavily cropped part of a larger, earlier image. The fact that many versions of the photograph have been circulating for almost a century is the only definite fact that can be established with any degree of certainty. In the *Fate* article Albert Brandt declared that his version of the photo was taken by Mildred Swanson, a Seattle, Washington, housewife, on a bright, sunny day in July 1920. His version of the story is similar to that reported from New Zealand in 1936:

> Mrs. Swanson wished to take a photo of her seven-year-old daughter Karin, and having loaded her Brownie camera with fresh film, put it down while Karin posed against a flower bank. Of its own accord the shutter clicked. Fearing she had ruined a frame, Mrs. Swanson advanced the film to the next frame. It clicked again on its own. The rest of the film behaved normally and she obtained the required photos of Karin except, when the film came back from the druggist in Rochester, NY, the two spoiled frames contained the image. Mrs. Swanson tried to duplicate the events with a second film, but that developed normally.

Bob Rickard discovered another variation of the same photograph was published by a Canadian newspaper during 1976. This version notably different from the Swanson photo and is distorted in a slightly different way.[3] Some 21 years later, journalist Julian North included the photo in an installment of his "Incredible but True" column in a Canadian newspaper, *The Victorian*. His version of Mildred Swanson's story is notably different and his version of the photo is distorted in a slightly different way. North traces its origins to 1937 and claims Swanson lived in Winnipeg. He says she wanted to send a snap of her flower garden to her daughter in Seattle. She put the camera down while she adjusted some flowers and heard it click on its own. Initially, she thought her cat might be responsible but it was not in sight. She continued to take pictures normally and, after development, was surprised to find the enigmatic image in place of a spoiled print. The manager of the store asked for and was given permission to sell reprints of "the picture that took itself," and several thousand were sold at a nickel each.

These stories, dated 1920 and 1937, say the background of Mildred Swanson's photo was a bank of flowers, not a snow scene. This leads Rickard to suspect that the idea of an image of Christ appearing miraculously in a photograph of a snow scene was invented by someone at a later date, in order to explain the contrasting black and white areas that appear on copies of the print. If you compare several versions of this image, and there are more than a dozen of them in existence, you immediately notice that the real cause of this high black/white contrast is successive copying. Every time the print has been copied and republished the contrast increased.[4]

But who took the original photograph and when? Maurice Barbanell told Bob Rickard that a print had been sent to Sir Arthur Conan Doyle in 1926 by someone who had obtained it in Vancouver, British Columbia, "where [even then] it was causing a sensation."[5] The photograph was displayed in the Conan Doyle Museum, then part of Sir Arthur's psychic bookshop in Victoria Street, London, for at least ten years and on the back of the print was an account which is identical to the Mildred Swanson story. *Psychic News* has reprinted the photo many times since its first outing in 1936, and each printing brought forth further variations of the same image, each accompanied by a unique claim as to how it was taken and by whom. Every time the photo is reproduced, its quality reduces, but it never fails to generate a new batch of impossible claims. A few examples include stories claiming the photograph was

- taken in a garden, either of a bank of flowers or a rose bush, versions reported from Canada, New Zealand, Australia, California and Britain.
- taken unexpectedly in a wood or of a bush or hedge covered in snow.

- taken during a snowstorm, or of a snow scene taken from the air.
- taken during thunderstorm, either of clouds or of a flash of lightning.
- as an example of spirit photography (in one case of the photographer's father, who died in 1919).
- taken by an atheist who exclaimed: "If God is everywhere, I'll take his picture." When the film was developed one negative contained the image of Jesus. As a result the skeptic either dies of shock, goes mad or is converted to Christianity.
- taken by someone either desperately seeking God or experiencing a spiritual crisis. The person is saved or healed as a direct result of taking the picture.

In one version of the tree story the photograph is taken at a prayer meeting by a group of Christians. They notice an exceptionally beautiful rose bush and take a picture of it. They explain the picture by reference to scripture: "For where two or three are gathered together in my name, there I am in the midst of them" (Matthew 18:20). However, in the vast majority of stories the photographer is either a woman taking a photograph of her daughter, or a group of girls on a ramble. Significantly, nothing is seen at the time but the camera (sometimes a Brownie) behaves mysteriously — either the shutter clicks of its own accord, or slips from the hands of the photographer.

In 1937 hundreds of *Daily Mirror* readers wrote to say they possessed identical copies of the print after columnist Godfrey Winn announced he had acquired the "genuine original." Other journalists have reported similar experiences. To celebrate their 5000th issue (on 13 November 1977), the London *Sunday People* printed one of the cropped versions showing just the face, saying it was "the most famous picture we have ever printed." It shows, they said, "a snow scene in the Alps, taken from an aircraft (in which) the face of Christ is etched in the melting snow." The editor explained how *People* had first published it on 10 October 1958, again the following week, and for a third time on 19 September 1965. As a result, the paper received 30,000 requests for copies of the picture "and sackfuls of requests more arrive almost every week." Just before Christmas 1977 the paper published a selection of letters from readers in response to yet another printing. One claimed that the photo was taken by a Chinese man troubled by the anti–Christian feelings in his country at that time. As he was walking through snow-covered mountains he called out: "Lord, if only I could see Thy face, I would believe." Then he heard a voice saying: "Take a photograph." Fortunately, he just happened to have his camera with him and snapped a hillside of melting snow and black earth. On seeing the "face" in the developed photo, he became a Christian.

One letter writer claimed the photo was "unexpectedly secured in the trenches in France" by a padre serving on the western front in World War I. This pushes the dating back to 1917 and links the photograph with the legends concerning apparitions seen during wartime such as the "Angels of Mons." Yet another story claimed the picture is "an aerial view of a WW2 snow scene" over London taken by an amateur photographer who was later killed in the bombing of the city during 1940.

These examples are just a sample of the many urban legends associated with the Jesus photograph that have been published and told by "friends of a friend" during the 20th century. The *Sunday People* newspaper claimed they had identified more than 40 different stories from the sacks full of letters they received in 1977. But the specific details, as few as they are, look more dubious the more closely they are examined. The names of the photographers involved are unknown and all attempts to trace their origins are frustrated at every turn.

The ubiquitous, perhaps even archetypal, nature of the Jesus photo legend suggests it may be an example of what the psychologist Carl Jung called *a visual rumor*, a phrase he applied to collective visions of phenomena such as the Angels of Mons and flying saucers. Its forms have spread far and wide and there are other examples of photos allegedly showing Eastern deities, allegedly taken in similar ambiguous circumstances by photographers in China and Korea. Where they turn up they seem to exert some strange amnesia over their owners. Precise details of how their copy was produced is replaced by a more personal origin legend which is often quite elaborate, while appealing to wider emotional, religious and mythical needs.

Another characteristic of visual rumors is their ability spawn myriad conflicting and contradictory accounts each time they are published. These are stories whose origin can never be satisfactorily pinned down. Each claimant believes, often very emphatically, their copy of the photograph is an original or that they know the true story of its origin. These accounts are always given on the authority of a "friend of a friend" or some even more esoteric chain of relationships. Each of these explanations is mutually exclusive, and therefore, not all of them can possibly be true."[6]

Despite the extraordinary claims, the photographic evidence falls far short of proof for anyone but the faithful. Like every phenomenon with a hint of the miraculous, the subject of miraculous photography appeals to frauds and fanatics. At the same time, it increases the happiness of large numbers of religious and spiritual people who are comforted by such images. One researcher who tried and failed to trace the original, Lewis Anthony, concluded: "There are several opinions one can take of this matter. One that I prefer is that the duplication of the pictures is further proof of the existence of Christ." And duplication it certainly does well. Back in the 1930s thousands of prints were made of the photograph and some versions even appeared as postcards. One account from 1958 describes how: "scores of young people carry copies of it in their wallets and handbags.... In universities and public schools it is passed on from hand to hand as the picture that turned the scoffing student to God."

Photos of the Gods remain one of the most popular in the "visual rumor" type of urban legend. In 1980 an advertisement in the U.S. *National Enquirer* offered a poster showing "The Hidden Face of Christ," already displayed in thousands of homes across the United States, at just $3 each or two copies for $5. The poster was promoted variously as "a conversation piece for every Christian home," "an optical illusion that will delight you and your friends," and was "ideal as a church fund-raiser."

Inevitably, copies of the image have now migrated onto the Internet where one was spotted in 1998 being sold "for healing purposes." Another variant of the image, in the form of a white-on-black negative, appeared in 2003 and was circulated as an e-mail forward with the title: "Optical Illusion." The London *Daily Mirror* published a version which it described as "an extraordinary miracle image [which] burns the face of Christ onto your mind's eye." The instructions were: "Concentrate on the set of four dots near the centre of this image for between 30 seconds and one minute. Then close your eyes and tilt your head back. Keep your eyes closed and you will see a circle of light. Keep staring at the circle of light: What do you see?" The widespread appearance of these and other so-called miracle images are a reminder of the propensity for human beings to see what they want to see. They would appear to be powerful reassuring symbols of hope and faith.[7]

Section Six

It Came from Everywhere

CHAPTER 28

The Satanic Cult Scare

> In the early 1980s, the fear of Satanic cults swept across the American landscape. Thousands of people eventually came forward to claim that they too had been the victim of Satanic ritual abuse. It soon became evident that the real culprit was a group of overzealous therapists who spread their fuzzy message with the aid of an unwitting media.

Starting in the early '80s, wild stories began circulating across America about a network of satanic cultists who were kidnapping and murdering children in ritual sacrifices. By the end of the decade, thousands of people had come forward with their own stories after attending psychotherapy sessions and revealing their own "hidden memories" of ritual abuse after being placed under hypnosis.

By the early '90s, it was clear that the accounts of organized ritual killing and abuse were imaginary, created from the fantasies of suggestive patients placed under hypnosis by overly aggressive therapists. Many journalists were unaware of the dubious techniques that were used to uncover these "hidden memories," instead relying on the views of certain "experts," as they helped to spread the Satanic cult myth nationwide. During the scare, there were absurd claims that upwards of 50,000 children a year were the victims of kidnapping and ritual sacrifice at the hands of covens. Incredibly, many journalists repeated these claims or suggested they were true, despite the glaring absence of even a single verified case. Sure, there was the odd story of satanic murder or kidnapping by wayward youths calling themselves satanists, but as part of an organized network, none.

At the height of the scare, researchers at the State University of New York at Buffalo surveyed clinical psychologists nationwide, asking them if they had treated victims of ritual abuse. Some 800 therapists reported over 5,700 cases.[1] An obvious question springs to mind: How could so many psychologists and patients be wrong? First, we must understand the scope of the problem. Eight hundred is a big figure, but the number of psychologists sampled was some 31,000.

Here's how the satanic cult scare happened. In 1980, Canadian psychiatrist Lawrence Pazder published *Michelle Remembers*, a heart-wrenching account of a woman who was brutally abused at the hands of a Satanic coven in Canada. Dr. Pazder describes how he began treating Michelle Smith in the late 1970s using regressive hypnosis, when he uncovered "repressed memories." *Michelle Remembers* was especially popular among Christians, and served as a cautionary tale against the evils people can do once led astray.

In the book, Michelle describes a tortured childhood at the hands of alcoholic parents. Her mother died when Michelle was 14, after which her father abandoned the family, leaving them to be raised by her grandparents. Michelle's story was nothing short of incredible. Over the next several months, Michelle told of being stripped naked and locked in a cage filled with snakes. She claimed to observe the butchering and burning of stillborn fetuses and the killing of kittens, and said she was forced to perform perverse sex acts. But this was tame compared to what she told Dr. Pazder next: that the cultists surgically attached horns to her head and a tail on her spine so she would resemble the devil! Dr. Pazder, who later married Michelle, was convinced that she had blotted these events from her conscious memory.[2]

Soon, based on publicity from *Michelle Remembers*, which sold over 100,000 copies, seminars and workshops began popping up across North America on satanic ritual abuse. At one point, satanism workshops were standard features for therapists, social workers and even police officers who thought they were keeping up with the latest developments in their fields. Armed with this information on the reality of satanic cults abusing children, therapists returned to their practices with lists of questions to ask their patients while under hypnosis. It comes as no surprise that a torrent of ritual abuse claims quickly followed.[3]

By the late '80s, hundreds of reports of satanic ritual abuse were being recorded in psychotherapy offices across the United States. Some victims appeared on such popular TV talk shows as *Geraldo Rivera*, *Oprah Winfrey*, and *Sally Jessy Raphael*. Sally aired such sensational shows as "Baby Breeders," "Devil Babies," "I Was Raised in a Satanic Cult," and "They Told Me I Have the Devil Inside Me."[4] Geraldo was even more sensational, with "Satanic Breeders," "Investigating Multiple Personalities," and the NBC special "Devil Worship."[5] *Larry King Live* also fueled the scare with "A Satanic Cult Survivor" and "Sex in the Name of Satan."[6]

Satanic cult stories also became a staple feature of many church revivals. The myth of satanic ritual abuse had entered the popular consciousness. A typical example was the story of Lauren Stratford, who was a guest on several

TV talk shows, promoting the publication of her book, *Satan's Underground*, which sold over 130,000 copies. Among her claims: Two of her babies were murdered in porn films, while a third died in a satanic ritual sacrifice. When journalists began delving into her story, they found it didn't check out: None of her friends, relatives, pastors, roommates or neighbors could confirm her pregnancies, but did verify that she had engaged in self-mutilation. In 1990, Harvest House Publishers withdrew the book from the market on the grounds that it was fraudulent.[7]

The entire foundation of the ritual abuse scare was based on dubious science, as there is no clear evidence that hidden memories exist. But if this is so, how could patients reveal such detailed accounts of ritual abuse? Easy. They were fantasies based on therapist suggestions and news reports of ritual abuse. During the satanic cult scare, the news media played a key role in publicizing what was often described as a hidden epidemic. Sociologist David Bromley notes that most media coverage of ritual abuse claims during the decade-long scare were "uncritical and sensationalist," and even where charges were filed but dropped, the early reports of satanic abuse "receive much greater fanfare than subsequent declaimers."[8] The satanism scare coincided with the explosion of the satellite and cable TV markets as more and more shows were competing for a smaller audience share. Lower advertising revenues translated into lower budgets, as many programmers turned to the economical talk show format, which can be done on a shoestring as it does not require elaborate equipment or sets.[9] During this period, there was a rise in fundamentalist Christians buying radio and TV stations, both of which became more talk-oriented, and satanism naturally was a common topic.[10] Also receiving significant media coverage during this time were testimonials from "survivors," and workshops and conferences on satanism.[11]

The satanism scare is reminiscent of other imaginary episodes that were cultivated by overzealous therapists. For instance, during the 1970s and '80s, regressive hypnosis in the hands of a small group of psychotherapists fueled reincarnation and UFO abduction manias.

Is it possible that some accounts of satanic ritual abuse are real? Perhaps, but not a single account has been confirmed. There are reports of "Satanists" killing people, but these are rare and usually involve attention-seeking youths who call themselves satanists in name only. The account of Michelle Smith was typically dubious. Despite claims of incredible abuse at the hands of so many people over so many years, neither of her two sisters could recall any of the "abuse."[12] Further, there was not a single shred of independent evidence to corroborate her claims. It shouldn't be too difficult to identify Michelle's abusers, since cultists supposedly amputated the middle fingers on their left hands to show their obedience to the devil.[13] This isn't to say that Michelle was lying. Like most people who saw therapists during the satanic cult scare, they didn't walk into offices with a conscious recall of abuse. Well-meaning therapists asked leading questions and placed their clients under hypnosis to release their suspected hidden memories. The result was an influx of abuse claims.

Even if hidden memories do exist, they do not appear to be common. Most child sex abuse victims *can* vividly recall their molestation. For them, the problem is "they can't forget what happened to them, not that they don't remember it."[14] The evidence for repression is not supported by any known theories of memory, which involves a rather straightforward process of encoding, storing and retrieving. Psychologist Terence Campbell observes: "Do traumatic experiences interfere with the encoding state of memory, and if so, how does this interference occur?" The same questions can be asked for the storage and retrieval stages of memory. Campbell says: "Current theories of trauma and memory loss neglect to answer these important questions. These theories suggest *why* people might engage in repression, but they fail to specify *how* repression supposedly occurs."[15]

Another important consideration in assessing the satanism scare is the Bugs Bunny factor. There is no evidence to suggest that memories are stored away like a DVD, waiting to be recalled and played back. On the contrary, it is easy to alter what we think we remember, especially when it comes to traumatic events. A dramatic example of this process occurred when psychologists Elizabeth Loftus and Jacquie Pickrell reported that they were able to get a significant number of people to believe they had met and shook hands with Bugs Bunny at Disneyland when they couldn't have. About one in three subjects exposed to a bogus print ad picturing Bugs Bunny at Disneyland said they had met the character. However, this scenario is impossible as the Bugs Bunny trademark is property of Warner Bros. Pickrell said she found the study frightening because "it suggests how easily a false memory can be created." Pickrell views the findings as potentially important for several areas of research. "It's not only people who go to a therapist who might implant a false memory or those who witness an accident and whose memory can be distorted who can have a false memory. Memory is very vulnerable and malleable. People are not always aware of the choices they make. This study shows the power of subtle association changes on memory."[16]

Most social scientists studying the satanic cult scare have come to a similar conclusion: There never was a network of satanic kidnappers and killers. The media eventually turned skeptical on the claims of ritual abuse given the absence of concrete evidence. But it took nearly a decade for many media outlets to figure out what was really going on: They were witnessing a dispute between a relatively small number of vocal therapists and the mainstream psychological community. There were many victims of what sociologist Jeffrey Victor termed the "new psychotherapy fad" of finding satanic ritual abuse patients. The patients themselves were given false hope as their underlying problems remained unaddressed. Equally bad were the mothers and fathers who, Victor observes, had to "live with painful confusion and distress after being falsely accused of ritual abuse by their adult offspring. Some parents ... found their personal and professional reputations in ruins."[17]

David Bromley notes just how absurd things got during the satanism scare — absurdities that were often not challenged by journalists. When confronted with where all the bodies were, he said proponents would argue that they were carefully disposed of in ways that would make it difficult to find, such as special graves. Bromley continues: "Challenges to this argument are met with assertions that bodies are burned. The observation that bodies cannot be burned in ordinary fires is then countered with the assertion that they are cremated. The problem of gaining access to crematoriums lead to contentions that satanists use special portable crematoriums." Near the end of the scare, the media, faced with such an overwhelming lack of confirming evidence, grew skeptical, as the claims grew more improbable, such as the use of mobile crematoriums. The tide had turned, but it was little consolation for the trail of shattered lives. Could better journalism have stopped the ritual abuse scare before it even began? Probably not. But more aggressive questioning of wild accusations and claims by proponents such as where all the bodies were, and verification by friends and relatives, would have gone a long way towards cutting the scare short. It's still hard to believe that trained journalists working in the most sophisticated country on Earth helped to foster a therapeutic witch hunt that persisted for a decade. The episode was tantamount to a modern-day incarnation of the infamous Salem witch hunts.

CHAPTER 29

Halloween Panics

> Each year on Halloween, politicians, police, and the news media join forces to scare parents and their children about the dangers posed by evildoers preying on children and poisoning candy. It turns out that the reality is far different than the perception.
>
> Talk of the devil and he is bound to appear.
>
> —*proverb*

Across the country, the big question for children at Halloween is that of picking the right costume: ghost, Spider-Man, witch, princess or pirate? For many parents and police, the question is far more serious: how to protect children from the unique threats and dangers that Halloween brings. Amid the make-believe witches, ghouls, and goblins, there are supposedly real-life villains who lay in wait all year, scheming about the death and mayhem they will wreak when October 31 comes around.

These threats involve innocent children — the most vulnerable among us — and stories about them circulate among concerned parents, helpful neighbors, and local police. The news media also play an important role in spreading word about the potential danger; newspapers and nightly newscasts are always eager for a story that worried parents will tune in for. The history of Halloween scares in America is too broad a subject to cover in this short chapter, but an examination of the most prevalent panics is instructive.

Poisoned Candy Panics

While Halloween costumes are fun for kids, they are simply a means to a much more important end: getting candy. The most familiar Halloween scares involve contaminated candy, and every year, police and medical centers across the country X-ray candy collected by trick-or-treaters to check for razors, needles, or contaminants that might have been placed there by strangers intending to hurt or kill children. Special school- and police-sponsored events are held that offer kids "a safe Halloween," suggesting that there are real lurking dangers.

Yet year after year, few if any sinister foreign objects are found. This threat is essentially an urban legend; the few cases that turn out to be false alarms often get front-page billing, though when they turn out to be duds, they often get buried on page 23. For instance, in 1975, when a 13-year-old Missouri boy collapsed and died with a bag of Halloween candy by his side, there were a flurry of media stories that the culprit was tainted sweets. After his death, police urged parents to destroy all of their Halloween candy. Several days later the Jackson County Medical Examiner announced: "The poison candy scare is over. Kevin Perry died from sniffing deodorant." The exact cause of death was heart failure. His brother admitted that he had a habit of sniffing such substances and a deodorant can was found shoved between the cushions of the couch near where he collapsed.[1] Yet another tainted candy scare turned out not to be what it first seemed.

Despite e-mail warnings, scary stories, and Ann Landers columns to the contrary, there have been only two confirmed cases of children being killed by poisoned Halloween candy, and in both cases the children were killed not in a random act by strangers but intentional murder by one of their parents. The best-known, "original" case was that of Texan Ronald Clark O'Bryan, who killed his son by lacing his Pixie Stix with cyanide in 1974.[2] In this instance, the holiday was used as a cover to throw off police to get them to look for a random attacker after the candy was given to other children who were trick-or-treating with Timothy O'Bryan, in an attempt to collect on a $70,000 insurance policy.[3]

Yet the fear continues. There have been a few instances of candy tampering over the years, and in most cases the victim turned out to be the culprit, children doing it as a prank or to draw attention. With the exceptions noted above, to date no child is known to have been killed or seriously harmed by contaminated Halloween candy. There are several problems with X-raying Halloween items to find harmful objects. For one thing, it would be obvious to even the most sugar-addled child or teen if a razor blade or pins were stuck in an apple or candy bar. Secondly, X-raying provides a false sense of security, since the process would reveal metal, and possibly glass, but would not detect poison. Third, and most obviously, it's unnecessary: If in doubt, throw it out! Like any other food, if you have even the slightest good reason to suspect that a piece of candy is not safe, it's easiest to simply toss it. There's no need to waste medical facility or police time making sure that a small free candy bar is safe to eat. X-raying candy helps parents feel like they are protecting their children, but in fact parents are simply wasting resources and feeding children's fears unnecessarily.

One infamous incident involving supposed tainted Halloween candy took place in Albany, New York, in 1905. Miss Elsie Smith received a box of poison candy after serving as the queen of a Halloween celebration — apparently from a girl who was not happy with the relationship she had struck of up the carnival's king, an apparently charming man by the name of Clayton McKinley. The tainted candy, which she had not eaten as the poison had oozed out, was given as a Christmas present and cannot be classified as a Halloween poisoning scare. Secondly, this was certainly no random act of malice but carefully targeted a single individual, although other people could have been inadvertently sickened.[4] In their investigation, police noted that Mr. McKinley was so popular that at least ten girls were suspects!

The Best and Horiuchi Study

In their review of news stories on Halloween sadists between 1958 and 1983, Joel Best and Gerald Horiuchi found the threat to have been "greatly exaggerated." The researchers discovered that the fear of razor blades in apples and poison candy was a scare fueled in part by the media, beginning in the early 1970s. As a response to this new exaggerated threat, laws were passed to punish Halloween sadists and children were trained to inspect their sweets carefully. As a result, what had once been a fun holiday filled with candy had become an event that was eyed by children and parents alike with fear and trepidation. In reality, the incidence of unprovoked, random attacks on small children during trick-or-treating, is rare, and deaths virtually unheard of.

Based on their examination of major newspapers of record — *The New York Times, Los Angeles Times, Chicago Tribune* and *Fresno Bee* — there were but two deaths during this period labeled as Halloween related. In 1970, it was reported that a five-year-old boy had died after eating heroin from tainted Halloween candy. It turned out that little Kevin Totson had died after finding heroin in the home of a relative, not from his Halloween cache. Of course, the other case, involving Timothy O'Bryan, which we have already discussed, also had nothing to do with Halloween sadists. Despite this, in 1975, *Newsweek* reported that "several children have died" at the hands of Halloween sadists. Best and Horiuchi concluded that "there were no reports where an anonymous sadist caused death or a life-threatening injury; there is no justification for the claim that Halloween sadism stands as a major threat to U.S. children."[5]

Best and Horiuchi concluded that most reports of Halloween sadism appear to be imaginary. They note that the dangers of tainted candy are well known to children, and the child who produces an adulterated treat stands to gain great sympathy and attention from friends, parents, police and the media. They believe that of the 76 reports, many were frauds, as 75 percent of children reporting bad candy were not even injured. They note that following Halloween in 1972, the newspaper and magazine industry conducted a study of Halloween sadism reported in local papers, concluding that virtually all were hoaxes! Indeed, according to a study on tainted Halloween candy reported during 1982, there were 270 supposed incidents. When the Food and Drug Administration analyzed the candy, it found that over 95 percent of the time, there was no evidence of tampering, leading an FDA official to characterize the situation as an episode of "psychosomatic mass hysteria."[6] In those cases where children weren't perpetrating deliberate hoaxes for mischief or attention, a knick on an apple or innocent tear of a candy wrapper was redefined as the work of the sadist.

Terrorist Candy

The media-fueled fear and panic over tainted candy has been a staple of American Halloweens for decades. However, following the September 11, 2001, terrorist attacks and the resulting hypervigilance about terrorism, the candy scare took an interesting twist in mid–October, when rumors circulated that two suspicious Arab men had purchased $35,000 worth of candy from a New Jersey wholesale store. E-mails spread across the country, warning parents that their children's candy might be tampered with by Middle Eastern terrorists. One person wrote, "I just personally found out through a police department that the FBI has taken over an investigation in our area. Arabs bought thousands of dollars worth of candy at a local CostCo [sic] store. Well, what's right around the corner??? Halloween!! BE CAREFUL!"[7]

Prompted by the public concern over potential terrorism, the FBI acknowledged that it was "investigating the cash purchase of 'large quantities' of candy from Costco stores in Hackensack and Wayne.... 'We have been advised and we are looking into the incident of a gentleman buying large quantities of candy,' said Sandra Carroll, an FBI spokeswoman in Newark. Carroll declined to identify the purchaser, but indicated that he is in federal custody for immigration law reasons not related to the purchase of the candy.... 'We have no evidence or information for us to suspect there is any reason to cancel scheduled events,' Carroll said when asked if the FBI had concerns about the safety of Halloween."[8]

A week before Halloween, on October 22, the FBI cleared up the rumors. It was one man, not two, who had bought $15,000 worth of candy, not

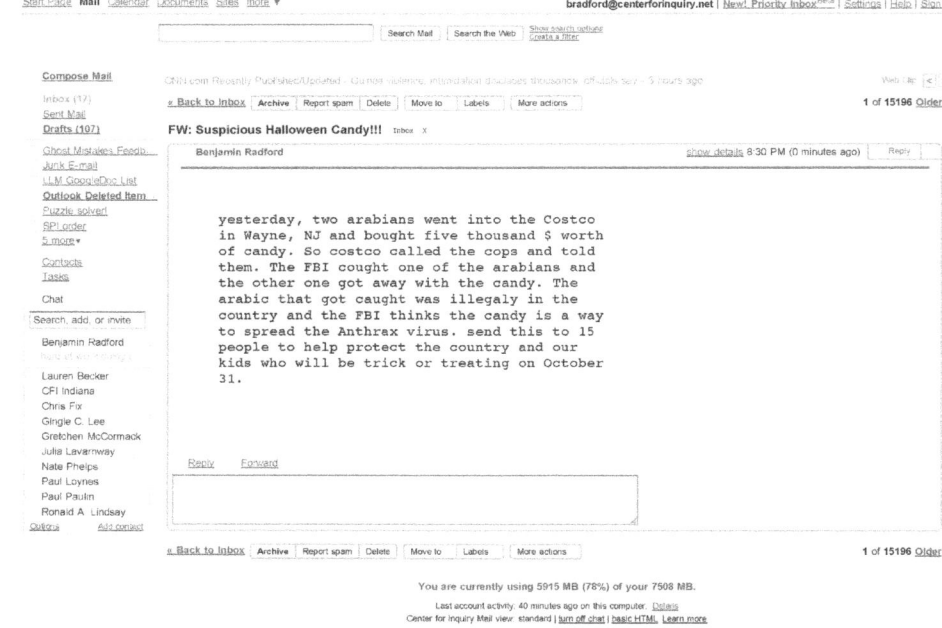

A widely forwarded e-mail from 2001 warning of suspicious Halloween purchases made at a Costco warehouse.

$35,000. The man's nationality was not revealed, so he may or may not have been Arab or dark-skinned or even had an ethnic name. The man was a wholesaler who planned to resell the candy, and the purchase was a routine, legitimate transaction that had nothing to do with terrorism.

Sex Offenders

Though the fears over poisoned candy (whether by malicious neighbors or foreign terrorists) never materialized into a real threat, the reputed Halloween evil took a new form in the 1990s: sex offenders. This scare, even more than the candy panics, was fueled by alarmist news reports and police warnings. In many states, convicted sex offenders were required not to answer the door if trick-or-treaters came by, or to report to jail overnight. In many states including Texas and Arkansas offenders were required to report to courthouses on Halloween evening for a mandatory counseling session.[9]

The theory behind such laws is that Halloween provides a special opportunity for sex offenders to make contact with children, or to use costumes to conceal their identities. This has been the assumption among many local politicians and police for years. Yet there is no reason to think that sex offenders pose any more of a threat to children on Halloween than at any other time. In fact, there has not been a single case of any child being molested by a convicted sex offender while trick-or-treating.

Ironically, a group of children dressed in costume at a sex offender's doorway are probably safer than at many other places they could be, including their own homes. This is because, contrary to popular belief, most attacks on children occur in their own home by someone they know. Furthermore, the simple logistics of trick-or-treating make an assault very unlikely. A sex offender would have great difficulty molesting a child who is in costume, outside his or her front door, and in front of other people.

A 2009 study confirmed that the public has little to fear from sex offenders on Halloween. The research, published in the September 2009 issue of *Sexual Abuse: A Journal of Research and Treatment*, examined 67,307 non-family sex offenses reported to law enforcement in 30 states over nine years. The researchers wanted to determine whether or not children are in fact at any greater risk for sexual assault around Halloween. The answer was a conclusive no: "There does not appear to be a need for alarm concerning sexual abuse on these particular days. Halloween appears to be just another autumn day where rates of sex crimes against children are concerned."[10]

Not only is the hype and fear unwarranted, but the study also suggests the taxpayer dollars spent monitoring sex offenders on Halloween are wasted. All the mandatory counseling sessions, increased police presence, and so on had no effect at all on the incidence of sexual abuse on Halloween. These measures provide a false sense of security, since there is no evidence that the policies actually make children any safer. As the study's authors note, traffic accidents are a far greater threat to trick-or-treaters than sex offenders. (Despite widespread popular belief, research has consistently shows that sex offenders are no more likely than other criminals to re-offend. The idea that sex offenders are incurable or likely to prey on children after their release simply has no basis in fact.)

So why all the fear, panic, and concern? As we have seen, much of it comes from well-meaning (but poorly informed) police, parents, and journalists who adopt an alarmist tone when talking about Halloween threats to children. These measures are popular and well-intentioned — but ultimately ineffective — publicity stunts offered by police and politicians to placate parents.

Texas housewife Helen Perez summed up the panic mentality when she said that she once let her kids trick-or-treat without worrying, but won't let the kids go out without adult supervision or to homes that she haven't per-

Cpl. Brandi Richardson of the Jasper County Sheriff's Department displays signs registered sex offenders are required by state law to display in their homes on Halloween (photograph by and courtesy of John Hacker/*The Carthage Press*).

sonally checked out first. Why? "All those stories of poison candy and razor blazes in cookies. Those things happen. We're not taking a chance with our kids," she said. Of course, no one can blame a parent for being safety conscious, but there must be a balance with reality, least we diminish the quality of our lives.[11]

The reality is, most kids are very safe at Halloween and have little to fear from strangers. Yet, our children are told the scary myth that their neighbors are likely to poison, hurt, molest or kill them. Poisoning *is* a real concern for our children, but not from Halloween sadists. According to the Centers for Disease Control, there has been an upswing in recent years in children dying after taking poison. It seems that so many people are taking medications these days, more and more children are dying after swallowing these drugs.[12] The real threat to children on Halloween isn't poisoned candy or sex offenders; it's being hit by a car crossing a dark street or wearing a flammable costume or taking a relative's medication. Each year hundreds of children drown in swimming pools across the United States. Unlike belief in the tooth fairy and the boogie man, some myths have real consequences. If there were more of a focus on car, pool, drug and fire safety instead of mythical strangers, without a doubt more of our children would be alive in order to enjoy their candy.

CHAPTER 30

Stranger Danger and the Predator Next Door

One of the most common panics in America over the past decade involves sexual predators. The news media feature a barrage of alarmist, misleading, and greatly exaggerated reports of the threat of predators.

If you believed many of the near-daily news reports that circulated in the mid–2000s, monsters who prey on children lurk everywhere: in parks, at schools, in the malls — even in bedrooms, through the Internet. An underground legion of predators supposedly lays in wait, hoping for the chance to abduct or sexually assault the most innocent among us.

While such horrific crimes certainly do occur, the news media (and therefore the public) have dramatically overestimated the actual threat posed by predators and sex offenders. Like all media scares, predator panics wax and wane over time. The most recent panic waxed in the mid–2000s, peaking in 2005 and 2006 when many media broadcast sensational news stories suggesting that predators were everywhere.

On the April 18, 2005, *CBS Evening News* broadcast, correspondent Jim Acosta reported that "when a child is missing, chances are good it was a convicted sex offender." Acosta is incorrect: If a child goes missing, a convicted sex offender is actually among the *least* likely explanations, far behind runaways, family abductions, and the child being lost or injured. On his hidden-camera "reality" series "To Catch a Predator," *Dateline NBC* reporter Chris Hansen claimed that "the scope of the [predator] problem is immense" and "seems to be getting worse." In fact, Hansen stated, Web-based predators are "a national epidemic." Hansen teamed up with a group called Perverted Justice to lure potential online predators to a house with hidden cameras. The program's ratings for the 2005 and 2006 seasons were so high that it spawned a half-dozen follow-up "To Catch a Predator" specials.

The New York Times helped launch the predator panic media scare. On December 19, 2005, reporter Kurt Eichenwald wrote a front-page article about Justin Berry, a California teen who earned money as an underage Webcam model, seduced by an online audience who paid to watch him undress. Berry's story made national news, and he appeared with Eichenwald on many television programs including *Oprah*, *Larry King Live*, the *Today Show*, and in front of a Senate committee. Berry's story was compelling and alarming, but was essentially an anecdote about one person, not an "epidemic." Was Berry's case unique, or did it represent just the tip of the sexual predation iceberg?

Eichenwald suggested that Berry's experience was typical of many children, but he was vague about how many other teen porn purveyors like Berry he found during his six-month investigation. Three or four? Dozens? Thousands? Eichenwald's article stated merely that "the scale of Webcam pornography is unknown."

Many journalists reporting on the predator panic often resorted to sensationalism, cobbling a few anecdotes and interviews together into a trend while glossing over data suggesting the problem may not be as widespread as they claim. But good journalism requires that personal stories — no matter how emotional and compelling — must be balanced with facts and context. Eichenwald's crusading investigation was widely criticized ("to many, it seemed alarmist and overblown, an invitation to a kind of sexual witch hunt," according to *New York* magazine writer David France[1]), and it was later revealed that he had violated *New York Times* journalism policies by paying Berry for his story. In the wake of questions about his conduct and research for his Internet predator investigation, Eichenwald resigned from the newspaper the following year.

Flawed Today Show *"Experiment" Spreads Fear*

A few months after Eichenwald's *New York Times* article suggested that Internet predators were everywhere, one of America's top morning news shows conducted an experiment designed to boost ratings and play on parents' fears of child abductors. In late March 2006, the *Today Show* broadcast a segment featuring security specialist Bill Stanton, who wanted to know if the public would help if a child was being kidnapped by a stranger. The experiment was filmed for the TV show so the viewers could see for themselves.

With the help of a seven-year-old named Rachelle, Stanton staged an abduction on a city street to see if the public would take action. Rachelle's mother watched from a surveillance van as Stanton approached the girl, who stood alone in the middle of a sidewalk playing a video game. Stanton walked up to Rachelle and took her by the arm, saying things like, "There you are, young lady! You come with me," while Rachelle protested, "No, no ... you're not my daddy!" Stanton and Rachelle repeated the scenario many times; as hidden cameras showed, rarely did bystanders intervene. Some kept walking, others glanced briefly at the scene, but few approached.[2]

The *Today Show* anchors called the results "shocking," and to Stanton, Rachelle's mother, the show's producers, and probably to much of the audience, this seemed a clear and tragic case of uncaring bystanders reluctant to help a child in need. "It's frightening that no one will help," Rachelle's mother said.

Yet there may be a very good, logical reason why people didn't get involved, a reason completely missed by Stanton and the *Today Show* producers: The bystanders didn't believe that they were actually seeing a child being abducted. Because the test abduction was poorly staged, it's more likely that those who witnessed the scene simply (and correctly) recognized that the child was not in danger. From the hidden camera footage that aired, it was clear that the girl they used was not an actress and didn't act scared or terrified when Stanton approached her. Her protests sounded like a typical child's whines instead of panicked pleas for help. The adult did not strike the child or hurt her in any way, and Rachelle didn't scream, kick at, or fight off the adult supposedly trying to abduct her. In short, other than her words, which weren't always clear, she didn't do anything that would convince the average person that she genuinely did not know the adult and was in danger.

The problem goes far beyond the seven-year-old's acting; the problem is that the test was badly conceived and conducted by Stanton and NBC News. The *Today Show*'s hidden camera test would be only valid if the bystanders actually believed that the child was in danger.

The *Today Show* test is a good example of a demonstration that seemed convincing on its face (and surely scared many parents), yet had no scientific validity. Bad science led to bad journalism, and the *Today Show* helped create a media scare. The episode aired as part of a series called "Who Can You Trust?" and the show's conclusion is exactly the opposite of the truth. The program suggested that strangers can't be trusted, that they are likely to either kidnap a child or fail to stop a real abduction. In fact, strangers are less likely to harm a child than a family member.

The "One in Five" Myth

In a social climate where parents and the public were already fearful of child abductions, the news media seemed to offer a steady stream of reports that confirmed their worst fears. Two months after the *Today Show*'s misleading and alarmist "abduction" test, the news media was abuzz with a new scary statistic. According to a May 3, 2006, ABC News report, "One in five children is now approached by online predators." This alarming statistic was widely cited in media stories about prevalence of Internet predators. Parents (quite understandably) wondered if their child was among the one in five.

But a closer look at the statistic reveals that the threat was greatly exaggerated. The claim can be traced back to a 2001 Department of Justice study issued by the National Center for Missing and Exploited Children ("The Youth Internet Safety Survey") that asked 1,501 American teens between 10 and 17 about their online experiences. Among the study's conclusions: "Almost one in five (19 percent) ... received an unwanted sexual solicitation in the past year." Not a single one of the reported solicitations led to any actual sexual contact or assault. Furthermore, almost half of the "sexual solicitations" came not from "predators" or adults but from other teens. When the study examined the type of Internet "solicitation" parents are most concerned about (e.g., someone who asked to meet the teen somewhere, called the teen on the telephone, or sent gifts), the number drops from one in five to 3 percent.[3]

This is a far cry from a "national epidemic" of children being "approached by online predators." As the study noted, "Much of the offending behavior comes from other youth [and] from females." Furthermore, "most youth are not bothered much by what they encounter on the Internet.... Most young people seem to know what to do to deflect these sexual 'come ons.'"

In fact, according to a study by researchers at the University of New Hampshire's Crimes against Children Research Center, this and other information about the threat posed to children regarding Web-based sex predators is wrong. The study concluded that "the stereotype of the Internet 'predator' who uses trickery and violence to assault children is largely inaccurate." Janis Wolak, lead author of the study, said, "To prevent these crimes, we need accurate information about their true dynamics. The things that we hear and fear and the things that actually occur may not be the same."[4]

Public Panic

These are only a few of the high-profile alarmist news stories that fueled the "stranger danger" fears. The panic generated by the scares quickly translated into public pressure on lawmakers and police to do something to keep America's children safe — no matter how remote the danger. States and communities across the country responded by passing a slew of laws aimed at protecting children. Every state has notification laws to alert communities about former sex offenders (also known as "Megan's Laws"). Many states have banned sex offenders from living in certain areas, and are tracking them using satellite technology. Other states have gone even further; Ohio lawmakers, for example, have suggested forcing some sex offenders to use specially colored license plates on their vehicles. State emergency leaders in Florida and Texas developed plans to route convicted sex offenders away from public emergency shelters during hurricanes. "We don't want them in the same shelters as others," Texas Homeland Security Director Steve McCraw said. (How exactly huge numbers of desperate and homeless storm victims are to be identified, screened, and routed in an emergency is unclear.) Other states locked them up overnight on Halloween night (see "Halloween Panics," Chapter 22).

Predator Panic in Perspective

Of course, there is a grain of truth to the claims; there are rare but high-profile horrible crimes against children. Despite popular belief, children are safer than ever. Sex assaults on teens dropped significantly (over 50 percent) between 1990 and 2005. Ironically, the news coverage of sex offenses jumped dramatically over the past decade — just as the attacks themselves plummeted.

While the abduction, rape, and killing of children by strangers is very, very rare, such incidents receive a lot of media coverage, leading the public to overestimate how common these cases are. Most sexually abused children are neither victims of convicted sex offenders nor Internet pornographers, and most sex offenders do not re-offend once released.

Indeed, according to a U.S. Bureau of Justice Statistics study (*Recidivism of Sex Offenders Released from Prison in 1994*), just five percent of sex offenders followed for three years after their release from prison in 1994 were arrested for another sex crime. A study released in 2003 by the Bureau found that within three years, 3.3 percent of the released child molesters were arrested again for committing another sex crime against a child. In the largest and most comprehensive study ever done of prison recidivism, the Justice Department found that sex offenders were in fact *less* likely to reoffend than other criminals. The 2003 study of nearly 10,000 men convicted of rape, sexual assault, and child molestation found that sex offenders had a re-arrest rate 25 percent lower than for all other criminals.

The news media's tendency toward alarmism only partly explains the panic; after all, many other media scares that appeared around the same time (such as shark attacks, heat stroke, and SARS disease) were relatively short-lived. The predator panic, by contrast, has shown a remarkable resilience because America was in the grip of a moral panic over sexual predators, and remains so, to a lesser degree, to this day. A defining characteristic of the panics is that the "concern about the threat posed by moral deviants and their numerical abundance is far greater than can be objectively verified, despite unsubstantiated claims to the contrary. Furthermore, during a moral panic "most of the figures cited by moral panic 'claims-makers' are wildly exaggerated."[5]

Indeed, this exact trend appears in the media scares over predators. News stories invariably exaggerate the true extent of sexual predation on the Internet, the magnitude of the danger to children, and the likelihood that sexual predators will strike.

One tragic result of these myths is that the panic over sex offenders distracts the public from a far greater threat to children: parental abuse and neglect. The vast majority of crimes against children are committed not by released sex offenders, but instead by the victim's own family, church clergy, and family friends. According to the National Center for Missing and Exploited Children, "based on what we know about those who harm children, the danger to children is greater from someone they or their family knows than from a stranger." If lawmakers and the public are serious about wanting to protect children, they should not be misled by "stranger danger" myths and instead focus on the much larger threat inside the home.

CHAPTER 31

The School Safety Panic

The odds of being killed at school in the United States are greater than a million to one. Yet, media portrayals give the impression that shootings are far more common than they really are. Occasionally the media even reports on school shootings that never happened.

Each day several American children are murdered at the hands of their parents — upwards of 3,000 each year. This statistic receives little fanfare despite family violence being the leading killer of kids under 13, and females of all ages. Yet, the issue is barely on the radar screen of most journalists.[1] On the other hand, murder at school — a much rarer event — takes center stage. From the early 1990s and into the first decade of the 21st century, the number of school shootings have actually declined despite media-generated images to the contrary. Forensic psychologist Dewey Cornell observes that the juvenile arrest rate for murder in the United States stood at 3,284 in 1993, yet by 2002, it had plunged to 973. During this same period there was a similar plunge in school homicides, which totaled 42 in 1993, but just eight in 2001, two the following year, and four in 2003. While the murder rate in schools varies from year to year and a single mass shooting can up the fatality rate dramatically, overall, the trend was clearly down. Dewey places the school homicide rate in perspective by using the infamous Columbine shootings in Colorado as an example. "In 1999 — the year of the Columbine shooting — 17 students were murdered at school.... In that same year, however, there were 21,373 deaths of persons 5 to 19 years old ... so that school homicides constituted .0008 percent of the total deaths."[2]

Schools are one of the safest places to be, and always have been; they are far safer than the home. The odds of a school-age child (ages five to 19) being murdered at school for any given one-year period are well over a million to one. In contrast, while many parents worry about their child being shot as they send them off to school, these same kids are at double the risk of being struck and killed by a flash of lightning.³ Well over 99 percent of school-aged deaths occur away from school. The average student has a 1 in 100 chance of dying of an automobile accident in his or her lifetime, and a 1 in 8,000 chance of dying in a motor vehicle crash in any given year. The odds of being murdered outside of school in a given year is one in 21,000; dying of cancer — one in 33,000; dying from an accidental fall — about 1 in 400,000.⁴

School shootings are exceptionally rare, but when they do occur, they make headlines, giving the impression that they are more common than they are. Of course, we should do everything we can to make our schools safer, and there is no acceptable number of school shootings, but let's get a handle on the extent of the problem. The media has always had to make choices about reporting tragedies; there are just too many to squeeze into news programs. For instance, according to the United Nations over 40,000 people starve to death every day. Yet, few people would know this from watching the evening news or reading their daily newspaper. The media will devote huge amounts of time to school shootings, making it appear that they are more common or likely to happen than they actually are. An analysis of the genocide in Darfur, Sudan, is a classic example. A 2004 study of the major American TV network's coverage of this tragedy revealed much more time being devoted to celebrities. ABC devoted 18 minutes to Darfur on its nightly news, and NBC just 5 minutes. As for CBS, it was 3 minutes — a figure which works out to roughly 100,000 deaths per minute. During the same period, food and home decor guru Martha Stewart received 130 minutes of coverage by the big three networks.⁵ A study of school-related violent deaths between 1992 and 2000 found a general decline.⁶ In 1992 the number peaked at 56, while in 2000 the number was at just 22. Between 2002 and 2003 the figure were essentially unchanged.⁷

The media has a remarkable capacity to make it seem that crime is spiraling out of control. Part of the problem is clearly caused by crime shows. Based on the dozens of popular TV crime shows that have bombarded the American public in recent decades, one could easily get an impression that violent crime in America is far worse than FBI statistics indicate. Shootings by police are a good example. How many times might a foreigner or even an American citizen guess that U.S. a police officer fires his or her gun in the line of duty over their 20-year career? The answer is zero. As hard as it may seem to believe, over 90 percent of cops in the United States go through their entire career without ever firing their gun unless it's on the practice range. Occasionally they may upholster it, but actually firing it is a rarity.

A 2010 study of American school shootings found that between 1996 and 2006, there was an average of 21 murders in U.S. schools per year. Considering that there are over 125,000 elementary and secondary schools across the country, "any given school can expect to experience a student homicide about once every 6,000 years." These 21 homicides represent less than 1 percent of the total of annual homicides among American youth between the ages of 5 and 18.[8]

The panic over school shootings and the widespread assumption that they are more common than they are has led to some embarrassing incidents, such as the shooting that never happened.

"Breaking news — possible school shooting!" It's every parent's worst nightmare. The story broke in San Antonio, on the morning of November 9, 1999. At 8:27 A.M., KENS-TV reported on the story that literally stopped people in their tracks. Possible shooting at a local elementary school. Within five minutes, KSAT-TV confirmed the initial account and said that there were at least 14 casualties. Other area media outlets quickly jumped on the story, based on these earlier reports. It wasn't long before parents began to swarm Coker Elementary School.[9]

How could professional news journalists with years of training and experience get the story so mixed up? It turned out to be a series of very unfortunate events. Journalism, like hand grenades and horseshoes, can be unforgiving.

Here is how the bungle unfolded. The journalists were doing what they normally do: routinely monitoring police and emergency service chatter. While driving to work, a custodian at Coker got into a confrontation with another driver whom, in a fit if rage, shot out his window. The custodian escaped with very minor cuts, then drove on to the school to phone police and report the incident. As police discussed the encounter over the radio waves, journalists got the story garbled. Some reporters then rang police dispatchers to confirm the shooting. Police responded that they were busy and couldn't talk. In the rush to break the story, they assumed the worst.

One of the reasons the San Antonio media assumed the worst is the intense coverage that shootings receive in the United States — and rightly so. These are tragic events. But it's important to put these incidents into perspective. When it comes to school shootings, perception is different than reality. Statistics tell the story.

CHAPTER 32

"Out of the Water!" Media Shark Frenzy

> During the Summer of 2001, American beachgoers were besieged by sharks — or so it seemed from the newspaper and TV blitz on the flurry of shark attacks. But a review of attack statistics portrays a normal summer — with above normal interest by the media.

It began with one of the most dramatic shark attacks on record. It ended two months later with a fizzle. In the summer of 2001, Americans went shark crazy. At the water cooler, in supermarket checkouts and in bank lines, people talked of little else. Cable TV, talk radio, newspapers and the Internet were abuzz with news of the latest attacks and sightings. Some TV stations even had Internet sharkcams so people could monitor hotspots any time of the day or night. It was a slow news summer and the media had to talk about something: Sharks fit the bill perfectly.

The frenzy began with a remarkable incident involving a little boy named Jessie Arbogast whose arm was ripped off by a bull shark in the shallow waters off Pensacola, Florida. Incredibly, his uncle grabbed the shark by the tail and wrestled it to shore, with Jessie's bloody arm still wedged in its mouth. A passing park ranger took out a gun and shot the fish dead, then grabbed his baton, jammed it into its mouth and began prying open its powerful jaws while a lifeguard pulled out the arm. Jessie, covered in blood and looking like a rag doll, was rushed to the hospital barely clinging to life. A team of surgeons worked feverishly in shifts for eleven hours, saving his life and reattaching the arm. Jessie remained in recovery for weeks, during which we received daily updates on his condition, where to donate money, and how to avoid being shark bait ourselves. It was an extraordinary story, and there were heroes everywhere. The trouble was, after news of Jessie's storybook rescue hit newsstands and airwaves, any shark-related incident, no matter how minor, became news fodder. *Time* magazine epitomized the hysteria with its cover story: "The Summer of the Shark." Even the ordinarily subdued Discovery Channel got into the act by announcing a series of programs during "Shark Week." Further fueling the scare was the release of two books recounting a series of infamous shark attacks off New Jersey in 1916: *Close to Shore* by Michael Capuzzo, and Richard Fernicola's *Twelve Days of Terror*.

The great shark scare of 2001 was a media-generated frenzy that had little grounding in reality. Statistically, shark attacks are rare events. To put the risk into perspective, between 1948 and 2005, there were eight shark fatalities in Florida. Eight. Twice as many Floridians died of alligator attacks during the same period.[1] Between 2000 and 2004, there were over 3,600 hunting accidents in the U.S. resulting in 354 deaths. During this same period, the sum total of shark-related deaths was just seven.[2] Or, how about this one: Between 1990 and 2005, there were over 10,000 U.S. bicycle fatalities. During this same span, just nine people died from sharks.[3] From 1959 to 2005, 1,900 Americans were struck and killed by lightning. The number of fatal shark attacks during this same period: 23.[4] There are many things to worry about, but clearly, shark attacks are not one of them.

In the wake of the media feeding frenzy by reporters desperate to latch onto a hot story during a slow news summer, people began to lose all sense of proportion. Shark expert George Burgess of the Florida Museum of Natural History observed that after the media shark blitz, he was receiving calls from people worried about sharks living in such remote areas as Montana and Idaho, where, he says, "there hasn't been a shark attack since the Miocene [Age]."[5]

Australia has a similar reputation for being a magnet for killer sharks attacking unsuspecting surfers. The reporting pattern is also similar: a few spectacular incidents followed by reports of sightings, "close calls," and endless speculation about how the beasts are on the rise and suddenly attacking humans. Yet, the threat of being killed by a shark down under is infinitesimal.[6] Between 1995 and 2005, the average number of shark attack deaths in Australian waters averaged just over one (1.3 to be exact).

Considering that each year millions of people spend billions of hours at the beach, one begins to realize just how rare these incidents are. Scientists estimate that there are about 370 species of sharks. Of these, just 32 have any interest in eating humans; fewer still are even capable of attacking and eating someone.[7] The vast majority of shark attacks can be traced to just four species: the great white, ocean whitetip, tiger and bull shark.[8] Sean Van Sommeran of the California-based Pelagic Shark Research Foundation compares the fear of all sharks to that of cats. He says when someone thinks of the word "cat," "typically people will conjure up the image of a Siamese cat or a Persian cat;

they don't necessarily jump to the image of a tiger or leopard or lion, which certainly are cats." In reality, only a small number of felines pose a danger to humans. Yet, when people think of sharks, most are "ignorant of the other vast number of species, which are not menacing or glamorous at all. And typically they will conjure up the image of a big white shark."[9]

Shark fatigue had set in by the first week in September as media reports started to dwindle. Then on September 11, stories of sharks and shark attacks suddenly dropped off media radar screens as the far more menacing threat of terrorism was thrust into the national media spotlight.

It could just as easily have been the summer of the bee sting, dog bite, or of a hundred other threats. One juicy story at the right time — during a news lull — and the media spotlight was focused on sharks as the new public enemy number one. A couple of spectacular rock slides or vicious coyote attacks could have led reporters sniffing in an entirely different direction.

Each year journalists fall in love with a handful of new media darlings. After a month or two, these scares usually run their course as the public grow weary. The problem is, few journalists are experts on the topics they write about. At first, reporters tend to focus on those experts making the most sensational claims. But after a while, once a number of experts have been interviewed, a more conservative consensus emerges and reality takes hold. Indeed, each year about 15 times more people around the world are killed by falling coconuts than sharks. In the end, killer coconuts engender little fear; sharks do, even though they account for remarkably few deaths.[10]

At the height of the scare, *Jaws* author Peter Benchley was asked by a pack of hungry reporters what he thought about the number of shark attacks. He didn't give the expected answer. Wondering instead what all the hoopla was about, Benchley noted that sharks aren't going to attack you in your home; you have to go out of your way to put yourself at risk.[11] But Howard Rosenberg summed it up best, observing that during the summer of 2001, bloodthirsty predators swarmed American beaches. "Following their primal instincts, they attacked ferociously, the size of their massive jaws and razorlike teeth creating waves of panic."[12] He was referring to the media, of course.

CHAPTER 33

The Great Puerto Rican Chupacabra Panic

> In 1995 Puerto Rico, sensational news reports on television and in tabloid newspapers helped launch a mythical vampire monster into global prominence.

Many people around the world believe in the existence of a terrifying, bloodthirsty beast called *el chupacabra*. Some refer to it as the Hispanic version of Bigfoot, but with a bizarre vampiric twist: The chupacabra is said to kill its prey and suck out its blood (chupacabra means *goat sucker* in Spanish). In addition to goats, it has also been blamed for attacks on sheep, rabbits, dogs, chickens, hogs, and other animals. Like Bigfoot, there is no hard evidence of its existence, making the popular belief in the legendary creature all the more curious. Descriptions of the chupacabra vary widely, but many believe the fearsome creature stands about four to five feet tall, with short but powerful legs, long claws, red eyes, and spikes down its back.

The chupacabra first gained international notoriety in Puerto Rico. Many believe it is the result of secret genetics experiments by the U.S. government, or that it's an extraterrestrial alien, or even a sign of the coming apocalypse. The Puerto Rican chupacabra panic began in March 1995 when some of the island's residents discovered farm animals that had apparently been drained of blood.[1] About five months passed before the chupacabra was finally sighted.

The first and best-known description of the bipedal creature was reported in August 1995 by eyewitness Madelyne Tolentino. In fact, that sighting provided much more than a glimpse; it was a detailed description of what became the world-famous chupacabra. As researcher Scott Corrales notes, "The first descriptions of this mysterious creature came about six months into the mutilation epidemic.... Sightings by Madelyne Tolentino, a housewife of Canovanas — a city to the east of the island's capital, San Juan — and others gave it a form and a name."² Another scholar noted that "The chupacabra craze had its own significance to the inhabitants of Canovanas who were at first flattered by the international attention they received; a mood which shifted to sour betrayal upon discovering just how quickly their narratives could escape their ownership and control."³

The News Media Scares Up a Story

Tolentino's chupacabra sighting might have remained a scary personal story, except that it found a very receptive audience. UFO promoters and tabloid reporters were keen to report the woman's dramatic, first-person account with the goat sucker. The Puerto Rican tabloid news media eagerly reported this and later chupacabra reports, warning their readers and audience about this new bloodthirsty monster with sensational stories.

Tolentino's account became the most important and influential eyewitness report of the Puerto Rican chupacabra. She worked with a UFO researcher named Jorge Martin to develop a widely circulated drawing of the creature that she'd seen. Martin's drawing was published on the front page of San Juan's *El Nuevo Dia* newspaper, and as Scott Corrales (1995) noted, it "prompted the [chupacabra] into global notoriety and perhaps a permanent place in Puerto Rican myth." Indeed, "by November 1995, the now-famous portrait by the island's leading UFOlogist, Jorge Martin, had flashed around the world courtesy of the Internet."⁴

The drawing, published with authority on the front page of the newspaper, had a powerful effect on Puerto Ricans who believed in the creature and who had followed the news (or rumor mill) about the beast. It told them what the chupacabra looked like, and therefore what to expect to see if they encountered it. In psychological terms, the public was primed to see Tolentino's version chupacabra — whether or not it existed.

Soon other people began reporting similar sightings that closely matched Tolentino's description, which is not surprising since widespread stress and panic can make people more vulnerable to "groupthink," conformity, and social imitation.⁵ As this relates to chupacabra reports, one writer notes that "these conditions lead people to mimic the beliefs and behaviors of their neighbors and friends in order to maintain a collective identity and strengthen vital social bonds."⁶

In Puerto Rico, many of the first chupacabra reports were spread through the typical folklore routes of rumor and gossip: over back fences and among neighbors and friends. But the creature's fame skyrocketed once local newspapers picked up the story and began printing sensational headlines. Among the four newspapers that served Puerto Rico in 1995, *El Vocero* was among the most popular. It was "a tabloid whose headlines, in bright, red, uppercase letters, often surmount a grotesque photograph of a murder or automobile accident [with] consistent UFO / paranormal coverage."[7] *El Vocero*, the *National Enquirer* of Puerto Rico, crassly promoted any lurid, shocking, or sensational story that would sell papers. And a mysterious animal-killing vampire was just the thing. No one was safe! What was this strange vampire beast? Would it soon hunt humans? Who would be next?

This strong bias toward sensationalism affected the information that most Puerto Ricans got about the monster. The mainstream newspapers largely ignored the chupacabra stories, leaving the tabloids to fill the void with their own dramatic reporting. While level-headed government officials were occasionally quoted as trying to quell the fear, panicked housewives and gun-toting farmers were always favored and highlighted. Fear and panic sell; skepticism does not. One scientist, Puerto Rican zoologist Edwin Velasquez, lamented the news media's role in fueling the chupacabra scare at the time: "When the humble, ignorant people of our rural areas hear there is a bloodsucking creature on the loose, they believe it. Hysteria sets in. We should not be so sensationalistic. The media, for whatever reason, only gives one part of the story rather than the whole story."[8]

A famous depiction of the terrifying vampire beast *el chupacabra*, based on an eyewitness sighting in Puerto Rico in 1995 (illustration by Benjamin Radford, after a drawing by Jorge Martin).

The majority of chupacabra news reports that circulated in Puerto Rico in 1995 were written by only a handful of people; one reporter for *El Vocero* tabloid accounted for nearly half of the news stories. This reporter made a cottage industry of the chupacabra, cranking out story after story, each more sensational than the last.

With the chupacabra hysteria in full swing on the small island, all reports, no matter how outlandish, were widely reported by the news media. People often jumped to illogical conclusions, attributing anything odd to the dreaded chupacabra. Take, for instance, the following report, from November 7, 1995: "Striking at a junkyard, it killed a cat and a sheep, and apparently swallowed an entire lamb, since the third animal being kept by the junkyard owner was never found." Exactly why the cat and sheep were assumed to have been chupacabra victims is not clear (no mention is made of drained blood), but in the case of the lamb, there was no evidence at all that the chupacabra, or any other creature, had even encountered it.

Some people reported merely finding dead animals; others claimed to have seen a gargoyle-like beast. One account states that "several witnesses swore that the goatsucker's eyes emitted beams of light that illuminated nocturnal landscape like flashlight beams.... Many who saw the chupacabras said it has a web of skin that connects its wrist to its knee or ankle, and this web forms a 'wing,' like that of a flying squirrel when it raises its arms, and that this structure allows it to glide like a hang glider.... One witness claimed that the extremely rapid movement of small, feather-like appendages along its backbone propelled it like a bumblebee."[9]

In one of the most outlandish chupacabra-related claims (yet one that was reported as a straight news story), "Although five chickens were found entirely drained of blood in the back yard of the property owned by Julio and Julia Gonzales, the most spectacular event appears to have been the strange mark placed on the forearm of the couple's daughter... Oralis Gonzales, five years old, was marked with a tattoo-like impression that read, 'OJO-10-OJO' after an alleged encounter with non-human entities. While the child is reluctant to discuss exactly what transpired ... it is generally acknowledged that this event has triggered the child's IQ, causing her father to describe her as a prodigy."[10] The story, which appeared in the November 13, 1995, issue of *El Vocero*, suggests that the story has been confirmed by a police officer, lending it some credibility. Despite this outlandish claim, nothing more is mentioned about the girl, her family, or the experience. If this story — which is almost certainly a hoax — is treated with the same seriousness as all the other chupacabra stories, what credibility do any of them have?

The public's reaction to the chupacabra panic varied widely. Some people ignored it, believing the stories to be merely rumor and gossip. Others (espe-

Dead chicken believed to have been attacked by the chupacabra, near El Paso, Texas, in 2010 (photograph by and courtesy of Jay Koester).

cially among the UFO-believer community) were certain that the sinister mystery was a very real threat to the Puerto Rican public. Many people perhaps fell in between these extremes, not quite believing all the stories, but suspecting that *something* strange was out there.

It is known that many people who believed the spoken and published rumors did panic, taking up arms against the chupacabra. Concerned citizens formed patrols and vigilante mobs, armed with rifles, machetes, pitchforks, and baseball bats, hoping to find and kill the chupacabra. In one case "a massive mobilization of searchers was outfitted with infrared lights, shotguns, electrical equipment, helmets, and riot shields."[11] Furthermore, local authorities "led 200-strong search parties on nightly forays" to capture the chupacabra. No sign of the creature was found.

The Puerto Rican chupacabra panic largely subsided by the end of 1995. Public interest in the beast waned, and therefore the news media reports declined as well, which in turn led to fewer sightings. The monster was soon reported in other countries, and eventually the Puerto Rican chupacabra reports dried up entirely. To this day chupacabra sightings still surface on occasion, even in North America — a lasting reminder of the power of the news media to create a panic around a non-existent threat.

CHAPTER 34

YouTube, Popcorn and the Killer Cell Phones

> Modern technology has brought us incalculable benefit: Computers and cell phones have become modern essentials. But are these technologies safe? Or do they harbor invisible killers, causing cancer and other dread diseases?

We take modern conveniences for granted. Microwave ovens, computers, and cell phones have become essentials for our everyday lives. But what if these necessities of modern life are secretly killing us? That's the basis for one of the greatest media scares of the past few decades, the panic over cell phones. Since the 1990s, some people have claimed that cell phones can cause cancer. One of the most vocal promoters of this idea is a man named George Carlo, an epidemiologist who built a career out of selling fear. Though he was never able to offer concrete evidence or proof of his claims, he insisted that more research was needed, and that the threat posed by cell phones was serious.

Carlo was the primary source for the ABC TV newsmagazine *20/20*, which in 1999 aired a sensationalized, alarmist report on the subject. As Dr. Ian K. Smith noted in *Time* magazine, "After spending six years and millions of dollars, Carlo produced only an inconclusive report offering no more than suspicions of health risks. Even so, *20/20* accepted it as medical fact. 'We have direct evidence of possible harm from cellular phones,' he told ABC's correspondent, who cast Carlo as an ultraethical scientist breaking ranks with his bosses because they wouldn't let him tell the truth."[1] Carlo cast himself as a persecuted hero, breaking a scientific conspiracy of silence.

Carlo's 2002 book added to the media scare over cell phones. Titled *Cell Phones: Invisible Hazards in the Wireless Age: An Insider's Alarming Discoveries about Cancer and Genetic Damage*, it contained much speculation and the claim that a study on cell phone safety published in the prestigious *Journal of the American Medical Association* (*JAMA*) had found that cell phone use tripled the risk of one type of brain cancer. The public was eager for information about the dangers of cell phones, and his book sold well.

There was just one problem. The lead author of that *JAMA* study, Joshua Muscat, noted that Carlo had his facts wrong. The study came to exactly the opposite conclusion of what Carlo claimed: "We found that regardless of how frequently the phones were used per month or how many years that the phones were used, there wasn't any relationship with the developments of brain cancer.... Radio frequency waves are low-energy waves. They are not like X-rays, which have been shown to cause genetic damage. They don't produce any harmful physiological effects that we know of."[2]

The scientific rebuttal did little to stem the public's fear, and the media scare continued to pick up steam and publicity. Larry King devoted a segment on his top-rated CNN show *Larry King Live* on August 9, 2000, to the case of a man named Larry Reynard, who told a scary story about how his wife had developed brain cancer several months after first using a cell phone. (Both King and Reynard missed the fact that brain cancers generally take years — not months — to develop, and that Reynard's wife probably had the cancer *before* she began using her cell phone. If using a cell phone for only three months is enough to cause brain cancer, nearly every American adult should be afflicted with the disease!)[3]

The Internet and the Popcorn Panic

For a while it seemed that scary cell phone stories were everywhere in the news media. The main panic calmed by the mid-2000s, but never went away. When the World Wide Web became ubiquitous, the Internet was soon used to spread the concern. Scary warnings about the dangers of cell phones circulated in the form of forwarded e-mails around the world. Some were cautious about the cancer dangers, but others contained new myths about the dangers of cell phones. According to Snopes, an urban-legend reference Web site, one warning that circulated in 2004 stated, "Don't answer a cell phone while it is being charged! A few days ago, a person was recharging his cell phone at home. Just at that time a call came through and he attended to it.... He was rushed to the nearby hospital, but was pronounced dead on arrival. A cell phone is a very useful modern invention. However, we must be aware that it can also be an instrument of death. FORWARD THIS TO THE PEOPLE THAT MATTER IN YOUR LIFE, I JUST DID!"

In June 2009, the cell phone panic jumped into a new medium, YouTube, and went viral. That's when, as Tracy King, a British media researcher, noted, "A series of videos on YouTube appeared to show four cell phone users popping a table full of corn kernels simply by pointing their ringing phones at them. The implication for the casual observer was clear: If cell phones emit enough radiation to pop corn, imagine what they are doing to your brain!" The video generated huge publicity, and was seen worldwide. Exactly as they had done with the earlier hoax e-mail warnings, friends who saw the video forwarded the link to other friends, either as a silly gag or out of sincere concern for their safety. Since the video was anonymous, many wondered if it was posted by a well-meaning cell phone scientist who wanted to warn the world but was afraid of repercussions for his career if his employers found out he was alerting the public to this horrific danger. These people were of course reading from a conspiracy theory script George Carlo had written a decade earlier.

As it turns out, the video was a hoax. Not only was it a hoax, it was an advertisement, a bit of clever marketing (or scare-mongering, depending on your point of view) by a company called Cardo Systems, which sold wireless Bluetooth headsets for cell phones. "The creative team at Cardo who created the popcorn videos exploited existing concerns about cell-phone radiation and made them legend. The 'anonymous' videos were viewed nearly 10 million times in just two weeks before Cardo stepped forward to take credit, although not, initially, to debunk the pseudoscience. Cardo claims that traffic to its Web site doubled in the days the videos were active."[4]

Despite the alarm and media scares, repeated studies have found no link between cell phone use and disease. In fact, as one physicist noted, the power in a standard cell phone would not be enough to cause problems: "The small amount of power being transmitted by the phone is traveling several kilometers to the tower. Also, the cell phone has to transmit this very little power in all directions. The small power in the direction of the tower passes through several walls and other obstructions, even people, without impeding the communication."[5] Thus, cell phone signals are everywhere — and probably passing through you as you read this. If the signals were carcinogenic, nearly everyone would have cancer. In the end, "unless one is willing to discard ... the entire body of quantum physics, it is simply not possible for the photons associated with a cell phone to cause cancer."

Though repeated studies have failed to find any link between cell phones and cancers, researchers are still doing tests to determine if there might be any long-term effects. Since cell phones are a relatively recent development, it is impossible for scientists to compare current health or cancer rates of cell phone users to those 20 or 30 years ago.

Fear of Technology

The cell phone scare, like all media scares, did not appear in a social vacuum. In fact it exploits one of the most common and ingrained anxieties in America: the public's fear of technology. People tend to be fearful of new technologies, especially devices that they don't fully understand. The public often rushes to embrace new scientific advances that make their life easier — but at the same time they distrust them. The efficacy of these new products can't be disputed: A microwave oven clearly heats food more quickly than a conventional oven. The visible benefits and results can't be denied, but it's the things we can't and don't see — such as radiation — that people fear.

Humans have always feared things they couldn't see. For thousands of years, one of the world's greatest threats was an invisible killer that could not be seen, smelled, tasted, or touched: disease. Humans naturally became fearful of invisible, undetectable forces that could harm or kill them. Of course, with modern technology we can now see and identify microscopic bacteria and viruses that killed off our forefathers, but people still fear things they cannot detect with their own bodily senses.

The public's fear of radiation is not irrational or illogical; indeed, radiation is carcinogenic and can be deadly under certain conditions and in high doses. It's not silly or stupid to be concerned about radiation and microwave exposure, but the public should be informed about what radiation is so they can understand the risks.

There is no way to avoid exposure to radiation, as it is everywhere. There is radiation in sunlight. People on airplanes are exposed to more radiation than people on the ground. And so on. Ideally, humans should be exposed to as little radiation as possible, but the exposure from power lines and cell phones is so low that it does not pose a significant health hazard.

The Cell Phone Panic Cools

As we have seen with other cases discussed in this book, politicians and lawmakers are often pushed by a panicky public to address scares they see in the media. Sometimes the politicians see themselves as crusaders, being proactive against an underreported threat. In December 2009, a state legislator from Maine, Rep. Andrea Boland, proposed that cell phones sold in her state should be required to include a printed warning about the health dangers of cell phone use. Taking a cue from graphic cigarette advertising, Boland also proposed that the phones include a full-color graphic of a child's brain, with the word WARNING in large red letters imposed over the picture.

There's no question that cell phones can be dangerous. Many scientific, reputable studies have proved that. In fact, cell phone use has been banned in many states for exactly this reason. But the chief threat of cell phones is the distraction they cause, not the electromagnetic fields they emit. Drivers who are busy texting on their cell phones are six times more likely to get in an accident than those who do not.[6] In one study, drivers needed 30 percent more reaction time while texting, and 9 percent more time when they were talking on a cell phone, compared to undistracted drivers. It is the non-chemical equivalent of drunk driving.

CHAPTER 35

Someone Stole My Kidney! Organ Theft Scares

> According to alarmist news media reports, body-snatchers lurk in the most unlikely places, waiting to lure the innocent into evil traps and steal their organs.

The idea of being murdered and butchered by a stranger is terrifying, a universal fear commonly exploited in gory horror and slasher films. Most of us know that only happens in the movies — but what about stories of people being killed for their organs? Are there really heinous murderers out there employing medical doctors who are happy to cut your heart, kidneys, liver, or any other vital organ and transplant it into the highest bidder, like some gruesome eBay auction?

Many people do believe this happens, because they hear horrific "true crime" news stories in the news media. While many people encounter incidences of organ theft as legitimate news stories in mainstream media, the horrific nature of the crime has inspired many fictional depictions as well. One of the earliest and most famous examples was the 1978 medical thriller *Coma*, which starred Michael Douglas as a young doctor who discovers a hospital taking organs from the comatose. An episode of the hit television show *Law and Order* also featured the theft of a kidney. Airing on April 2, 1991, it was titled "Sonata for Solo Organ." The show's writer said he had heard it from a friend, and the friend assured him that the story was a true account that had come from a newspaper.[1] The following year, a film titled *The Harvest* involved a screenwriter in Central America who uncovers a black market in kidneys. Organ-snatching was also an element in Walter Salles's acclaimed 1998 Brazilian film *Central do Brasil* (*Central Station*) in which a young boy escapes an "adoption agency" that actually uses children for their organs. Guillermo del Toro's 2001 Mexican horror film *El Espinazo del Diablo* (*The*

Devil's Backbone) also makes reference to bodily theft, when a character suggests the fate of a missing boy: "They sell the blood to rich people to cure their tuberculosis." The line between fact and fiction can be blurry, and for people whose fears are fed on a steady diet of sensationalized crime stories in the news media, any outrageously evil act may seem plausible.

News Media Spreads the Panic

When rumors of organ thefts first emerged, the stories were met with some skepticism. After all, the idea that ruthless, evil gangs would kidnap and murder innocent children for their organs was too terrible to be true. Surely no humane person could slit a young boy's throat just before a doctor—a trained man or woman of ethics and medicine—carefully removed his small organs. Of course, the organ theft stories (whether true or not) were too lurid and sensational for the news media—and especially the tabloids—to pass up. Fear and sensationalism sells newspapers and increases TV audiences; the pressure of the marketplace launched the organ theft panic into the global sphere. Children who claimed to have been victims (or attempted victims) of organ theft were tracked down by newspaper or television reporters looking for a sensational story. One famous case was that of Pedro Reggi, an Argentine boy who claimed that his corneas had been forcibly removed during his stay at a mental institution. The claim surfaced in a British/Canadian television program titled "The Body Parts Business," and was later broadcast on a French television program titled "Organ Snatchers." On November 25, 1993, four days after the original claim was broadcast, Reggi and his half-brother, Mario Barretto, went on the Argentine television program *Hora Clave* to retract the allegation. Barretto revealed that an ophthalmologist examined Reggi earlier that day and found that his corneas were in fact intact, but they had been damaged by disease. Subsequent investigation uncovered Reggi's medical records, which confirmed that the sight loss was due to natural causes.[2]

A second claim that aired on the "Body Parts Business" was that of eight-year-old Honduran Charlie Alvarado. The boy claimed that he had been kidnapped by foreigners who wanted to sell his organs, but he managed to escape after four days. The documentary aired the claims without a hint of skepticism, and panicked many viewers. Eventually investigative journalists from Germany's Spiegel television examined the claims, including that of Charlie Alvarado. As Todd Leventhal, formerly of the United States Information Agency (USIA), reported, "According to a June 20, 1993, Spiegel television broadcast on this subject, an investigation of Alvarado's claims by the Honduran courts 'revealed that Charlie's story was a fabrication.' Alvarado could not remember the day on which he was allegedly kidnapped, he had no bruises from the ropes with which he claimed he had been bound tightly for days, and the two foreign workers he accused of kidnapping him were released for lack of evidence."[3]

The "Organ Snatchers" documentary also featured a Colombian woman, Mrs. Luz Dary Vargas, who claimed that her young son Weinis Jeison had also been the victim of this horrible crime. She said that when Jeison became ill she took him to a local hospital, where his corneas were taken from him. But when the Colombian Office of Human Rights investigated the theft, the story began to unravel. In a report issued February 4, 1994, the office found that in fact Jeison had gone blind due to natural causes. In early February 1993, the boy was hospitalized with numerous health problems including "severe bilateral eye infection," which led to complete blindness well before the allegations of cornea theft were made. The report also found that, in a clear breach of journalistic ethics and protocol, a French journalist paid his mother for the story.[4]

Over and over, a close examination proved that the organ theft claims were myths. Yet, as often happens with such sensational claims, the original inaccurate stories received widespread international attention, while the debunking follow-ups refuting the claims were little noticed.

The organ-snatching legend reached a peak of popularity in the mid–1990s, when several prominent organizations gave the rumors credibility. As noted earlier, several media outlets ran stories about child organ trafficking, including the Brazilian newspaper *Correio Braziliense* and a book published in Spain titled *Niños de Repuesto (Spare-Parts Children)*. Further credibility was lent when the World Organization against Torture issued a report by its director, Eric Sottas, in March 1994. The paper, titled "Trade in Organs and Torture," listed six Latin American countries as confirmed traffickers in child organs. Sottas rehashed numerous accounts, many of them long since disproven, of organ trafficking. Sottas included, for example, the case of Pedro Reggi, the Argentine boy mentioned earlier who had lost his sight to disease, not cornea thieves.[5]

Consequences of Organ Theft Panics

Beliefs about organ theft are alive and well — especially in Latin America — and not just in cinematic fiction. Slayings in several places including Juarez, Mexico, and Altamira, Brazil, have been attributed to organ traffickers and Satan worshippers. At times, innocent people have been attacked and killed by those who fear organ thieves; in fact several unprovoked attacks on foreigners occurred in the mid-1990s. In March 1994, Melissa Larson, a woman from New Mexico, was hiking in Guatemala when she was taken to a police station for routine questioning. Rumors quickly spread in the town of Santa Lucia Cotzumalguapa that she had been detained for selling babies and baby organs. When she was transferred to a larger jail, townspeople rioted, believing that she had bribed guards to be let free. The riot left sixty people hospitalized and led to fifty arrests.[6] The following month, Alaska native June Weinstock was beaten unconscious and stabbed by a mob of about 300 angry villagers in western Guatemala. The 52-year-old woman suffered multiple stab wounds, three skull fractures, a broken arm, and a broken leg. She fell into a coma shortly thereafter and remains disabled. Weinstock was accused of abducting an eight-year-old boy who was actually at a religious procession and later returned home safe and oblivious to the village's concern.[7]

In the Guatemalan highlands, an elderly Japanese tourist was killed in 2000 after stroking a baby's head. The baby's mother panicked, believing that the foreigner was a bloodthirsty satanist who might stab her child and rip out its heart for use in a ritual. Perez Mendoza, a street vendor, incited a mob to kill not only the tourists but the Guatemalan police who tried to protect them. Another Japanese tourist and a Guatemalan bus driver were hacked to death with machetes; the bus driver's remains were then burned with gasoline. Such is the fear that rumors can create.

First-World Organ Theft Panics

While many of the organ theft rumors are set (and spread in) Latin American third-world countries,[8] sometimes the organ theft stories appear elsewhere. One high-profile allegation of an organ-theft case made headlines in December 1989 when a Turkish man named Ahmet Koc claimed that three months earlier, he had been brought to London, England, with the promise of a job. When he went in for a medical check, he was given an injection which he believed to be a blood test, but he woke up the next day to find that a kidney had been removed. He was told that he should not go to the police because he would be well paid for his kidney.

The story hit the British tabloids like wildfire, and once again the ugly "reality" of organ theft and bodily violation was exposed. Yet, once again, predictably, there was less to this story than met the eye. Under police questioning and mounting public pressure to explain his story, Koc soon admitted he lied. He had not been the victim of organ theft; he had voluntarily sold his kidney, but wanted more money and went to the press with his fictional story when he was refused. Although transplanting brokered kidneys was legal at the time in Britain, three London doctors who participated in the transplant were found guilty of professional misconduct.[9]

In late 2009, a Swedish tabloid journalist claimed that Israeli soldiers and doctors in Tel Aviv killed Palestinians for their organs. The story was immediately refuted as anti–Semitic propaganda, but the Israeli government was eventually forced to acknowledge that there was some truth to the claims when an American anthropologist released an interview she had conducted in 2000 with the former head of Israel's main forensic institute, Dr. Jehuda Hiss. Hiss stated that body parts were taken from the dead (not just Palestinians, but Israelis and others as well) without consent during the 1990s and transplanted into wounded soldiers. The Israeli military then admitted the procedures had been done but stated that the practice had ended a decade earlier.

Yet the claims about Israel's organ theft are not quite rumor, but not quite fact. There is no evidence that the premise of the original newspaper story—that Israeli soldiers killed Palestinians for the purpose of harvesting their organs—is true. Often the very act of killing the victims would render many of their organs unusable. However, the admission by Dr. Hiss, especially in light of previous governmental denials, exposes a very real (and unethical) organ scandal. Were body parts taken from victims without their consent? Yes. Were people killed for their body parts? No.[10] Especially in the polarized world of Middle East politics, such nuances are often ignored in favor of sensationalized claims of body-parts theft.

Like all media scares, the organ-theft panics come and go. They appear now and then, fueled by anti–Western sentiment, political agendas, hoaxes, bad journalism, misunderstandings, and tabloid sensationalism. These horrific stories tell us nothing about the trade in stolen organs, but much about the social and cultural climate in which these panics appear.

Chapter 36

Killer Vaccines

by Felicity Goodyear-Smith
and *Helen Petousis-Harris*

Vaccines are good and have spared hundreds of millions of people around the world from the ravages of disease. The social and economic benefits resulting from the development and wide-scale introduction of vaccines is well documented and undeniable. It has been calculated that as a direct result of immunization, every dollar spent to purchase measles-containing vaccine in the United States has saved $10.30 in direct medical costs and $3.20 in indirect societal costs.[1] The ten vaccines universally recommended and funded for New Zealand children, offering protection against diseases which previously have decimated human populations, have led to dramatic declines in numbers of cases. New Zealand has been free of poliomyelitis (polio) for many decades.[2] Prior to its development in the 1950s, just the mention of the word would send chills through the spines of schoolchildren around the world as classmates would be suddenly and inexplicably stricken by this crippling illness. Vaccines are the biggest area of investment for the Bill and Melinda Gates Foundation (over $800 million every year). They write, "Vaccines are one of the most effective health interventions ever developed. We are committed to research on new vaccines, and the delivery of existing and future vaccines to those who need them."[3]

Felicity Goodyear-Smith *is an associate professor and Goodfellow Postgraduate Chair in the Department of General Practice and Primary Health Care, University of Auckland. The author of more than 150 journal articles, she is an active member of the New Zealand skeptics.*

Helen Petousis-Harris *is the director of research at the Immunization Advisory Centre, Department of General Practice and Primary Health at the University of Auckland. Her specializations include molecular medicine and vaccinology.*

The First Vaccine

In 1721 the practice of varioation was introduced, whereby someone was inoculated with smallpox to produce immunity to the disease. As might be expected, this was not an exact science and serious illness and death from varioation was common. In 1774, English farmer Benjamin Jesty used a needle to transfer material from a cow pustule to a scratch on the arms of his family as an inoculation against smallpox. His neighbors were disgusted by his introducing an animal disease into humans and some feared that they would metamorphosis into horned beasts. He was assaulted for this inhumane act.[4]

A few years later scientist Edward Jenner was consulted by Sarah Nelmes, a dairymaid, about a rash on her hand. Jenner suspected cowpox rather than smallpox and Sarah confirmed that one of her cows, Blossom, had recently had cowpox. This led to the first official vaccination. Jenner made scratches on the arm of James Phipps, the eight-year-old son of his gardener, into which

The Cow Pock; Or, the Wonderful Effects on the New Inoculation. Edward Jenner among patients in the Smallpox and Inoculation Ward. Colored etching after J. Gillray, 1802 (courtesy Wellcome Images).

he rubbed material from Sarah's pock. A few days later James became mildly ill but soon recovered. Jenner learned that cowpox could pass both from cow to person and from person to person. The next step was to see if this would protect young James from the dreaded smallpox. He boldly inoculated James with smallpox on several occasions but the boy did not develop the disease.[5]

Jenner conducted several similar experiments and published his findings.[6] Initially this new proven method to protect against smallpox did not catch on as Jenner had hoped. Firstly, cowpox was not common and doctors had to obtain the material from Jenner. Secondly, cowpox samples often became contaminated with smallpox, leading to claims that cowpox was no safer than smallpox and thirdly, variolation was a profitable business which was threatened by Jenner's safer, more effective cowpox method. It took an Act of Parliament in 1840 outlawing variolation to establish vaccination and make it free for the poor. In 1853 smallpox vaccination was made compulsory for all babies, with fines or imprisonment for defaulting parents. Vaccination against smallpox has proved immensely successful. In the 20th century between 300 and 500 million people died from smallpox.[7] Vaccination resulted in the worldwide eradication of smallpox in 1979,[8] the only successful globally eradicated infectious disease.

Vaccines and the Media

Despite overwhelming evidence of their general efficacy and safety (the benefits of preventing illness and death from vaccine-preventable diseases greatly outweighing any rare adverse effects), there has always been an anti-vaccination lobby. Mandatory smallpox vaccination sparked protests and violent riots from those who wanted the freedom of choice. The Anti-Vaccination League was founded in 1853 and the Anti-Compulsory Vaccination League in 1867, with many others to follow. In 1878 the *National Anti-Compulsory Vaccinator Reporter* in the UK claimed that the smallpox vaccine contained dangerous poisons, caused serious illnesses, represented wicked medical despotism, reduced neither the incidence nor the severity of smallpox, and was a futile substitute for healthy living.[9] History has proved this wrong. However, the same claims that vaccines are dangerous, that they do not work, or that mandatory vaccination violates civil liberties are still promoted in the media by the anti-immunization lobby today.[10] At the end of this chapter, in Table 1, we outline some of the arguments against vaccination and their modern-day equivalents found in New Zealand media.

Most people obtain information about health issues from the mass media in various modalities including radio, television, print and the Internet.[11] The media can have either positive or negative influence on immunization uptake.[12] In New Zealand the mainstream print media reaches all homes in all regions, including free, regional newspapers, at least weekly, although these papers may not be read in every home. A recent review concluded that the mass media is a tool which might promote the use of health services proven to be effective and discourage those of unproven effectiveness.[13] However, this result depends on accurate reporting.

The media is a powerful agent in influencing public opinion about controversial health concerns.[14] When a topic affects most of the population, as opposed to a small sector, it becomes relevant to the media and, from a news perspective, immediately "hot." If one moves from a health topic relevant to a smaller segment of society, such as a new treatment for a rare cancer, to one with more universal appeal, such as a mass childhood immunization program, then the number of people to whom the story is relevant increases exponentially. If one adds personal adventure/mishap, controversy such as two sides that can pit one against another and graphic or emotive images, then immunization becomes an excellent topic for media attention.

Media reports which question the safety of vaccines may greatly increase the concerns of parents.[15] Vaccine opposition typically expands as the prevalence of the diseases declines, and the experience of epidemics leading to disability and death recedes from social memory over time. Typically the media focus shifts from a fear of disease to a fear about vaccine safety.[16] Other areas of opposition relate to religious concerns around interfering with God's will and issues around individual choice.[17]

Measles and Mumps

Children are vaccinated against English measles (morbilli), mumps and German measles (rubella) in a triple vaccine called MMR, typically given between age one to two, with a second shot before starting school at age five.

Effects of Measles and Mumps

In the past, epidemics of measles have decimated populations. The *Times* records the rapidly rising death rate in English children through such an epidemic in 1922.[18] Measles was even more devastating for populations such as New Zealand Maori and Pacific people in Polynesia, introduced through immigration by Europeans from the 1840s onwards. With no natural immunity, measles ravaged populations of both children and adults. While German measles is a relatively benign disease, it can cause serious damage to the unborn child if a woman catches it during the first three to four months of her pregnancy. It may cause miscarriage, stillbirth, or birth defects such as deafness, brain damage and heart defects. Mumps is seldom fatal but can have complications such as inflammation of the brain (meningitis), miscarriage if contracted in pregnancy, and, if contracted in young men, inflamed testicles with subsequent infertility.

The Wakefield Saga

In 1998 Andrew Wakefield and colleagues published an article in the esteemed medical journal *The Lancet*. Their paper described 12 children with gastrointestinal and developmental problems. According to the parents of eight of them, the onset of their symptoms had followed their MMR vaccine.[19] On the day of publication Wakefield began a media campaign against the continued use of MMR. The mass media rapidly disseminated the message that MMR was causing autism and the story grew over the next decade. Internationally the media was rife with stories of healthy children suddenly becoming autistic following MMR. Prior to this scare, the vaccination rate for two-year-olds receiving MMR in the United Kingdom (UK) was about 91 percent. Parental fear led to this rate plummeting. The resulting measles outbreaks resulted in the death or permanent disability of a number of children in the UK and Ireland.

In 2004, 10 of the 12 original authors of *The Lancet* paper published a retraction to clarify that no causal link had been established between MMR vaccine and autism.[20] That year it was made public that Wakefield had received £55,000 of funding from solicitors seeking evidence to use against the manufactures of vaccines, and by 2006 it was revealed that he had received over £400,000 and that payments had started two years before the 1998 paper. Additionally, several of the parents in *The Lancet* study claiming that MMR had caused their children autism were litigants. Wakefield had not declared this conflict of interest to his co-investigators nor to *The Lancet*. Additionally, in 1997 Wakefield had filed for a patent for a single vaccine against measles (without the mumps and rubella components) and for a treatment of inflammatory bowel disease and then set up a company to produce and sell it. Apparently the managing director was the father of one of the children in the study. Wakefield had tried his new vaccine on the child without ethical permission and arranged for friends of his son to give blood samples at a birthday party for which he paid them each £5.

Finally in 2010 the General Medical Council declared that Wakefield had abused his position of trust as a medical practitioner, failed in his duties and brought the medical profession into disrepute. He and two colleagues were charged with serious professional misconduct. The editors of *The Lancet* announced that the 1998 paper had been fully retracted from the published record.[21]

Numerous robust studies, some involving hundreds of thousands of individuals, have been conducted and all demonstrate that there is no causal association between MMR vaccine and autism nor any other developmental disorder. Tragically, there is continued widespread public belief that MMR causes autism.

The New Zealand Meningococcal B Story

In the 1990s New Zealand experienced a ghastly epidemic of meningococcal B disease. Caused by the bacterium *Neisseria meningitidis*, infection leads to blood poisoning (septicemia) characterized by a rash, sometimes progressing to gangrene and limb loss and/or to infection of the lining of the brain (meningitis). The epidemic resulted in significant death and disability, including brain damage, deafness and limb amputation in around 11 to 19 percent of cases. At its height, 648 cases were reported in one year, with over 5500 cases throughout the course of the epidemic. Pacific (Polynesian) children were at greatest risk, with a 1 in 68 chance of contracting the disease by age five.

Although there are a number of different strains of meningococcal bacteria (A, B, C, W...), most of the New Zealand disease was caused by a single subtype of group B. There are vaccines against other strains of meningococcal bacteria, but group B poses more difficulty. There is no vaccine available for general meningococcus B. After a meeting of New Zealand health authorities and the World Health Organization in Geneva in 1998, it was proposed that a vaccine be produced to control the epidemic. In 2000 manufacturers were invited to submit proposals to develop and bring to licensure a tailor-made vaccine against the meningococcal strain causing most of the New Zealand disease. The vaccine would not work against other strains. In 2004, following successful phase 1 and 2 clinical trials proving the safety and capacity of the vaccine to protect against disease, the MeNZB vaccine was rolled out in a staggered fashion to the whole New Zealand population aged 20 years and under. The objective was to bring the epidemic under control.

The Media Response

The prospect of a vaccine to control this devastating disease was discussed with excitement in the mass media during the time leading up to the roll-out of the vaccine. The illness was severe and often graphically horrific. Many stories were told of children battling the disease in intensive care units around the country while traumatized parents stood on watching helplessly as their children's blackened limbs were amputated and their brains suffered permanent damage. The fact that medical science had developed a vaccine to end this scourge was viewed in a positive light. Analysis of the press clippings shows stories to be scientifically accurate and not misleading.

Predictably this "honeymoon" of accurate reporting came to an abrupt halt on the day that the vaccine became publicly available. In 2004 there were over 1000 articles discussing MeNZB in the New Zealand print media and in 2005 this increased to over 4000 articles. Sadly, instead of all press reporting being scientifically accurate, 42 percent contained at least some unsubstantiated information.

Even though a journalist may have crafted a well written and accurate article, the headline often bore little resemblance to the story. Two cases below illustrate this practice.

Case Study 1

On 8 November 2004 the launch of the mass meningococcal B vaccination campaign starting that day was publicized. The vaccine was being offered to children under five in Central Auckland, a large New Zealand urban area. Essentially, the story announced the launch, discussed vaccine safety (the independent safety board, adverse reaction monitoring and clinical trials findings all had reported no major safety issue), then quoted the opinion of an anti-immunization lobbyist who told stories of children reputed to have had reactions to the vaccine. This story generated eight articles on the same day for which there were three accurate ("Preschoolers get jabs," "Meningitis jabs begin" and "Vaccinations begin") and five misleading headlines ("Dispute over vaccine risk goes on," "Mass vaccination proceeding despite concerns," "Vaccine debate continues, 25,000 face needle," "Vaccine row rages" and "Meningococcal vaccine risk dispute goes on").

Case Study 2

In November 2004 two toddlers fully vaccinated with MeNZB™ were admitted to hospital with meningococcal C disease. The Ministry of Health was quoted that the vaccination is only against the strain specific B type, and that children need three doses. The story went national via the New Zealand

Press Association distribution. This release generated 30 print media stories between November 22 and December 2, 2004. There were nine accurate headlines, six ambiguous headlines and 15 misleading headlines.

The accurate headlines included "Vaccinated boy sick with another strain of killer bug," "Vaccinated child catches different strain of disease," "Vaccinated child catches different meningitis strain," "Immunised tot catches another strain of disease," "Vaccinated boy struck by another strain" and "Jabs can't protect against all strains."

Included in the misleading headlines were "Toddler struck down," "Vaccine fails," "Vaccine fails to protect," "Two children develop meningococcal disease despite being immunised," "Sick children no surprise to anti-jab campaigner" and "Two meningococcal cases, despite immunisation."

Common Fallacies

Some techniques are used with monotonous regularity to mislead the reader. One is the error of omission, where information is cherry-picked and only a selected part of the truth is presented, ignoring data that may contradict the position. For example: "The Norwegian government decided against the use of this vaccine after researchers concluded it wasn't effective enough to justify a national campaign." In fact, the Norwegian government did not use the meningococcal vaccine because their meningococcal B epidemic was waning by the time the vaccine became available.

Another technique is the non sequitur, for example, assuming because one event follows another in time it was caused by the first (called *post hoc ergo propter hoc*). For example, "An Oamaru pupil says the meningitis vaccine caused him to collapse and spend a night in hospital." Emotive language is often used to provoke fear: for example, about the MeNZB™ vaccination program: "How a nation can be so totally swayed by officials and advisors into spending quarter of a billion dollars for such a gamble that has delivered false hope to trusting New Zealanders."

Perhaps of greatest frustration to health professionals and those who have some expertise in vaccination is the false attribution. This is the appeal to irrelevant, unqualified, biased or fabricated source: "Ron Law a risk and policy analyst and former Ministry consultant, [said] that using the formula the Ministry proposed before the vaccine was rolled out, the effectiveness for the past 6 months is only 9%." Law is a vocal anti-immunization lobbyist whose qualifications are a certificate gained working in a medical laboratory for 20 years and a Master of Business Administration degree.

On the Television

While there was considerable coverage about this vaccine in the national and local print media, television and radio also provided stories. By the end of 2006 the epidemic had waned and the school vaccination program was complete. The commitment by New Zealand's health professionals had been staggering, the achievement admirable. New Zealand's most at-risk children had been immunized. Hospital emergency staff were no longer seeing admissions for meningococcal disease. This cause for celebration was missed. Nobody congratulated themselves for a job well done. No stories about the absence of disease appeared. Instead, in early November 2006 a shockumenatry screened on TVNZ Channel 1.

Opening Transcript

"Researchers dressed in white. Our guardian angels. In the service of the holy, the common science in an eternal battle against dangerous microorganisms, they are there to protect us against disease and death. A contract of faith for the good of public health. One of the researchers' great feats is the development of vaccines. This is the story of a vaccine which Norwegian researchers call a success, and which they have been internationally recognised for. The story starts with a hope of saving the world from a fatal disease. It continues with a vaccine which was tested on Norwegian college children, but which was never used in Norway, and it ends in New Zealand, with accusations of low medical morals and claims that the Norwegian Institute of Public Health has been the guarantor of a mass experiment on more than a million New Zealand children." The program included misleading material such as stating that 27 fully vaccinated people had contracted the disease, failing to mention that 158 unvaccinated or incompletely vaccinated people had contracted the disease; and making claims around serious adverse events, omitting to mention that a study around serious adverse events included 350,000 teenagers and compared vaccinated (145,000) with unvaccinated (110,000). There were 14 serious adverse events in the vaccine recipients and 43 in those who had not received the vaccine. The follow-up period for these events was over three years.

Grassroots and the Internet

In addition to print, radio and television media there is also the Internet. Although difficult to analyze, it is possible that the use of this tool by opponents of the MeNZB™ vaccination program played the greatest role in the generation of public outrage and fear about the vaccine. An example of Internet scares around this vaccine was a series of newsletters written by opponents to the program. Although the authors had no relevant medical or scientific qualifications, they were able to publish their opinions widely. The newsletters made claims around conspiracy and cover-up of the facts and generally used fallacies of omission and commission to paint a picture of a vaccine that was both dangerous and wouldn't work. Rabid statements such as how New Zealand had enlisted hundreds of thousands of small kids into a gigantic experiment and how the vaccine program would lead to 95,000 adverse reactions severe enough to warrant going to a GP were made with impunity.

What Was the Result of All of This?

All in all, the negativity around the meningococcal B program left a nasty taste in the mouths of both the public and many health professionals. The myths perpetuated throughout the media gave an impression of a vaccine that was not tested thoroughly, did not work, and was not very safe. The reality is that the MeNZB™ strategy has been admired internationally as a gold standard approach. The safety monitoring of the vaccine was one of the best the world has ever seen. In 2008 vaccination with the MeNZB™ vaccine ceased. In 2009 there were a total of 31 cases of the epidemic strain of disease. The epidemic is over.

The Latest Controversy: HPV

Since the quadrivalent human papillomavirus (HPV) vaccine Gardasil was added to schedules around the world in 2007, new media scares have emerged. As with any anti-vaccination campaign, there was a beginning. In the case of Gardasil this came from personal injury lawyers in the United States, presumably eager to obtain some of the considerable funds set aside for vaccine injury claims. Little time was wasted in disseminating a report making baseless claims about the vaccine.[22] This material traveled fast and provided the basis for an evolving campaign which includes claims about idiopathic illnesses, unholy alliances for profit, poisonous chemicals, cover-ups, totalitarianism, duration of immunity, lack of effectiveness and the role of healthy lifestyle behavior as an alternative to vaccination.

Initially media reporting about the vaccine against the cancer-causing HPV contained positive and accurate information about the science and the purpose of the vaccine. Almost immediately after introduction of the vaccine, negative reporting started to appear, along with inaccuracies and pseudoscience. The considerable evidence behind the vaccine was twisted in creative ways. One example is the evidence around the duration of protection of the vaccine. At the time it had been about five years since the first recipients received the vaccine; therefore, it was known the vaccine lasted *at least* five years. Additionally it was demonstrated that the immunity generated by the vaccine was still strong with no signs of waning. It was also known that based on other very similar vaccines, immunity was very likely to be very long-lasting, possibly for life. Unfortunately, opponents of the vaccine took the opportunity to claim that the vaccine only lasted five years. This was circulated widely in print, radio and Internet and rapidly became a popular belief among the public.

Balance in the Media

The media often claims the need to "give balance" to their reporting. In reality this may result in balancing evidence from 15 to 20 years of scientific research followed by pivotal, large, randomized, controlled trials (RCTs) against one person's opinion or anecdote. A graph that shows a dramatic drop in disease or an RCT demonstrating the safety profile of a vaccine balances poorly against a personal story of an individual who develops a dreadful neurological condition soon after receiving a vaccine, regardless of whether this is likely to be coincidence not effect.

Misunderstanding between causality and coincidence creates many of the scares around vaccines. Whenever there is widespread introduction of vaccination campaigns into a community, it is inevitable that many adverse events happen after the vaccine is given. An example of a temporal association is eating cornflakes for breakfast and then being hit by a bus on your way to work that morning. The cornflakes are associated in time with the bus incident. Most people are sensible enough not to blame the cornflakes. An example of causality is reading the newspaper while walking in the middle of the road on the way to work and being hit by a bus. The accident was probably caused by not looking where you were going and walking on the road instead of the sidewalk.

In September 2009 the BBC News reported that a 14-year-old girl had died in hospital following a cervical cancer vaccine at school.[23] A subsequent postmortem found that the cause of death was a malignant tumor in her chest and was unrelated to the vaccine she had received, but by then the international media had reported that the girl "had appeared to be healthy before being given the jab," that "a few other girls also reported being unwell after receiving the vaccine and some were sent home"[24] and that this was the first reported death from the vaccine. A similar case in New Zealand involved the death of an 18-year-old girl who died six months after receiving her third dose of Gardasil. While the postmortem results are still to be released, there has been considerable media exposure that her death was caused by the vaccine and her family are convinced that the vaccine killed her.[25] Media coverage includes a TV documentary "Close-Up."

The possible dangers of Gardasil are also prominent in advertising. In March 2010 a huge billboard in central Auckland advertising *Fitness Life Magazine* showed the picture of an attractive young woman wearing a scanty bikini beside a headline that said, "Will Gardasil Leave Your Daughter Infertile?" The article in question contained misleading information about the fact that the vaccine contains polysorbate 80 which, when injected into the abdominal cavity in four-day-old mice, results in infertility. Whether or not the vaccine causes infertility is easily answered by the fact that during the large clinical trials there were equal rates of pregnancy, equal rates of live births and equal

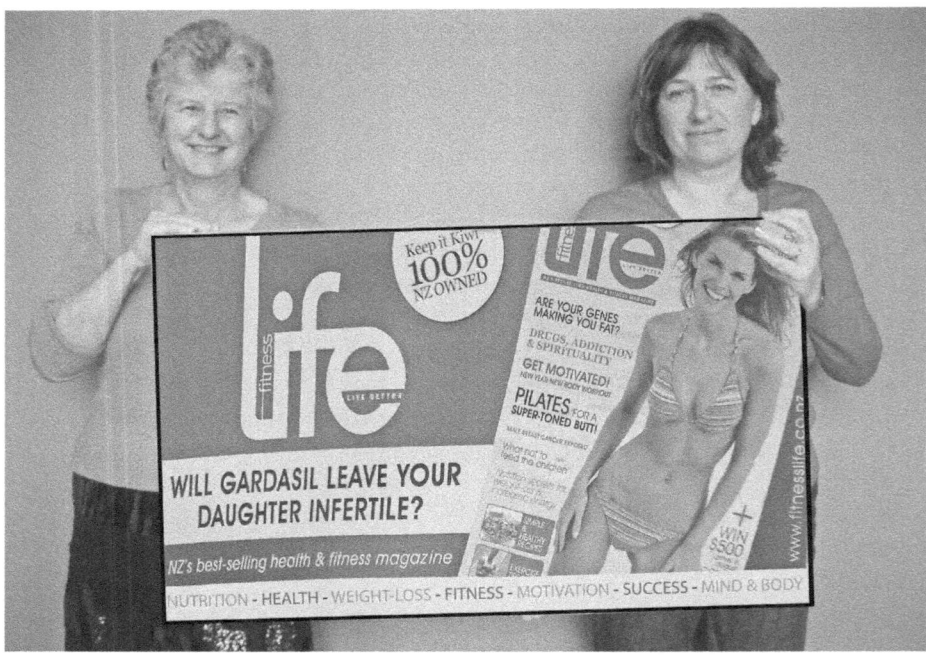

Researchers Felicity Goodyear-Smith and Helen Petousis-Harris display an image from *Fitness Life* magazine that spreads fear of vaccines (image by and courtesy of Felicity Goodyear-Smith).

rates of birth defects in both the group that received the vaccine and the group that did not. However, the infertility myth has now circulated both in New Zealand and internationally.

Surveys asking people where they prefer to get information about vaccines and vaccination consistently show that the general practice is the source of choice.[26] In contrast, surveys asking people where they heard about the Gardasil vaccine found that news items and unpaid media was the most common source. An analysis of this media, including print, radio and television, found that overall, 32 percent of articles were anti–Gardasil, 10 percent were neutral and 5 percent were mixed. Just over half (53 percent) were accurate and positive. Given that this is the primary source of information for most people, it is little wonder that public perceptions of this vaccine are at odds with the science.

Conclusion

For 150 years public health has battled against a passionate and vocal lobby which continue to use the same tired arguments aimed at derailing immunization programs. In the 19th century there may have been valid concerns regarding civil liberty and vaccination practices which were fraught with risk. However, these arguments hold less weight in today's world of informed consent and modern vaccination procedures.

It is also important to recognize that medicine is based on the best evidence of the time, which is an evolving, not a static, situation. Medical errors have occurred, and will continue to do so. "Watchdogs" who review and challenge the dogma of the day have an important role in our society. While it can be frustrating to be beset by anti-scientific nonsense we must be mindful of the importance of genuinely listening to criticism and to continue to critique and re-critique the clinical data and analysis behind the decisions for immunization programs.

TABLE 1. ARGUMENTS PUT FORWARD BY ANTI-IMMUNIZATION LOBBYISTS HAVE CHANGED LITTLE BETWEEN THE 19TH CENTURY AND TODAY

Arguments	Reasons to Support the National Anti-Vaccination League	Recent New Zealand Print Media Anti-immunization Arguments*
Vaccines cause idiopathic illness	That since Vaccination has been rendered obligatory, infantile syphilis (under one year old) has been increased in England, according to a Parliamentary return, dated February 25, 1880, from 472 per million of births in 1847, to 1,736 per million in 1877, or fourfold; and that other inoculable diseases, such aspyaemia, scrofula, erysipelas, and bronchitis, were also augmented in infants. In England, the increase of inoculable diseases was 20 percent, notwithstanding an expenditure of 200 millions sterling since 1850 in sanitary works. Another Parliamentary return (No. 443, Session 1877) demonstrates that 25,000 babies are yearly sacrificed by diseases excited byVaccination.[29]	"I have seen case historie of children, and spoken to other doctors whose children decompensated [regressed] so drastically after the MMR that you can't deny that in some cases it happened." *New Zealand Herald, 2006*
Cover up	The popularity of Vaccination has disappeared.The practice has been unable to face free discussion, and the only support of vaccinal tyranny, in the present day, is the dead weight of State-officialism, and the advocacy of an interested professional trades-unionism. The SCIENCE which occupies itself with providing substitutes for Municipal and Personal Cleanlinessis foredoomed to failure.[30]	"They (health officials) don't know if the vaccine works at all." *Northern Advocate News, 2004*
Vaccines are ineffective	BECAUSE as fast as the numbers of those vaccinated in the United Kingdom have decreased, the smallpox death rate has fallen.[31]	"Statistics show the risk of vaccination damage is greater than the risk of the disease." *Ashburton Guardian, 2005*
Unholy alliance for profit	BECAUSE the League has no large endowments or Government grants.[32]	"The people who are making these vaccines and drugs are getting millions of dollars a year and I'm sure they love it." *Gisborne Herald News, 2005*

*Reported although not necessarily endorsed by the referenced newspaper.

Arguments	Reasons to Support the National Anti-Vaccination League	Recent New Zealand Print Media Anti-immunization Arguments*
Towards totalitarianism	BECAUSE by doing so you will help to free our soldiers and sailors from the burden of compulsion, which they detest, which frequently causes serious illness, occasionally even death, and hinders recruiting.[33]	"Epidemic is a word health authorities utilise to scare parents into vaccinating." *Nelson Mail News, 2004*
Vaccines as poisonous chemical cocktails	BECAUSE those who will not take animal flesh into their mouths should not allow animal poisons to be inserted into their blood.[34]	"Vaccines contain toxic and entirely unnatural ingredients. *Ashburton Guardian, 2005*
Health lifestyle alternative	BECAUSE by the abolition of vaccination, the way is made clear for attending to sanitation, and adopting a better way of living.[35]	"The Society says breastfeeding for at least 6 months and a healthy diet and environment for children provide better protection [than immunization]." *The Press, 2006*
Vaccines are an abomination	BECAUSE it works for the abolition of one of the most absurd, yet disgusting, superstitions that has ever plagued mankind.[36]	"Worldwide controversies about autism, MS neurological diseases, depressed immune systems and the presence of heavy metals and formaldehyde and many more allegedly caused by vaccines; at least the public has the right to know that some of us have made a link, and can do their own research and questioning." *Kapiti Observer News, 2004*

Notes

Chapter 1

1. Ronald A. Knox, *Essays in Satire* (New York: E. P. Dutton, 1930), 285.
2. "The Radio Joke That England Took Seriously," *Syracuse Herald*, 23 March 1926.
3. "Britain Is Alarmed by Burlesque Radio 'News' of Revolt in London and Bombing of Commons," *New York Times*, 18 Jan. 1926, p. 3.
4. Knox, *Essays in Satire*, 281.
5. "The Radio Joke That England Took Seriously."

Chapter 2

1. "Hoax Spreads Terror Here," *Trenton Evening Times*, 31 Oct. 1938, p. 1.
2. Scott Marvin, "The Halloween Radio Spoof That Shook a Nation," *Parade Magazine* (29 Oct. 1975): 5.
3. "Radio Listeners in Panic, Taking War Drama as Fact," *New York Times*, 31 Oct. 1938, p. 1.
4. "Boo!" *Time* (7 Nov. 1938), 40.
5. Photocopy of the actual police log, accessed at http://www.war-ofthe-worlds.co.uk.
6. "Scare Is Nation-Wide," *New York Times*, 31 Oct. 1938, p . 4.
7. "Geologists at Princeton Hunt 'Meteor' in Vain," *New York Times*, 31 Oct. 1938, p. 4.
8. "Scare Is Nation-Wide."
9. "Nasty Monsters from Mars Give Radio Listeners Uneasy Moments," *Nebraska State Journal*, 31 Oct. 1938, p. 1.
10. "Scare Is Nation-Wide."
11. *Ibid*.
12. "Women Faint as Lights Go Out at Concrete," *Seattle Post-Intelligencer*, 31 Oct. 1938, p. 1; "Radio 'Invasion' Throws Listeners into Hysteria," *Seattle Post-Intelligencer*, 31 Oct. 1938, pp. 1, 2.
13. "Bus Delayed," *Iowa City Press-Citizen*, 31 Oct. 1938, p. 1.
14. "Too-Real Radio Drama Gives Nation a Bad Case of War Jitters," *The Clearfield Progress* (Clearfield, PA), 3 Nov. 1938, p. 2.
15. "Even Author H. G. Wells Was Deeply Perturbed," *Trenton Evening News*, 31 Oct. 1938, p. 1.
16. Hadley Cantril, Hazel Gaudet, and Herta Herzog, *The Invasion from Mars: A Study in the Psychology of Panic* (Princeton, NJ: Princeton University Press, 1940), 4.
17. Frank Brady, *Citizen Welles: A Biography of Orson Welles* (New York: Charles Scribner's Sons, 1989), 169.
18. Barbara Leaming, *Orson Welles: A Biography* (New York: Penguin, 1986), 198.
19. *Ibid.*, 193.
20. Cantril, Gaudet, and Herzog, *The Invasion from Mars*, 77.
21. *Ibid.*, 5.
22. Orson Welles, *The War of the Worlds*, uncut original broadcast, 30 Oct. 1938 (Metacom Incorporated, 1938).
23. Cantril, Gaudet, and Herzog, *The Invasion from Mars*, 18–19.
24. *Ibid.*, 30.
25. *Ibid.*, 31.
26. "Realistic Dramatization of 'Invasion' by Men from Mars Causes Panic Through U.S.," *Iowa City Press-Citizen*, 31 Oct. 1938, p. 1.

27. Justin Levine, "History and Analysis of the Federal Communications Commission's Response to Radio Broadcast Hoaxes," *Federal Communications Law Journal* 52, no. 2 (1999): 286.
28. *Ibid.*
29. Cantril, Gaudet, and Herzog, *The Invasion from Mars*, 55–58.
30. James Milio, Melissa Jo Peltier, and Mark Hufnail (producers), *Martian Mania: The True Story of The War of the Worlds* (hosted by James Cameron), Science Fiction Channel, USA, 30 Oct. 1998.
31. William Bainbridge, "Collective Behavior and Social Movements," in Rodney Stark (ed.), *Sociology* (Belmont, CA: Wadsworth, 1987), 544–576.
32. David L. Miller, *Introduction to Collective Behavior* (Belmont, CA: Wadsworth, 1985), 100; James Naremore, *The Magic World of Orson Welles* (New York: Oxford University Press, 1978).
33. Miller, *Introduction to Collective Behavior*, 107.
34. Brady, *Citizen Welles*, 176; Timothy Crook, "The Psychological Impact of Radio," *Independent Radio Drama Production*, http://www.irdp.co.uk/hoax.html.
35. Correspondence from Justin Levine to Robert Bartholomew, 26 Nov. 2003.
36. Editorial item, no title, *Chicago Daily Tribune*, 10 Nov. 1938, p. 16.
37. "What Radio Cannot Do," *St. Louis Post-Dispatch*, 1 Nov. 1938, p. 20.
38. "Probe on as Protests Mark Program That Spread Panic," *Trenton Evening Times*, 31 Oct. 1938, p. 2.
39. Orson Welles, Peter Bogdanovich, and Jonathan Rosenbaum, *This Is Orson Welles* (New York: HarperCollins, 1992). The book is comprised of revealing interviews between Welles and his close friend Peter Bogdanovich over a 15-year period and was published after Welles's death in 1985.
40. Brady, *Citizen Welles*, 167.
41. "Geologists at Princeton Hunt 'Meteor' in Vain," *New York Times*, 31 Oct. 1938, p. 4.
42. Eric Fettmann, "'The Martians Have Landed!' In Radio Show 60 Years Ago, America Lost its Innocence," *New York Post*, 28 Oct. 1988, p. 41.
43. Leaming, *Orson Welles*, 198.
44. Levine, "History and Analysis of the Federal Communications Commission's Response to Radio Broadcast Hoaxes," 286.

Chapter 3

1. "Those Men from Mars," *Newsweek* (27 Nov. 1944): 89.
2. *Ibid.*
3. *Ibid.*
4. *Ibid.*
5. "Mars Raiders Caused Quito Panic; Mob Burns Radio Plant, Kills 15," *New York Times*, 14 Feb. 1949, pp. 1, 7. Quote appears on p. 1.
6. *Ibid.*
7. *Ibid.*
8. "Mob Kills 15 Over Radio Station, Kills 15 After War Scare," *The Modesto Bee* (Modesto, CA), 14 Feb. 1949, p. 1.
9. "Wolf, Wolf," *Newsweek* 33, no. 8 (21 Feb. 1949): 44.
10. "Mob Kills 15 Over Radio Station, Kills 15 After War Scare."
11. "Radio Program Starts Riot; 7 Die," *The Independent* (Long Beach, CA), 14 Feb. 1949, p. 22.
12. "Invasion from Mars," *Times of London*, 14 Feb. 1949, p. 4; "When You Say That, Smile," *The Commonweal* 49, no. 20, pp. 483–484.
13. "Radio: Boomerang in Ecuador: A Mob Takes Revenge," *The Independent Record* (Sedalia, MO), 20 Feb. 1949; "Mob Kills 15 Over Radio's Mars 'War.'"
14. "Two Officials Indicted," *Times of London*, 15 Feb. 1949, p. 4.
15. "Mars Raiders Caused Quito Panic."
16. Enrique Tovar, "The Martians Cause Panic," *La Nación*, 3 March 1996.
17. "20 Dead in Quito Riot," *New York Times*, 15 Feb. 1949, p. 5; "Quito Holds 3 for 'Mars' Script," *New York Times*, 15–16 Feb. 1949.
18. Walter Lippman, *Public Opinion* (New York: Harcourt, Brace, 1922), cited in F. MacDonnell, *Insidious Foes* (New York: Oxford University Press, 1995), 2.

Chapter 4

1. Justin Levine, "History and Analysis of the Federal Communications Commission's Response to Radio Broadcast Hoaxes," *Federal Communications Law Journal* 52, no. 2 (1999): 274–320; see 291–295. I would like to thank Justin Levine for his support in writing this chapter.

2. Levine, "History and Analysis," 293.
3. "Newspaper Exposes Radio Hoax," *Editor & Publisher* 124, no. 17 (27 April 1991): 17.
4. "FCC Investigating Station's Role in Murder Confession Hoax," *The Post-Standard* (Syracuse, NY), 23 April 1991, p. D1.
5. "Sheriff's Dept. Bills KROC $12,000 for Hoax," *Los Angeles Times*, 1 May 1991, p. F2; Sean Ross, Craig Rosen, and Phyllis Stark, "Postwar Arbs Show N/T Stations in Retreat; Hoax Costs KROQ Jocks," *Billboard* 103, no. 21 (25 May 1991): 10.
6. Levine, "History and Analysis," 303–305; "KROQ Receives a Slap on the Wrist for Hoax," *Los Angeles Times*, 4 Dec. 1991, p. F7.
7. Bill Holland, "FCC Lets Infinity Off the Hook After KROQ Hoax," *Billboard* 103, no. 50 (14 Dec. 1991): 71; Reed E. Bunzel, "FCC Admonishes KROQ-FM for Murder Hoax," *Broadcasting* 121, no. 24 (9 Dec. 1991): 31.
8. Levine, "History and Analysis," 300; "FCC Take Action on Phony Radio Hoaxes," *The Intelligencer and the Record* (Doylestown, PA), 15 May 1992, p. A9.
9. Levine, "History and Analysis," 305–306.
10. Ibid., 312–313.
11. Jim Sullivan, "Radio Hoaxes Stung Bosses into Action," *Sunday Star-Times*, 18 March 1999, p. A13.
12. Craig Rosen, "KSHE, KROQ Hoaxes No Joke to FCC," *Billboard* 103, no. 18 (4 May 1991): 12.

Chapter 5

1. Karl E. Rosengren, Peter Arvidson, and Dahn Sturesson, "The Barseback 'Panic': A Radio Programme as a Negative Summary Event," *Acta Sociologica* 18, no. 4 (1975): 303–321, see 310.
2. Rosengren, Arvidson, and Sturesson, "The Barseback Panic," 311.
3. Ibid., 312.
4. Ibid., 307–308.
5. "Radio Hoax Program Halted Early," *Chronicle-Telegram* (Elyria, OH), 10 Nov. 1982, p. D2.
6. Serge Schmemann, "Soviet Furor Mounts Over Reagan's Bombing Quip," *The New York Times*, 16 Aug. 1984, p. A5.

7. Justin Levine, "History and Analysis of the Federal Communications Commission's Response to Radio Broadcast Hoaxes," *Federal Communications Law Journal* 52, no. 2 (1999): 274–320, see 301–303.

Chapter 6

1. "Mythical Anti-Nuclear Attack Riles Thousands of Viewers," *The Post* (Frederick, MD), 22 March 1983, p. B14.
2. "WDAF Gets Calls on 'Special Bulletin,'" *The Chillicothe Constitution* (Chillicothe, MO), 21 March 1983.
3. Ibid.
4. Ibid.
5. Tom Jory, "NBC Hopes Warning Will Avert Panic During 'Special Bulletin,'" *Syracuse Herald-Journal*, 19 March 1983, p. B6.

Chapter 7

1. Jon Burlingame, "'Bulletin' Feels Like Real Event," *Syracuse Herald-Journal* (Syracuse, NY), 29 Oct. 1994, p. A6; "Worried TV Viewers Call During Drama," *Syracuse Herald-Journal* (Syracuse, NY), 31 Oct. 1994, p. C4.
2. "Worried TV Viewers Call During Drama."
3. "TV Movie on Asteroid Crash Causes Real Fear in Viewers," *Daily Herald* (Chicago, IL), 31 Oct. 1994, pp. 1, 6.
4. Ibid., 6.
5. "War of the Worlds Revisited—Almost," *The Chronicle-Telegram* (Elyria, OH), 31 Oct. 1994, p. A3.
6. Ted Cox, "'Without Warning' No 'War of the Worlds,'" *Daily Herald*, 1, 7 Nov. 1994.
7. Ibid.
8. Interview with Dr. Rachael Webster on 28 March 2006. Webster is the chair of astronomy at Melbourne University.
9. Interview with Dr. Webster on 28 March 2006.
10. Gretchen Vogel, "Asteroid Scare Provokes Soul-Searching," *Science* 279, no. 5358 (1998).
11. Terence Dickinson, "Why Does NASA Cry Wolf About 'Killer' Asteroids?" *Toronto Star*, 2 Jan.2005, p. A18.

Chapter 8

1. "'Pocket Monsters' Shocks TV Viewers into Convulsions," *Japan Times*, 17 Dec. 1997; "Govt Launches Probe of 'Monster' Cartoon," *Yomiuri Shimbun*, 18 Dec. 1997; "Psychiatrists Seek Animation Probe," *Yomiuri Shimbun*, 19 Dec. 1997; Y. Yamashita, T. Matsuishi, S. Ishida, T. Nishimi, and H. Kato, "Pocket Monsters Attacks Japanese Children Via Media," *Annals of Neurology* 44, no. 3 (1998): 428; T. Hayashi, T. Ichiyama, M. Nishikawa, H. Isumi, and S. Furukawa, "Pocket Monsters, a Popular Television Cartoon, Attacks Japanese Children," *Annals of Neurology* 44, no. 3 (1998): 427; S. Tobimatsu, Y. M Zhang, Y. Tomoda, A. Mitsudome, and M. Kato, "Chromatic Sensitive Epilepsy: A Variant of Photosensitive Epilepsy," *Annals of Neurology* 45, no. 6 (1999): 790.
2. J. Snyder, "Cartoon Sickens Children," *Reuters News Agency*, 17 Dec. 1997; J. Snyder, "'Monster' TV Cartoon Illness Mystifies Japan," *Reuters News Agency*, 17 Dec. 1997; "Govt Launches Probe of 'Monster' Cartoon."
3. "Pocket Monsters Attacks Japanese Children Via Media."
4. Tobimatsu et al., "Chromatic Sensitive Epilepsy," 790.
5. Brenda Stardom (pseud.), "Portuguese Teen Soap Cause for Real-life Virus Hysteria," *The BS Report*, 19 June 2006, http://www.wayodd.com/teens-suffer-from-soap-opera-virus/v/2838/.
6. "Teens Suffer Soap Opera Virus," *Reuters News Agency*, 25 May 2006, http://go.reuters.com/newsArticle.jhtml?type=oddlyEnoughNews&storyID=12254563&src=rss/oddlyEnoughNews.
7. Quotation from "Austria Gripped by a Fear of Spider," *BBC News*, 4 Aug. 2006, http://news.bbc.co.uk/go/pr/fr/-/2/hi/europe/5244840.stm; Toby Moore, "Did You Hear?" *The Times* (London), 7 Aug. 2006, Features Section, p. 2; "Doctor, Doctor," *New Statesman*, 14 Aug. 2006, p. 18.
8. Jonathan Banks, Phil Sirvid, and Cor Vink, "White-Tailed Spider Bites — Arachnophobic Fallout?" *The New Zealand Medical Journal* 117, no. 1108 (2004): 1–7, see 4.
9. Ibid., 4.
10. Ibid., 7.
11. Figures were for 2002, obtained from the Seattle Biomedical Research Institute, 4 Nickerson Street, Suite 200, Seattle, Washington. Refer to: http://www.sbri.org/Mission/disease/Chagas.asp.
12. *Ibid.*
13. Leland O. Howard, "Spider Bites and 'Kissing Bugs,'" *Popular Science Monthly* 56 (Nov. 1899): 31–42, see 34.
14. James F. McElhone, "Bite of a Strange Bug." *Washington Post*, 20 June 1899.
15. Howard, "Spider Bites and 'Kissing Bugs,'" 34.
16. *Ibid.* Italics in original.
17. W. J. F., editorial, *Entomological News* 10 (Sept. 1899): 205–206.
18. Eugene Murray-Aaron, "The Kissing Bug Scare," *Scientific American* 81 (22 July 1899): 54.
19. "Weird Tales of Kissing Bug," *Chicago Daily Tribune*, 11 July 1899, p. 2.
20. Howard, "Spider Bites and 'Kissing Bugs,'" 34.

Chapter 9

1. D. Simons and W. R. Silveira, "Post-Traumatic Stress Disorder in Children After Television Programmes," *British Medical Journal* 308, no. 6925 (1994): 389–390.
2. Stephen Volk, "Faking It: Ghostwatch," *Fortean Times* 166 (Jan. 2003).
3. *Ibid.*
4. Robert Rickard, "Whatever Possessed Parkinson?" *The Fortean Times* 67 (1992): 38–41.
5. Kim Newman, "Kim Newman on Ghostwatch" [review], *Mssv*, http://www.mssv.net/realityart/bfinewman.html.
6. *Ibid.*
7. Harrison, "Tales from the Screen: Enduring Fright Reactions from Scary Media," *Media Psychology* (Spring 1999): 106.

Chapter 10

1. R. Catalanello and C. Pittman, "At the Edge of Anarchy," *St. Petersburg Times*, 21 Sept. 2005, p. 1.
2. Robert Pierre and Anne Gerhart, "News of Pandemonium May Have Slowed Aid," *The Washington Post*, 5 Oct. 2005, p. A8; Matt Welch, "They Shoot Helicopters, Don't They? How Journalist Spread Rumors During Katrina," *Reason* 37, no. 7 (2005): 16–18.

3. Pierre and Gerhart, "News of Pandemonium."
4. Jennifer Harper, "Media, Blushing, Takes a Second Look at Katrina," *The Washington Times* (Washington, DC), 29 Sept. 2005, p. A1.
5. Susannah Rosenblatt and Jamers Rainey, "Katrina Takes a Toll on Truth, News Accuracy," *The Los Angeles Times*, 27 Sept. 2005.
6. Welch, "They Shoot Helicopters, Don't They?" 18.
7. Pierre and Gerhart, "News of Pandemonium."
8. Brian Thevenot, "Myth-Making in New Orleans," *American Journalism Review* 27, no. 6 (2005/2006): 30–37, quote from page 32.
9. Harper, "Media, Blushing, Takes a Second Look at Katrina."
10. Pierre and Gerhart, "News of Pandemonium."
11. Patricia Donovan, "New Orleans — What Urban Myths Say About U.S.," press release issued by the State University of New York at Buffalo, 2005, http://www.buffalo.edu/news/fast-execute.cgi/article-page.html?article=75960009.
12. *Ibid.*
13. *Ibid.*
14. Paul Pawlaczyk, "Officials Debunk One of the Most Disturbing Katrina Stories," *Knight Ridder Tribune* (Washington, DC, Bureau), 11 Nov. 2005.
15. David Brown, "Floods' Pollutants Within the Norm. Oil Spills Seen as the Only Exception," *The Washington Post*, 15 Sept. 2005, p. A15.
16. *Ibid.*
17. *Ibid.*
18. *Ibid.*
19. Harper, "Media, Blushing, Takes a Second Look at Katrina."
20. "NOAA Attributes Recent Increase in Hurricane Activity to Naturally Occurring Multi-Decadal Climate Variability," *NOAA Magazine Online*, 29 Nov. 2005, http://www.magazine.noaa.gov/stories/mag184.htm.
21. Brian Handwerk, "Eye on the Storm: Hurricane Katrina Fast Facts," *National Geographic News*, 6 Sept. 2005, http://news.nationalgeographic.com/news/2005/09/0906_050906_katrina_facts.html.
22. *Ibid.*
23. Thevenot, "Myth-Making in New Orleans," 37.

Chapter 11

1. "Bird Flu Movie Should Not Lead to Panic," United States Federal News Service, Washington DC, 9 May 2006.
2. "Key Facts About Pandemic Influenza," 17 Oct. 2005, http://www.cdc.gov/flu/pandemic/keyfacts.htm. This site is operated by the Centers for Disease Control and Prevention.
3. "Key Facts About Avian Influenza (Bird Flu) and Avian Influenza A (H5N1) Virus," 25 Nov. 2005, http://www.cdc.gov/flu/avian/gen-info/facts.htm. This site is operated by the Centers for Disease Control and Prevention.
4. Michael Fumento, "Fuss and Feathers Pandemic Panic Over the Avian Flu," *The Weekly Standard* (21 Nov. 2005): 24–30, see 24; Paul Mickle, "1976: Fear of a Great Plague," *The Trentonian*, n.d., http://www.capitalcentury.com/1976.html.
5. Fumento, "Fuss and Feathers Pandemic Panic," 24.
6. *Ibid.*
7. *Ibid.*
8. *Ibid.*, 25.
9. *Ibid.*, 26.
10. Greg Szymanski, "Avian Flu May Come to America," *The American Free Press* 41 (10 Oct. 2005), http://www.americanfreepress.net/html/avian_flu.html.
11. Fumento, "Fuss and Feathers Pandemic Panic."
12. Wendy Orent, "We'll Survive the Bird Flu, Chicken Little," *The New Republic*, 12 Sept. 2005, http://www.tnr.com/docprint.mhtml?i=20050912&s=orent091205.
13. *Ibid.*
14. *Ibid.*
15. Frank Furedi, "Bird Flu Prophets of Doom Spread Nothing but Needless Alarm," *Daily Express*, 18 Oct. 2005, http://www.frankfuredi.com/articles/birdflu-20051018.shtml.
16. *Ibid.*
17. Diane Chun, "Experts Dismiss Scare Over Bird Flu," *The Gainesville Sun* (Florida), 1 Nov. 2005, http://www.gainesville.com/apps/pbcs.dll/article?AID=/20051101/LOCAL/51101021/1078/news.
18. *Ibid.*
19. Lianne George, Karin Marley, and Danylo Hawaleshka, "Forget Sars, West Nile, Ebola and Avian Flu: The Real Epidemic Is Fear," *Maclean's* 118, no. 40 (3 Oct. 2005): 46–52.

20. Marc K. Siegel, "Afraid of the Bird Flu? The Worse Virus Is Fear," *Fortune* 152, no. 11 (2005): 61.

Chapter 12

1. Ivan Watson, "Fake Russian Invasion Broadcast Sparks Georgian Panic," *CNN News*, 14 March 2010, http://www.cnn.com/2010/WORLD/europe/03/14/georgia.invasion.scare/index.html.
2. "False Report of Russian Invasion Spurs Panic," *Reuters News Agency*, 14 March 2010.
3. Sarah Marcus, "Panic and Fury Over Fake Television Report on Russian Invasion of Georgia," *The Telegraph*, 15 March 2010.
4. Robert Siegel, "Georgia 'Invasion' Report Stirs Panic," *All Things Considered*, National Public Radio, 15 March 2010.

Chapter 13

1. New Zealand Chief Film Censor's instructions to Warner Bros Ltd., 28 Aug. 1973. Copy obtained by the author from the film censor's office.
2. "Nasty Videos 'like Peddling Drugs,'" *The Auckland Star*, 3 Jan.1984.
3. Katharine Whitehorn, "Child Video Menu Hard to Swallow," *New Zealand Herald*, 5 Jan. 1984.
4. Peter Enos, "British MPs Want 'Video Nasties' Curbed," *The Auckland Star*, 12 Jan. 1984.
5. Graham Murdock, "Figuring Out the Arguments," in Martin Barker (ed.), *The Video Nasties* (London: Pluto Press, 1984), 64.
6. "MP Pleads: Shops Bar Texas Chainsaw," *The 8 O'Clock*, 19 Jan.1985.
7. "Violent Videos on Agenda," *New Zealand Herald*, 18 June 1985.
8. "Violent Video Seen as Prod," *New Zealand Herald*, 23 June 1985.
9. "'Violence' Videotape Will Be Investigated," *The Auckland Star*, 24 June 1985.
10. "Move to Have Videos Censored," *New Zealand Herald*, 28 June 1985.
11. "Video Nasties: Loose in Your Living Room?" *Grapevine*, Aug. 1985, pp. 10–17.
12. Nigel Andrews, "Nightmares and Nasties," in Martin Barker (ed.), *The Video Nasties* (London: Pluto Press, 1984), 42.
13. "Video Decision Is Disputed," *New Zealand Herald*, 4 Oct. 1985.
14. Simon Kilroy, "MPs Leave Video Nasty Off Agenda," *The Auckland Star*, 9 Oct. 1985.
15. Colin Hogg, "Driller Killer ... the Horrible, Boring Truth," *The Auckland Star*, 12 Oct. 1985.
16. Marianne Norgaard, "Driller Killer ... the Horrible, Boring Truth," *The Auckland Star*, 12 Oct. 1985. This is certainly not your everyday reference but it is correct. There were two articles on the same page with the exact same title. One gave a female perspective; the other gave a male perspective.
17. "Publicity Boosts Video Nasty," *The Auckland Star*, 23 Oct. 1985.
18. "Child Video Protection," *New Zealand Herald*, 15 Oct. 1985.
19. *Ibid.*
20. "Clamping Down on Video Nasties," *New Zealand Women's Weekly*, 25 Nov. 1985.
21. *Ibid.*
22. *Ibid.*
23. *Ibid.*
24. "Videotapes to be Classified and Labelled," *New Zealand Herald*, 13 Dec. 1985.
25. Geoffrey Pearson, "Falling Standards: A Short, Sharp History of Moral Decline," in Martin Barker (ed.), *The Video Nasties* (London: Pluto Press, London, 1984), 88–103.
26. Jenny Ashford, "Tiny Paris Theater Became Synonymous with Grisley Horror," 27 July 2009, http://theatrehistory.suite101.com/article.cfm/le_thetre_du_grandguignol.
27. *Ibid.*
28. "Titus Has Them Rolling in Aisle," *The Age* (Melbourne, Australia), 25 Oct. 1955.
29. P. K. Bock, *Modern Cultural Anthropology* (New York: Knopf, 1979).

Chapter 14

1. Edward Rosen and Johannes Kepler, *Kepler's Somnium; The Dream, or Posthumous Work on Lunar Astronomy* (1634; Madison: University of Wisconsin Press, 1967).
2. Francis Godwin and Grant McColley (ed.), *The Man in the Moone and Nuncius Inanimatus; for the first time edited, with an introduction and notes, from the unique copies of the first editions of London, 1629 and London, 1638* (Northhampton, MA: Smith College, 1937).
3. George Tucker, *A Voyage to the Moon: With Some Account of the Manners and Cus-*

toms, Science and Philosophy, of the People of Morosofia, and Other Lunarians (New York: E. Bliss, 1827).

4. de Bergerac, Cyrano (1649). *A Voyage to the Moon.* Also titled *The Comical History of the States and Empires of the World of the Moon.* London.

5. Paul Maliszewski, "Paper Moon," *The Wilson Quarterly* 29, no. 1 (2005): 26–34.

6. "GREAT ASTRONOMICAL DISCOVERIES Lately Made by SIR JOHN HERSCHEL, L.L.D, F.R.S, &c. at The Cape of Good Hope." *The Sun* (New York), 25 Aug. 1835, p. 2.

7. *Ibid.*, 26 Aug. 1835.
8. *Ibid.*, 27 Aug. 1835.
9. *Ibid.*, 28 Aug. 1835.
10. *Ibid.*, 29 Aug. 1835.
11. *Ibid.*, 31 Aug. 1835.

12. Joseph Bulgatz, *Ponzi Schemes, Invaders from Mars & More Extraordinary Popular Delusions and the Madness of Crowds* (New York: Harmony Books, 1992), 147.

13. Vicky Hallett, "Extra! Extra! Life on Moon!" *U.S. News & World Report*, 26 Aug. 2002, p. 53.

14. Bulgatz, *Ponzi Schemes*, 150.
15. *Ibid.*

16. Edward Mitchell, "The Story of the Sun," *The Sun*, 3 Sept. 1883, p. 1.

17. Hallett, "Extra! Extra! Life on Moon!"
18. *Ibid.*
19. Maliszewski, "Paper Moon," 33.
20. *Ibid.*
21. *Ibid.*, 34.

Chapter 15

1. Carl Sifakis, *Hoaxes and Scams: A Compendium of Deceptions, Ruses and Swindles* (New York: Facts on File, 1993), 283.

2. *Ibid.*

3. "Practical Jokes" [editorial], *The New York Times*, 10 Nov. 1874, p. 4.

4. Sifakis, *Hoaxes and Scams*, 283.
5. "Practical Jokes," p. 4.
6. *Ibid.*

7. No title, *The Morning Oregonian*, 24 Nov. 1874.

8. "A 'Herald Sell,'" *The Galveston Daily News* (Texas), 15 Nov. 1874, p. 1.

9. "A Celebrated Hoax," *The Newark Daily Advocate* (Newark, NJ), 27 June 1893, citing a detailed interview with T.B. Connery.

10. Untitled editorial, *Daily Sentinel* (Fort Wayne, IN), 15 Feb. 1875, p. 2; untitled editorial, *The Daily Republican* (Decatur, IL), 17 Feb. 1875, p. 2.

11. Alex Thio, *Sociology: An Introduction* (New York: Harper & Row, 1986), 499, citing Duane Schultz, *Panic Behavior* (New York: Random House, 1964); Davis Wallechinsky and Irving Wallace (eds.), *The People's Almanac* (Garden City, NY: Doubleday, 1975), 557.

12. Scott Gabriel Knowles, "Lessons in the Rubble: The World Trade Center and the History of Disaster Investigations in the United States," *History and Technology* 19, no. 1 (2003): 9–28, quotation from page 21.

Chapter 16

1. "Discuss Halley's Comet," *The Washington Post*, 6 Feb. 1910, p. 15.

2. *Ibid.*

3. "Comet's Poisonous Tail. Yerkes Observatory Finds Cyanogen in Spectrum of Halley's Comet," *The New York Times*, 7 Feb. 1910, p. 1.

4. *Ibid.*

5. Richard Flaste, Holcomb Noble, Walter Sullivan, and John Noble Wilford, *The New York Times Guide to the Return of Halley's Comet* (New York: Times Books, 1985), 68.

6. *Ibid.*, 68–69.

7. "Comet Quits Its Path," *The Washington Post*, 11 May 1910, p. 1.

8. D. J. McAdam, "The Menace in the Skies: I. The Case for the Comet," *Harper's Weekly* 54 (14 May 1910): 12.

9. Patrick Moore and John Mason, *The Return of Halley's Comet* (New York: W. W. Norton, 1984), 71; Flaste et al., *The New York Times Guide to the Return of Halley's Comet*, 61.

10. Carl Sagan and Ann Druyan, *Comet* (New York: Random House 1985), 140.

11. "Southern Negroes in a Comet Frenzy," *The New York Times*, 19 Feb. 1910, p. 1.

12. "Comet Jerusalem's Omen," *The Washington Post*, 11 May 1910, p. 1.

13. "Miners Refuse to Work," 1.

14. Alter Dinsmore, "Comets and People," *Griffith Observer* 20, no. 7 (1956): 82.

15. Mark Littmann and Donald K. Yeomans, *Comet Halley: Once in a Lifetime* (Washington DC: American Chemical Society, 1985), 43; Flaste et al., *The New York Times Guide to the Return of Halley's Comet*, 58.

16. Flaste et al., *The New York Times Guide to the Return of Halley's Comet*, 75.
17. Ibid.
18. Sagan and Druyan, *Comet*, 140.
19. Flaste et al., *The New York Times Guide to the Return of Halley's Comet*, 80.
20. Sagan and Druyan, *Comet*, 140.
21. "Pope Not Impressed by Halley's Comet," *The New York Times*, 29 May 1910, p. 2.
22. "Parisians Feared Comet Would Kill," *The New York Times*, 22 May 1910, p. 3.
23. Brian Harpur, *The Official Halley's Comet Book* (London: Hodder and Stoughton, 1985), 48–49.
24. "Berlin Comet Picnics," *The New York Times*, 19 Feb. 1910, p. 1.
25. "Rush to Alpine Heights," *The New York Times*, 19 Feb. 1910, p. 1.
26. "Alarm on the Rand," *The New York Times*, 19 Feb. 1910, p. 1.
27. "Night Services in Russia," *The New York Times*, 19 Feb. 1910, p. 1.
28. "Mexicans Pray, Then Dance," *The New York Times*, 19 Feb. 1910, p. 1.

Chapter 17

1. Reconstruction of the initial "attack" on Mrs. Kearney is taken from the following sources which include firsthand interviews by Mattoon police and Chicago psychiatrist Harold S. Hulbert. *The Daily Journal-Gazette* (1944). "Anesthetic Prowler on Loose," *Daily Journal-Gazette*, 2 Sept. 1944, p. 1; "Show How They Were Gassed," *Chicago Herald-American*, 10 Sept. 1944, p. 10; E. Alley, "Illness of First Gas 'Victim' Blamed for Wave of Hysteria in Mattoon," *Chicago Herald-American*, 17 Sept. 1944, p. 3; "Chicago Psychiatrist Analyzes Mattoon Gas Hysteria," *Chicago Herald-American*, 17 Sept. 1944, p. 3; Donald Max Johnson, "The 'Phantom Anesthetist' of Mattoon: A Field Study of Mass Hysteria," *Journal of Abnormal Psychology* 40 (1945): 175–186.
2. The skull cap implies that he was Jewish, possibly reflecting rural Midwestern anti-Semitism of the time where Judaism was often associated with the "evils" of the secularism of big-city life. Ironically, during this same period, millions of Jews were gassed to death in Europe.
3. "Anesthetic Prowler on Loose," 1.

4. Johnson, "The 'Phantom Anesthetist' of Mattoon," 180.
5. "Anesthetic Prowler on Loose," 1.
6. "Mattoon's Phantom 'Suggestive' Fear," *Chicago Herald-American*, 21 Sept. 1944, p. 2.
7. Ibid.
8. Ibid.
9. Ibid.
10. Ibid.
11. "Mattoon's Mad Anesthetist" [editorial], *The Daily Journal-Gazette*, 8 Sept. 1944, p. 2.
12. Robert Ladendorf and Robert E. Bartholomew, "The Mad Gasser of Mattoon: How the Press Created an Imaginary Chemical Weapons Attack," *The Skeptical Inquirer* 26, no. 4 (Jul–Aug. 2002): 53.
13. "'Mad Gasser' Adds Six Victims! 5 Women and Boy Latest Overcome," *The Daily Journal-Gazette*, 9 Sept. 1944, p. 1.
14. "Safety Agent to Aid Police in 'Gas' Case," *The Daily Journal-Gazette*, 6 Sept. 1944, p. 6.
15. "Chemists Trace Mattoon Mad Man's 'Gardenia Gas,'" *The News-Gazetteer* (Champaign, IL), 9 Sept. 1944, p. 3.
16. C. Ballenger, "Mattoon's Gas Fiend Attacks Girl, 11, in Home," *Chicago Daily Tribune*, 9 Sept. 1944, p. 10.
17. "Mattoon Gets Jitters from Gas Attacks," *Chicago Herald-American*, 10 Sept. 1944, p. 1; "'Chasers' to Be Arrested," *The Daily Journal-Gazette*, 11 Sept. 1944, p. 1; "Sidelights of 'Mad Gassers' Strange Case," *The Daily Journal-Gazette*, 12 Sept. 1944, p. 4.
18. "'Chasers' to Be Arrested," 1.
19. "To All Citizens of Mattoon," *The Daily Journal-Gazette*, 11 Sept. 1944, p. 1.
20. "Sidelights of 'Mad Gassers' Strange Case," 4.
21. "'Mad Gasser' Adds Six Victims!"
22. "Mattoon Gets Jitters from Gas Attacks," 1.
23. "Two Women Believed Victims Examined at Hospital," *The Daily Journal-Gazette*, 11 Sept. 1944, p. 1.
24. "Many Prowler Reports; Few Real…," The *Daily Journal Gazette* (Mattoon, Illinois), September 11, 1944, p. 1.
25. C. Ballenger, "FBI at Mattoon as Gas Prowler Attacks 5 More," *Chicago Daily Tribune*, 10 Sept. 1944, p. 15; "Many Prowler Reports…," 1.
26. "'Mad Gasser' Case Limited to 4 Sus-

pects," *The Daily Journal-Gazette*, 12 Sept. 1944, p. 1.

27. Johnson, "The 'Phantom Anesthetist' of Mattoon," 177.

28. G. Erickson, "Mad Gasser Called Myth," *Chicago Herald-American*, 13 Sept. 1944, p. 1.

29. "'Gasser' Case 'Mistake,'" *The Daily Journal-Gazette*, 12 Sept. 1944, p. 4; "Police Chief Says Sprayer Tales Hoax," *Illinois State Journal*, 13 Sept. 1944, p. 1; "Cole Amplifies Statement," *The Daily Journal-Gazette*, 13 Sept. 1944, p. 1.

30. "Police Get Two False Alarms During Night," *The Daily Journal-Gazette*, 13 Sept. 1944, p. 1.

31. "No Gas, Not Even Madman Seen During Night," *The Daily Journal-Gazette*, 15 Sept. 1944, p. 6.

32. *Ibid.*

33. "Debunk Mattoon Gas Scare," *Chicago Herald-American*, 13 Sept. 1944, p. 4; Erickson, "Mad Gasser Called Myth," 1; E. Alley, "Illness of First Gas 'Victim' Blamed for Wave of Hysteria in Mattoon," 3; "Chicago Psychiatrist Analyzes Mattoon Gas Hysteria," 3; "Study Terror in Mattoon," *Chicago Herald-American*, 18 Sept. 1944, p. 1; E. Alley, "Credulity Seat of Mattoon's Terror," *Chicago Herald-American*, 20 Sept. 1944, p. 4; "Mattoon's Phantom 'Suggestive' Fear," 2.

34. "The 'Perfumed City' Speaks" [editorial], *The Daily Journal-Gazette*, 20 Sept. 1944, p. 2.

35. "At Night in Mattoon," *Time*, 18 Sept. 1944, p. 23; "Letter to the Editor," *The Daily Journal-Gazette*, 26 Sept. 1944, p. 2.

36. "Letter to the Editor," *The Daily Journal-Gazette*, 26 Sept. 1944, p. 2.

37. "Letter to the Editor," *The Daily Journal-Gazette*, 29 Sept. 1944, p. 2.

38. E. K. Lindley, "Thoughts on the Use of Gas in Warfare," *Newsweek* 22 (20 Dec. 1943): 24; V. Sanders, "Our Army's Defense against Poison Gas," *Popular Science* 146 (Feb. 1945): 106–111; E. W. Scott, "Role of the Public Health Laboratory in Gas Defense," *American Journal of Public Health* 34 (March 1944): 275–278.

39. J. Marshall, "We Are Ready with Gas if the Axis Turns on the Gas," *Collier's* 112 (7 Aug. 1943): 21.

40. F. J. Brown, *Chemical Warfare: A Study in Restraints* (Princeton, NJ: Princeton University Press, 1968), 244.

Chapter 18

1. Phillip Knightley, *A Hack's Progress* (London: Vintage Random House, 1998); Philip Knightly, personal communication with Robert Bartholomew, Aug. 2005.

2. Knightly, *A Hack's Progress*, 51.

3. *Ibid.*, 52.

4. Phillip Knightley, transcript of an address to the Melbourne Press Club, 23 March 2001, Quill Awards Dinner, Grand Hyatt Hotel (Melbourne, Victoria), 1.

5. Knightly, transcript of an address, 1.

6. Knightly, *A Hack's Progress*, 52–53.

7. *Ibid.*, 53.

Chapter 19

1. Norman Jacobs, "The Phantom Slasher of Taipei: Mass Hysteria in a Non-Western Society," *Social Problems* 12 (1965): 320.

2. *Ibid.*, 320.

3. *Ibid.*, 319.

4. *Ibid.*, 320–321.

5. *Ibid.*, 320.

6. *Ibid.*, 325.

7. *Ibid.*, 322.

8. *Ibid.*

9. *Ibid.*, 322, 324.

10. *Ibid.*, 324.

11. *Ibid.*

Chapter 20

1. Loren Coleman, "Phantom Clowns," *Fate* 35, no. 3 (March 1982): 53–54.

2. Loren Coleman, *Mysterious America* (New York: Faber & Faber, Inc., 1983), 211–215; Christopher Callahan, "Beware 'Clown,' Pupils Told," *The Boston Globe*, 7 May 1981, p. 21.

3. Lucinda Smith, "Parents, Cops Quell False Rumors of 'Killer Clowns,'" *Montclair Times*, 6 June 1991. Cited in Jan Harold Brunvand, *The Encyclopedia of Urban Legends* (New York: Norton, 2001), 313–315.

4. Jerry Taylor, "Police Discount Reports of Clowns Bothering Kids," *The Boston Globe*, 9 May 1981, p. 18.

5. For more on this, see chapter 12 in Benjamin Radford, *Media Mythmakers: How*

Journalists, Activists, and Advertisers Mislead Us (New York: Prometheus Books, 2003).
 6. Brunvand, "Phantom Clowns," 313–315.
 7. Jan Harold Brunvand, "Take Away Kidnapping Clowns," *The Post-Standard* (Syracuse, NY), 5 Aug. 1991, p. A7.
 8. *Ibid.*
 9. *Ibid.*
 10. Gillian Bennett, *Bodies: Sex, Violence, Disease and Death in Contemporary Legend* (Jackson, MS: University Press of Mississippi, 2005), 199–200.
 11. Loren Coleman, *Phantom Clowns Are Back*, Nov. 2008, http://copycateffect.blogspot.com/2008/10/phantom-clowns-are-back.html.

Chapter 21

 1. William Thomas, "Stolen Skies: The Chemtrail Mystery," *Earth Island Journal* (Summer 2002): 34–35.
 2. *Ibid.*, 35.
 3. *Ibid.*
 4. Thomas Schlatter, "Weather Queries," *Weatherwise* (Nov–Dec. 2000): 36–39.
 5. Thomas Schlatter, "Weather Queries." *Weatherwise* (Sept.–Oct. 2002): 53.
 6. Mike Blair, "Military Behind Mystery Chemtrails," *The Spotlight*, http://www.libertylobby.org/articles/2001/20010611chemtrails.html
 7. "ChemTrails — 80% Population Reduction of Earth?????" *Details Here*, 2009, http://www.detailshere.com/chemtrails.htm.
 8. Traci Watson, "Conspiracy Theorists Read Between Lines in the Sky," *USA Today*, March 7, 2001, http://www.chemtrailcentral.com/usatoday.shtml.
 9. Letter from M. Kim Johnson to the New Mexico State Attorney General dated 31 Oct. 1999, *New Mexicans for Science and Reason*, http://www.nmsr.org/mkjrept.htm.

Chapter 22

 1. J. Koo and C. S. Lee, "Delusions of Parasitosis: A Determologist's Guide to Diagnosis and Treatment," *American Journal of Clinical Dermatology* 2 (2001): 285–290.
 2. Benjamin Chertoff, "Making Their Skin Crawl," *Popular Mechanics* 182, no. 6 (2005): 62.
 3. Virginia R. Savely, Mary M. Leitao, and Raphael B. Stricker, "The Mystery of Morgellons Disease. Infection or Delusion?" *American Journal of Clinical Dermatology* 7, no. 1 (2006): 1–5; Debbie Gilbert, "Morgellons: Is Skin Rash Real or Imagined?" *The Gainesville Times*, 20 Aug. 2006, http://www.gainesvilletimes.com/news/stories/20060820/localnews/118795.shtml.
 4. Gilbert, "Morgellons."
 5. *Ibid.*

Chapter 23

 1. Barbara Mikkelson, "Utah Evacuees," *Snopes*, 8 Oct. 2005, http://www.snopes.com/katrina/personal/utah.asp.
 2. *Ibid.*
 3. *Ibid.*
 4. *Ibid.*
 5. *Ibid.*
 6. *Ibid.*
 7. *Ibid.*
 8. *Ibid.*

Chapter 24

 1. Ray Tomlinson, *The First Network Email*, n.d., http://openmap.bbn.com/~tomlinso/ray/firstemailframe.html.
 2. Dave Crocker, *Email History*, 2 Nov. 2009, http://www.livinginternet.com/e/ei.htm.
 3. Alan Solomon, *A Brief History of PC Viruses*, 8 May 2009, http://www.cknow.com/cms/vtutor/dr-solomon-history.html.
 4. Steve Ragan, "Malware Then and Now — A Look Back on the Anniversary of the Melissa Virus," *The Tech Herald*, 26 March 2009, http://www.thetechherald.com/article.php/200913/3308/Malware-then-and-now-%E2%80%93-a-look-back-on-the-anniversary-of-the-Melissa-Virus?page=2. While widely reported and attributed to an interview published in *Insight Magazine*, I was unable to find any source that gave the original citation. There are several magazines with "Insight" in the title, most with a religious theme, though *CIO Insight* regularly publishes articles on computer developments.

It's possible that the quote is in itself an urban myth. Even so, however, it accurately expresses the initial incredulity that the first computer virus reports inspired among many technicians.

5. Charles Schmidt and Tom Darby, *The What, Why, and How of the 1988 Internet Worm*, July 2001, http://www.snowplow.org/tom/worm/worm.html. The creator, Robert Morris, cooperated with authorities, received a suspended sentence and fine, and soon after was hired as a professor by MIT's department of Computer Science.

6. Solomon, *A Brief History of PC Viruses*.

7. Rob Rosenberger, "Michelangelo Fiasco: A Historical Timeline," *VMyths*, 1 June 1992, http://vmyths.com/column/1/1992/6/1/.

8. Ragan, "Malware Then and Now."

9. Les Jones, *Good Times Virus Hoax FAQ*, 27 April 1995, http://www.cityscope.net/hoax1.html.

10. *Ibid*.

11. Bill Ellis, "Legend/AntiLegend: Humor as an Integral Part of the Contemporary Legend Process," in Veronique Campion-Vincent, Chip Heath, and Gary Alan Fine (eds.), *Rumor Mills: The Social Impact of Rumor and Legend* (New Brunswick: Aldine Transaction, 2005), 126.

12. *Ibid*., 127.

13. For instance, CIAC Notes 95–05d (11 Jan.1995) reads in part: "It is possible to create a file that remaps keys when displayed on a PC/MS-DOS machine with the ANSI.SYS driver loaded. However, this only works on PC/MS-DOS machines with the text displayed on the screen in text mode. It would not work in Windows or in most text editors or mailers. A key could be remapped to produce any command sequence when pressed, for example DEL or FORMAT. However, the command is not issued until the remapped key is pressed and the command issued by the remapped key would be visible on the screen. You could protect yourself by removing ANSI.SYS from the CONFIG.SYS file, but many DOS programs use the functionality of ANSI.SYS to control screen functions and colors. Windows programs are not effected [sic] by ANSI.SYS, though a DOS program running in Windows would be."

14. Bill Ellis, "'Good Times Cathy' Computer Virus," *FOAFTale News* 36 (Jan.1995): 5.

15. Ellis, "Legend/AntiLegend," 131–132.

16. Symantec, *Wscript.KakWorm*, 13 Feb. 2007, http://www.symantec.com/security_response/writeup.jsp?docid=2000-121908-3951-99.

Chapter 25

1. Jan Harold Brunvand, *The Vanishing Hitchhiker: American Urban Legends and Their Meanings* (New York: W. W. Norton, 1981).

2. Jan Harold Brunvand, *Encyclopedia of Urban Legends* (Santa Barbara, CA: ABC-CLIO, 2001), xxix.

3. Hal Morgan and Kerry Tucker, *Rumor!* (New York: Penguin, 1984), 82.

4. Jean-Noel Kapferer, *Rumors: Uses, Interpretations, and Images* (New Brunswick, NJ: Transaction Publishers, 1990), 22; Ralph L. Rosnow and Gary Allen Fine, *Rumor and Gossip* (New York: Elsevier, 1976), 14.

5. Rosnow and Fine, *Rumor and Gossip*, 22.

6. *Ibid*., 14–20; Kapferer, *Rumors*, 22–23.

7. Morgan and Tucker, *Rumor!*, 87.

8. John Neary, "The Magical McCartney Mystery," *Life*, 7 Nov. 1969, p. 104.

Chapter 26

1. Martin Sharpe, "The Curse of the Crying Boy: Picture Is a Fire Jinx," *The Sun*, 4 Sept. 1985, p. 13.

2. Peter Chippindale and Chris Horrie, *Stick It Up Your Punter! The Uncut Story of the Sun Newspaper* (New York: Simon & Schuster, 1990).

3. *Ibid*.

4. Georgina Boyles, *Perspectives on Contemporary Legend* (vol. 4) (Sheffield, UK: Sheffield University, 1989).

5. *Ibid*.

6. Tim Slemen, *Haunted Liverpool* (Liverpool: Bluecoat Press, 2000).

7. *Ibid*.

8. *Ibid*.

Chapter 27

1. Bob Rickard and John Michell, *Unexplained Phenomena: A Rough Guide Special* (London: Rough Guides Ltd., 2000).

2. Ibid.
3. Ibid.
4. Ibid.
5. Ibid.
6. Ibid.
7. General information from the following source was also used in this chapter: David Clarke, *The Angel of Mons: Phantom Soldiers and Ghostly Guardians* (London: Wiley, 2004).

Chapter 28

1. Jeffrey S. Victor, "Satanic Cult's Ritual Abuse of Children: Horror or Hoax?" *USA Today* 122, no. 2582 (1993).
2. Mark Pendergrast, *Victims of Memory: Incest Accusations and Shattered Lives* (Hinesburg, VT: Upper Access, Inc., 1995), 49.
3. Brian Siano, "All the Babies You Can Eat," *The Humanist* 53, no. 2 (1993): 40–41.
4. "Baby Breeders," *The Sally Jessie Raphael Show*, Journal Graphics Transcripts, 28 Feb. 1989; "Devil Babies," *The Sally Jessie Raphael Show*, Journal Graphics Transcripts, 24 July 1991; "They Told Me I Have the Devil Inside Me," *The Sally Jessie Raphael Show*, Journal Graphics Transcripts, 14 July 1992.
5. "Satanic Breeders," *Geraldo*, Journal Graphics Transcripts, 24 Oct. 1998; *Devil Worship*, Geraldo Rivera (producer), 25 Oct. 1988, NBC, New York; "Investigating Multiple Personalities," *Geraldo*, Journal Graphics Transcripts, 10 Sept. 1991.
6. "Sex in the Name of Satan," *Larry King Live*, Journal Graphics Transcripts, 13 May 1991; "A Satanic Cult Survivor," *Larry King Live*, Journal Graphics Transcripts, 2 Aug. 1991.
7. Ken Sidey, "Publisher Withdraws Satanism Story," *Christianity Today* 34, no. 3 (19 Feb. 1990): 34–35.
8. David G. Bromley, "The Satanic Cult Scare," *Society* (May–June 1991): 62.
9. James T. Richardson, "The Social Construction of Satanism: Understanding an International Social Problem," *Australian Journal of Social Issues* 32, no. 1 (1997): 68.
10. Ibid.
11. Bromley, "The Satanic Cult Scare."
12. Pendergrast, *Victims of Memory*, 49.
13. David Alexander, "Giving the Devil More Than His Due," *The Humanist* 50, no 2 (Mar/April 1990): 5–14, http://users.cybercity.dk/~ccc44406/smwane/Devildue.htm.
14. Dennis Coon, *Introduction to Psychology: Exploration and Application* (8th ed.) (Pacific Grove, CA: Brooks/Cole Publishing, 2000), 343.
15. Terence W. Campbell, *Smoke and Mirrors: The Devastating Effect of False Sexual Abuse Claims* (New York: Plenum Press, 1998).
16. "'I Tawt I Taw' a Bunny Wabbit at Disneyland: New Evidence Shows False Memories Can Be Created," *Science Daily News Release*, University of Washington, 12 June 2001, http://www.sciencedaily.com/releases/2001/06/010612065657.htm.
17. Victor, "Satanic Cult's Ritual Abuse of Children."

Chapter 29

1. "Spray Deodorant Killed Boy," *Adirondack Daily Enterprise*, 6 Nov. 1975, p. 2.
2. Benjamin Radford, "Candy Fears Are Mere Halloween Phantoms," *Bad Science at Live Science*, 25 Oct. 2005, http://www.livescience.com/strangenews/051025_halloween_candy.html.
3. "Wife's Testimony Part of Poison Candy Case," *Dallas Morning News*, 14 Dec. 1974, p. A17.
4. "Receives Poisoned Candy," *Los Angeles Herald*, 27 Dec. 1905, p. 3; "Miss Smith's Poisoned Candy," *The Sun* (New York), 28 Dec. 1905, p. 2.
5. Joel Best and Gerald T. Horiuchi, "The Razor Blade in the Apple: The Social Construction of Urban Legends," *Social Problems* 32, no. 5 (1985): 491.
6. Ibid.
7. W. Jocelyn, "Suspicious Halloween Candy Purchases at Costco," *About.com Urban Legends*, http://urbanlegends.about.com/library/blcostco-terror2.htm.
8. Mitchell Maddux and Peter Pochna, "Large Candy Purchases Investigated by FBI," *Bergen County Record*, 20 Oct. 2001.
9. Benjamin Radford, "Sex Offenders Not a Halloween Scare," *Bad Science at Live Science*, 2009, http://www.livescience.com/health/091030-sex-offenders-halloween.html.
10. Mark Chaffin, Jill Levenson, Elizabeth Letourneau, and Paul Stern, "How Safe Are Trick-or-Treaters?: An Analysis of Child Sex Crime Rates on Halloween," *Sexual Abuse: A*

Journal of Research and Treatment 21, no. 3 (2009): 363–374.

11. Maryln Schwartz, (1976). "All Fun Gone in Halloween," *Dallas Morning News*, 30 Oct. 1976, p. A1.

12. Centers for Disease Control, "Age-Adjusted Death Rates Per 100,000 Population for the Three Leading Causes of Injury Death — United States, 1979–2006," *MMWR Weekly* 58, no. 24 (25 June 2009), 675.

Chapter 30

1. David France, "Saving Justin Berry," *New York*, 28 Oct. 2007.

2. Benjamin Radford, "Stranger Danger: How Real Is It?" *Skeptical Briefs*, 7 April 2006.

3. Benjamin Radford, "Predator Panic: A Closer Look," in Kendrick Frazier (ed.), *Science Under Siege: Defending Science, Exposing Pseudoscience* (Amherst, NY: Prometheus Books, 2009), 207.

4. Janis Wolak, David Finkelhor, and Kimberley J. Mitchell, "Online 'Predators' and Their Victims: Myths, Realities, and Implications for Prevention and Treatment," Crimes Against Children Center at the University of New Hampshire, *American Psychologist* 63, no. 2 (2008).

5. For more on moral panics, see Ehrich Goode and Nachman Ben-Yehuda, *Moral Panics: The Social Construction of Deviance* (Malden, MA: Wiley-Blackwell, 1994).

Chapter 31

1. M. Males, "Who's Really Killing Our School Kids?" *Los Angeles Times*, 31 May 1998, p. M1.

2. Dewey G. Cornell, *School Violence: Fear Versus Facts* (Mahwah, NJ: Lawrence Erlbaum Associates, 2006), 21.

3. "School Safety Report Released," 20 Nov. 2005, press release issued by the United States Department of Education's National Center for Education Statistics, Washington DC.

4. *What Are the Odds?*, School Violence Resource Center, Little Rock, AR.

5. Nicholas D. Kristof, "When Brad Pitt Gets More Coverage Than Genocide," *New York Times Upfront* 138, no. 2 (19 Sept. 2005): 27.

6. Larance Johnson, *Fact Sheet on School Crime Statistics*, School Violence Resource Center, Little Rock, AR, 2001.

7. "Federal Report: School Still the Safest Place for Young People," *National Education Association*, 2006, http://www.nea.org/schoolsafety/research-schoolsafety.html.

8. Randy Borum, Cornell Dewey, William Modzeleski, and Shane Jimerson, "What Can Be Done About School Shootings? A Review of the Evidence," *Educational Researcher* 39, no. 1 (2010): 27–37.

9. Natalie Pompilio, "Going for the Fake," *American Journalism Review* 22, no. 1 (2000): 29.

Chapter 32

1. *International Shark Attack File*, Florida Museum of Natural History, University of Florida, http://www.flmnh.ufl.edu/fish/sharks/attacks/relariskgator.htm.

2. "Shark Attack Fatalities Compared to Hunting Incident Fatalities in the U.S. and Canada: 2000–2004." *International Shark Attack File*, Florida Museum of Natural History, University of Florida, http://www.flmnh.ufl.edu/fish/sharks/attacks/relariskhunting.htm.

3. "Comparison of Shark Attack and Bicycle-Related Fatalities 1990–2005." *International Shark Attack File*, Florida Museum of Natural History, University of Florida, http://www.flmnh.ufl.edu/fish/sharks/attacks/relariskbike.htm.

4. "A Comparison with the Number of Lightning Fatalities in Coastal United States: 1959–2005." *International Shark Attack File*, Florida Museum of Natural History, University of Florida, http://www.flmnh.ufl.edu/fish/sharks/attacks/2004lightning.html.

5. John Elvin, "Here Comes Summer; Are the Sharks Far Behind?" *Insight on the News* 18, no. 23 (2002): 34.

6. Julia Baird, "Just When You Think It's Unsafe to Go into the Water," *The Sydney Morning Herald*, 12 Jan.2006, p. 11.

7. Juan Williams, "Analysis: Human Perception of Sharks," *Talk of the Nation*, National Public Radio, 15 Aug. 2001; "American Elasmobranch Society (Global Shark Attack Statistics)," *Student British Medical Journal* (Oct. 2001): 398.

8. "Statistics on Attacking Species of Shark," *International Shark Attack File*,

Florida Museum of Natural History, University of Florida, http://www.flmnh.ufl.edu/fish/sharks/statistics/species2.htm.
9. Williams, "Analysis: Human Perception of Sharks," 4.
10. "Relax: You're Not That Tempting," *New Scientist* 174, no. 2345 (1 June 2002): 25.
11. John Elvin, "Sorry, No Sharks ... but Lots of Media," *Insight on the News* 17, no. 35 (17 Sept. 2001): 35.
12. Howard Rosenberg, "Reality Bites," *Animal's Agenda* 21, no. 5 (Sept.–Oct. 2001): 35.

Chapter 33

1. Scott Corrales, "How Many Goats Can a Goatsucker Suck?" *Fortean Times* 189 (1996): 34–37.
2. Ibid.
3. Lauren Derby, "Imperial Secrets: Vampires and Nationhood in Puerto Rico," *Past and Present* 199, suppl. 3 (2008): 292.
4. Corrales, "How Many Goats Can a Goatsucker Suck?"
5. I. L. Janis, "Group Identification under Conditions of External Danger," *British Journal of Medical Psychology* 36 (1963): 227–238.
6. Robert Michael Jordan, "El Chupacabra: Icon of Resistance to U.S. Imperialism" (master's thesis, University of Texas, 2008).
7. Corrales, "How Many Goats Can a Goatsucker Suck?" 70.
8. Ibid., 27.
9. Ibid., 4.
10. Ibid., 78.
11. Ibid., 142.

Chapter 34

1. Ian K. Smith, "Cell Phone Scare," *Time* (1 Nov. 1999): 8.
2. Susan Dentzer, "Cell Phone Safety," transcript interview with Joshua Muscat on *The NewsHour with Jim Lehrer*, 28 Dec. 2000, http://www.pbs.org/newshour/bb/health/july-dec00/cell_phones.html.
3. Michael Fumento, "Is the Cell Phone Scare Finally Over?" *Townhall* column, 26 Jan. 2006, fumento.com.
4. Tracy King, "Viral Video Cell-Phone Scare," *Skeptical Inquirer* 33, no. 5 (Sep/Oct. 2009): 34–35.
5. S. T. Lakshmikumar, "Power Line Panic and Mobile Mania," *Skeptical Inquirer* 33, no. 5 (Sept./Oct. 2009): 32.
6. David Strayner and Frank A. Drews, *Effects of Cell Phone Conversations on Younger and Older Drivers* (Salt Lake City: University of Utah, 2004), http://www.psych.utah.edu/AppliedCognitionLab/Aging.pdf.

Chapter 35

1. Barbara Mikkelson and David Mikkelson, "You've Got to Be Kidneying," *Snopes: Urban Legends Reference Page*, 1998, http://snopes.simplenet.com.
2. Todd Leventhal, "The Child Organ Trafficking Rumor: A Modern 'Urban Legend,'" *U.S. Information Agency Report to the United Nations Special Rapporteur* (Washington DC: U.S. Information Agency, 1994).
3. Ibid., 24
4. Ibid., 28
5. Eric Sottas, *Trade in Organs and Torture*, presentation, Geneva, Switzerland, World Organization Against Torture, 1994.
6. Carol Morello, "Baby Theft Panic Cools Guatemalan Tourism, Adoptions," *Albuquerque Journal* 17 April 1994.
7. Minerva Canto, "Rumors Nearly Killed N.M. Traveler," *Albuquerque Journal* 17 April 1994.
8. Veronique Campion-Vincent, "The Baby-Parts Story: A New Latin American Legend," *Western Folklore* 49 (1990): 9–25.
9. Benjamin Radford, "The Truth About Sensational Kidney Thefts," *Bad Science at Live Science*, 2008, http://www.livescience.com/health/080219-bad-kidney-theft.html.
10. Benjamin Radford, "Body Part Theft: Truth Vs. Myth," *Bad Science at Live Science*, 2009, http://www.livescience.com/strangenews/091222-body-part-organ-theft.html.

Chapter 36

1. *Impact of Vaccines Universally Recommended for Children in the United States, 1990–1999* (Ottawa, ON: Public Health Agency of Canada, 1999), 122–127.

2. Q. S. Huang, G. Greening, M. G. Barker, et al., "Persistence of Oral Polio Vaccine Virus After Its Removal from the Immunisation Schedule in New Zealand," *Lancet* 366, no. 9483 (2005): 394–396.

3. "Vaccines," *Bill and Melinda Gates Foundation*, 1999, http://www.gatesfoundation.org/vaccines/Pages/default.aspx.

4. S. Plotkin, W. Orenstein, and P. Offit, *Vaccines* (5th ed.) (St. Louis, MO: Saunders Elsevier, 2008).

5. M. Wensing, "Evidence-based Patient Empowerment," *Quality and Safety in Health Care* 9, no. 4 (2000): 200–201.

6. E. Jenner, *An Inquiry into the Causes and Effects of the Variolae Vaccine A Disease Discovered in Some of the Western Counties of England, Particularly Glousectershire, and Known by the Name of the Cow Pox* (1789; Cambridge; The Harvard Classics, 1909–1914), 94.

7. D. Koplow, *Smallpox: The Fight to Eradicate a Global Scourge* (Berkeley: University of California Press, 2003), 274.

8. S. Bhattacharya, "World Health Organization and Global Smallpox Eradication," *Journal of Epidemiology and Community Health* 62, no. 10 (2008): 909–912; "Conclusions and Recommendations of the Advisory Committee on Poliomyelitis Eradication," *Weekly Epidemiological Record* 84, no. 3 (Nov. 2008): 17–28.

9. R. M. Wolfe and L. K. Sharp. "Anti-Vaccinationists Past and Present," *British Medical Journal* 325, no. 7361 (2002): 430–432.

10. Ibid.

11. J. K. Blackford, "Immunization Controversy: Understanding and Addressing Public Misconceptions and Concerns," *The Journal of School Nursing* 17, no. 1 (2001): 32–37; J. Leask and P. McIntyre, "Public Opponents to Vaccination: A Case Study," *Vaccine* 21 (2003): 4700–4703; M. K. Pitts, S. J. Dyson, and D. A. Rosenthal, "Knowledge and Awareness of Human Papillomavirus (HPV): Attitudes Towards HPV Vaccination Among a Representative Sample of Woman in Victoria, Australia," *Sex Health* 4, no. 3 (2007): 177–180.

12. M. C. Danovaro-Holliday, A. L. Wood, and C. W. LeBaron, "Rotavirus Vaccine and the News Media, 1987–2001," *Journal of the American Medical Association* 287, no. 11 (2002): 1455–1462.

13. R. Grilli, C. Ramsay, and S. Minozzi, "Mass Media Interventions: Systematic Review," *Cochrane Database of Systematic Reviews* 1 (2005): 1–27.

14. E. Gangarosa, A. Galazka, C. Wolfe, et al., "Impact of Anti-vaccine Movements on Pertussis Control: The Untold Story," *The Lancet* 351 (1998): 356–360.

15. O. Mansoor, D. Sarfati, and G. Durham, "Is Confidence in Immunisation Declining?" *New Zealand Medical Journal* 111, no. 1071 (1998): 300.

16. J. Leask, "Vaccination and Risk Communication: Summary of a Workshop, Arlington Virginia, USA, 5–6 October 2000," *Journal of Paediatrics and Child Health* 38, no. 2 (2002): 124–128.

17. M. Nelson and J. Rogers, "The Right to Die? Anti-vaccination Activity and the 1874 Smallpox Epidemic in Stockholm," *Social History of Medicine* 5, no. 3 (1992): 369–388.

18. "Measles Epidemic: Rising Death Rate," *The Times* (London), 31 March 1922.

19. A. J. Wakefield, S. H. Murch, A. Anthony, et al., "Ileal-Lymphoid-Nodular Hyperplasia, Non-Specific Colitis, and Pervasive Developmental Disorder in Children," *The Lancet* 351, no. 9103 (1998): 637–641.

20. S. H. Murch, A. Anthony, D. H. Casson, et al. "Retraction of an Interpretation," *The Lancet* 363, no. 9411 (2004): 750.

21. "Ileal-Lymphoid-Nodular Hyperplasia, Non-Specific Colitis, and Pervasive Developmental Disorder in Children" [Retraction of A. J. Wakefield et al., *The Lancet* 351, no. 9103 (1998): 637–641], *The Lancet* 375, no. 9713 (2010): 445.

22. Judicial Watch, *Judicial Watch Investigates Side-Effects of HPV Vaccine*, http://www.judicalwatch.org/gardasil, Washington DC, 2007.

23. "Cancer Jab Alert After Girl Dies," *BBC News*, 29 Sept. 2009.

24. "British Girl, 14, Dies After Receiving Cervical Cancer Vaccine Cervarix," *New York Daily News*, 29 Sept. 2009.

24. M. Johnston, "Grieving Mother Blames Cancer Vaccine," *New Zealand Herald*, 9 Jan.2010.

26. J. H. Cossar and D. Reid, "Immunisation and Health Advice for Travellers: The Role of the General Practitioner," *Health Bulletin* (Edinburgh) 50, no. 6 (1992): 428–432.

27. Executive Committee of the International Anti-Vaccination League, *Chief Points*

Against Vaccination by International Anti-Vaccination League (Paris, 1880).
  28. *Ibid.*
  29. M. L. Loat, "Some Reasons Why You Should Support the National Anti-Vaccination League (1919)," *Wikipedia, the Free Encyclopedia*, http://en.wikisource.org/wiki/Some_Reasons_Why_You_Should_Support_the_National_Vaccination_League.
  30. *Ibid.*
  31. *Ibid.*
  32. *Ibid.*
  33. *Ibid.*
  34. *Ibid.*

Bibliography

"Alarm on the Rand." *The New York Times*, 19 Feb. 1910, p. 1.

Alexander, David. "Giving the Devil More Than His Due." *The Humanist* 50, no. 2 (1990): 5–14, http://users.cybercity.dk/~ccc44406/smwane/Devildue.htm.

Alley, E. "Credulity Seat of Mattoon's Terror." *Chicago Herald-American*, 20 Sept. 1944, p. 4.

———. "Illness of First Gas 'Victim' Blamed for Wave of Hysteria in Mattoon." *Chicago Herald-American*, 17 Sept. 1944, p. 3.

Andrews, Nigel. "Nightmares and Nasties." In *The Video Nasties*, edited by Martin Barker, 42. London: Pluto Press, 1984.

"Anesthetic Prowler on Loose." *The Daily Journal-Gazette*, 2 Sept. 1944, p. 1.

Ashford, Jenny. "Tiny Paris Theater Became Synonymous with Grisley Horror," 27 July 2009, http://theatrehistory.suite101.com/article.cfm/le_thetre_du_grandguignol

"At Night in Mattoon." *Time*, 18 Sept. 1944, p. 23.

"Austria Gripped by a Fear of Spider," *BBC News*, 4 Aug. 2006, http://news.bbc.co.uk/go/pr/fr/-/2/hi/europe/5244840.stm.

"Baby Breeders." *The Sally Jessie Raphael Show*. Journal Graphics Transcripts, 28 Feb. 1989.

Bainbridge, William. "Collective Behavior and Social Movements." In *Sociology*, edited by Rodney Stark, 544–576. Belmont, CA: Wadsworth, 1987.

Baird, Julia. "Just When You Think It's Unsafe to Go into the Water." *The Sydney Morning Herald*, 12 Jan. 2006, p. 11.

Ballenger, C. "FBI at Mattoon as Gas Prowler Attacks 5 More." *Chicago Daily Tribune*, 10 Sept. 1944, p. 15.

———. "Mattoon's Gas Fiend Attacks Girl, 11, in Home." *Chicago Daily Tribune*, 9 Sept. 1944, p. 10.

Banks, Jonathan, Phil Sirvid, and Cor Vink. "White-tailed Spider Bites — Arachnophobic Fallout?" *The New Zealand Medical Journal* 117, no. 1108 (2004): 1–7.

Bennett, Gillian. *Bodies: Sex, Violence, Disease and Death in Contemporary Legend*. Jackson: The University Press of Mississippi, 2005.

"Berlin Comet Picnics." *The New York Times*, 19 Feb. 1910, p. 1.

Best, Joel, and Gerald T. Horiuchi. "The Razor Blade in the Apple: The Social Construction of Urban Legends." *Social Problems* 32, no. 5 (1985): 488–499.

Bhattacharya, S. "World Health Organization and Global Smallpox Eradication." *Journal of Epidemiology and Community Health* 62, no. 10 (2008): 909–912.

"Bird Flu Movie Should Not Lead to Panic." United States Federal News Service, Washington, DC, 9 May 2006.

Blackford, J. K. "Immunization Controversy: Understanding and Addressing Public Misconceptions and Concerns." *The Journal of School Nursing* 17, no. 1 (2001): 32–37.

Bock, P. K. *Modern Cultural Anthropology*. New York: Knopf, 1979.

"Boo!" *Time*, 7 Nov. 1938, p. 40.

Boyles, Georgina. *Perspectives on Contemporary Legend*, vol. 4. Sheffield, UK: Sheffield University, 1989.

Brady, Frank. *Citizen Welles: A Biography of Orson Welles*. New York: Charles Scribner's Sons, 1989.

"Britain Is Alarmed by Burlesque Radio

"News' of Revolt in London and Bombing of Commons." *New York Times*, 18 Jan. 1926, p. 3.

"British Girl, 14, Dies After Receiving Cervical Cancer Vaccine Cervarix. *New York Daily News*, 29 Sept. 2009.

Bromley, David G. "The Satanic Cult Scare." *Society* (May-June 1991): 55-66.

Brown, David. "Floods' Pollutants Within the Norm. Oil Spills Seen as the Only Exception." *The Washington Post*, 15 Sept. 2005, p. A15.

Brown, F. J. *Chemical Warfare: A Study in Restraints*. Princeton, MJ: Princeton University Press, 1968.

Brunvand, Jan Harold. "Phantom Clowns." In *The Encyclopedia of Urban Legends*, 313-315. New York: Norton, 2001.

———. "Take Away Kidnapping Clowns." *The Post-Standard* (Syracuse, NY), 5 Aug. 1991, p. A7.

———. *The Vanishing Hitchhiker: American Urban Legends and Their Meanings*. New York: W.W. Norton, 1981.

Bulgatz, Joseph. *Ponzi Schemes, Invaders from Mars & More Extraordinary Popular Delusions and the Madness of Crowds*. New York: Harmony Books, 1992.

Bunzel, Reed E. "FCC Admonishes KROQ-FM for Murder Hoax." *Broadcasting* 121, no. 24 (9 Dec. 1991): 31.

Burlingame, Jon. "'Bulletin' Feels Like Real Event." *Syracuse Herald-Journal* (New York), 29 Oct. 1994, p. A6.

Burns, Ronald, and Charles Crawford. "Shootings, the Media, and Public Fear: Ingredients for a Moral Panic." *Crime, Law & Social Change* 32 (1999): 147-168.

"Bus Delayed." *Iowa City Press-Citizen*, 31 Oct. 1938, p. 1.

Callahan, Christopher. "Beware 'Clown,' Pupils Told." *The Boston Globe*, 7 May 1981, p. 21.

Campbell, Terence W. *Smoke and Mirrors: The Devastating Effect of False Sexual Abuse Claims*. New York: Plenum Press, 1998.

Campion-Vincent, Veronique. "The Baby-Parts Story: A New Latin American Legend." *Western Folklore* 49 (1990): 9-25.

"Cancer Jab Alert After Girl Dies." *BBC News*. 29 Sept. 2009.

Canto, Minerva. "Rumors Nearly Killed N.M. Traveler." *Albuquerque Journal*, 17 April 1994.

Cantril, Hadley, Hazel Gaudet, and Herta Herzog. *The Invasion from Mars: A Study in the Psychology of Panic*. Princeton, NJ: Princeton University Press, 1940.

Catalanello, R., and C. Pittman. "At the Edge of Anarchy." *St. Petersburg Times*, 2 Sept. 2005, p. 1.

"A Celebrated Hoax." *The Newark Daily Advocate* (New Jersey), 27 June 1893, citing a detailed interview with T. B. Connery.

Chaffin, Mark, Jill Levenson, Elizabeth Letourneau, and Paul Stern. "How Safe Are Trick-or-Treaters?: An Analysis of Child Sex Crime Rates on Halloween." *Sexual Abuse: A Journal of Research and Treatment* 21, no. 3 (2009): 363-374.

"'Chasers' to Be Arrested." *The Daily Journal-Gazette*, 11 Sept. 1944, p. 1.

"Chemists Trace Mattoon Mad Man's 'Gardenia Gas.'" *The News-Gazetteer* (Champaign), 9 Sept. 1944, p. 3.

Chertoff, Benjamin. "Making Their Skin Crawl." *Popular Mechanics* 182, no. 6 (2005): 60-62.

"Chicago Psychiatrist Analyzes Mattoon Gas Hysteria." *Chicago Herald-American*, 17 Sept. 1944, p. 3.

"Child Video Protection." *New Zealand Herald*, 15 Oct. 1985.

Chippindale, Peter, and Chris Horrie. *Stick It Up Your Punter! The Uncut Story of the Sun Newspaper*. New York: Simon & Schuster, 1990.

Chun, Diane. "Experts Dismiss Scare Over Bird Flu." *The Gainesville Sun* (Florida), 1 Nov. 2005, http://www.gainesville.com/apps/pbcs.dll/article?AID=/20051101/LOCAL/51101021/1078/news.

"Clamping Down on Video Nasties." *New Zealand Women's Weekly*, 25 Nov. 1985.

Clarke, David. *The Angel of Mons: Phantom Soldiers and Ghostly Guardians*. London: Wiley, 2004.

"Cole Amplifies Statement." *The Daily Journal-Gazette*, 13 Sept. 1944, p. 1.

Coleman, Loren. *Mysterious America*. New York: Faber & Faber, 1983.

———. "Phantom Clowns." *Fate* 35, no 3 (Mar. 1982): 53-54.

———. *Phantom Clowns Are Back*, Nov. 2008, http://copycateffect.blogspot.com /2008/10/phantom-clowns-are-back.html.

"Comet Jerusalem's Omen." *The Washington Post*, 11 May 1910, p. 1.

"Comet Quits Its Path." *The Washington Post*, 11 May 1910, p. 1.

"Comet's Poisonous Tail. Yerkes Observatory Finds Cyanogen in Spectrum of Halley's

Comet." *The New York Times*, 7 Feb. 1910, p. 1.

"Comparison of Shark Attack and Bicycle-Related Fatalities 1990–2005." *International Shark Attack File*, Florida Museum of Natural History, University of Florida, http://www.flmnh.ufl.edu/fish/sharks/attacks/relariskbike.htm.

"Comparison of Shark Attacks and Fatalities with the American Alligator," *International Shark Attack File*, Florida Museum of Natural History, University of Florida, http://www.flmnh.ufl.edu/fish/sharks/attacks/relariskgator.htm.

"A Comparison with the Number of Lightning Fatalities in Coastal United States: 1959–2005." *International Shark Attack File*, Florida Museum of Natural History, University of Florida, http://www.flmnh.ufl.edu/fish/sharks/attacks/2004lightning.html.

Coon, Dennis. *Introduction to Psychology: Exploration and Application*, 8th ed. Pacific Grove, CA: Brooks/Cole, 2000.

Corrales, Scott. "How Many Goats Can a Goatsucker Suck?" *Fortean Times* 189 (1996): 34–37.

Cossar, J. H., and D. Reid. (1992). "Immunisation and Health Advice for Travellers: The Role of the General Practitioner" [Edinburgh]. *Health Bulletin* 50, no. 6 (1992): 428–432.

Cox, Ted. "'Without Warning' No 'War of the Worlds.'" *Daily Herald*, 1 Nov. 1994, p. 7.

Crocker, Dave. *Email History*. 2 Nov. 2009, http://www.livinginternet.com/e/ei.htm.

Crook, Timothy. "The Psychological Impact of Radio," *Independent Radio Drama Production*, http://www.irdp.co.uk/hoax.html.

Danovaro-Holliday, M. C., A. L. Wood, and C. W. LeBaron. "Rotavirus Vaccine and the News Media, 1987–2001." *Journal of the American Medical Association* 287, no. 11 (2002): 1455–1462.

de Bergerac, Cyrano. *A Voyage to the Moon. Also titled The Comical History of the States and Empires of the World of the Moon*. London, 1649.

"Debunk Mattoon Gas Scare." *Chicago Herald-American*, 13 Sept. 1944, p. 4.

Dentzer, Susan. "Cell Phone Safety." Transcript interview with Joshua Muscat on *The NewsHour with Jim Lehrer*, 28 Dec. 2000, http://www.pbs.org/newshour/bb/health/july-dec00/cell_phones.html.

Derby, Lauren. "Imperial Secrets: Vampires and Nationhood in Puerto Rico." In *Past and Present* 199, suppl. 3 (2008): 290–312.

"Devil Babies." *The Sally Jessie Raphael Show*. Journal Graphics Transcripts, 24 July 1991.

Devil Worship. Geraldo Rivera (producer), 25 Oct. 1988, NBC, New York.

Dickinson, Terence. "Why Does NASA Cry Wolf About 'Killer' Asteroids? *Toronto Star*, 2 Jan. 2005, p. A18.

Dinsmore, Alter. "Comets and People." *Griffith Observer* 20, no. 7 (1956): 82. Published by the Griffith Observatory, Los Angeles, CA.

"Discuss Halley's Comet." *The Washington Post*, 6 Feb. 1910, p. 15.

"Doctor, Doctor." *New Statesman*, 14 Aug. 2006, p. 18.

Donovan, Patricia. "New Orleans—What Urban Myths Say About U.S." Press release issued by the State University of New York at Buffalo, 2005, http://www.buffalo.edu/news/fast-execute.cgi/article-page.html?article=75960009.

Ellis, Bill. "'Good Times Cathy' Computer Virus." *FOAFTale News* 36 (Jan. 1995): 4–5.

_____. "Legend/AntiLegend: Humor as an Integral Part of the Contemporary Legend Process." In *Rumor Mills: The Social Impact of Rumor and Legend*, edited by Veronique Campion-Vincent, Chip Heath, and Gary Alan Fine, 123–140. New Brunswick: Aldine Transaction, 2005.

Elvin, John. "Here Comes Summer; Are the Sharks Far Behind?" *Insight on the News* 18, no. 23 (2002): 34.

_____. "Sorry, No Sharks ... but Lots of Media." *Insight on the News* 17, no. 35 (17 Sept. 2001): 35.

Enos, Peter. "British MPs Want 'Video Nasties' Curbed." *The Auckland Star*, 12 Jan. 1984.

Erickson, G. "Mad Gasser Called Myth." *Chicago Herald-American*, 13 Sept. 1944, p. 1.

"Even Author H. G. Wells Was Deeply Perturbed." *Trenton Evening News*, 31 Oct. 1938, p. 1.

"False Report of Russian Invasion Spurs Panic." *Reuters News Agency*, 14 March 2010.

"FCC Investigating Station's Role in Murder Confession Hoax." *The Post-Standard* (Syracuse, NY), 23 April 1991, p. D1.

"FCC Takes Action on Phony Radio Hoaxes."

The Intelligencer and the Record (Doylestown, PA), 15 May 1992, p. A9.
Fettmann, Eric. "'The Martians Have Landed!' In Radio Show 60 Years Ago, America Lost Its Innocence." *New York Post*, 28 Oct. 1988, p. 41.
Flaste, Richard, Holcomb Noble, Walter Sullivan, and John Noble Wilford. *The New York Times Guide to the Return of Halley's Comet*. New York: Times Books, 1985.
France, David. "Saving Justin Berry." *New York*, 28 Oct. 2007.
Fumento, Michael. "Fuss and Feathers Pandemic Panic Over the Avian Flu." *The Weekly Standard* (21 Nov. 2005): 24–30.
_____. Is the Cell Phone Scare Finally Over? *Townhall* column, 26 Jan. 2006, fumento.com.
Furedi, Frank. "Bird Flu Prophets of Doom Spread Nothing but Needless Alarm." *Daily Express*, 18 Oct. 2005, http://www.frankfuredi.com/articles/ birdflu-20051018.shtml.
Gangarosa, E., A. Galazka, C. Wolfe, et al. "Impact of Anti-vaccine Movements on Pertussis Control: The Untold Story." *The Lancet* 351 (1998): 356–360.
"'Gasser' Case 'Mistake,'" *The Daily Journal-Gazette*, 12 Sept. 1944, p. 4.
"Geologists at Princeton Hunt 'Meteor' in Vain." *New York Times*, 31 Oct. 1938, p. 4.
George, Lianne, Karin Marley, and Danylo Hawaleshka. "Forget Sars, West Nile, Ebola and Avian Flu: The Real Epidemic Is Fear." *Maclean's* 118, no. 40 (3 Oct. 2005): 46–52.
Gilbert, Debbie. "Morgellons: Is Skin Rash Real or Imagined?" *The Gainesville Times*, 20 Aug. 2006, http://www.gainesvilletimes.com/news/stories/20060820/localnews/118795.shtml.
Godwin, Francis, and Grant McColley (ed.). *The Man in the Moone and Nuncius Inanimatus; for the first time edited, with an introduction and notes, from the unique copies of the first editions of London, 1629 and London, 1638*. Northhampton, MA: Smith College, 1937.
"Govt Launches Probe of 'Monster' Cartoon." *Yomiuri Shimbun*, 18 Dec. 1997.
"Great Astronomical Discoveries Lately Made by Sir John Herschel, L.L.D., F.R.S., and co. at the Cape of Good Hope." *The Sun* (New York), 25–31 Aug. 1835.
Grilli, R., C. Ramsay, and S. Minozzi. "Mass Media Interventions: Systematic Review." *Cochrane Database of Systematic Reviews* 1 (2005): 1–27.
Hallett, Vicky. "Extra! Extra! Life on Moon!" *U.S. News & World Report*, 26 Aug. 2002: 53.
Handwerk, Brian. "Eye on the Storm: Hurricane Katrina Fast Facts." *National Geographic News* (6 Sept. 2005), http://news.nationalgeographic.com/news/2005/09/09 06_050906_ katrina_facts .html.
Harper, Jennifer. "Media, Blushing, Takes a Second Look at Katrina." *The Washington Times* (Washington, DC), 29 Sept. 2005, p. A1.
Harpur, Brian. *The Official Halley's Comet Book*. London: Hodder and Stoughton, 1985.
Harrison, Kristen. "Tales from the Screen: Enduring Fright Reactions from Scary Media." *Media Psychology* (Spring 1999): 97–116.
Hayashi, T., T. Ichiyama, M. Nishikawa, H. Isumi, and S. Furukawa. "Pocket Monsters, a Popular Television Cartoon, Attacks Japanese Children." *Annals of Neurology* 44, no. 3 (1998): 427.
"A 'Herald Sell.'" *The Galveston Daily News* (Texas), 15 Nov. 1874, p. 1.
"Hoax Spreads Terror Here." *Trenton Evening Times*, 31 Oct. 1938, p. 1.
Hogg, Colin. "Driller Killer ... the Horrible, Boring Truth." *The Auckland Star*, 12 Oct. 1985.
Holland, Bill. "FCC Lets Infinity Off the Hook After KROQ Hoax." *Billboard* 103, no. 50 14 Dec. 1991): 71.
Howard, Leland O. "Spider Bites and 'Kissing Bugs.'" *Popular Science Monthly* 56 (Nov. 1899): 31–42.
Huang, Q. S., G. Greening, M. G. Barker, et al. "Persistence of Oral Polio Vaccine Virus After Its Removal from the Immunisation Schedule in New Zealand." *Lancet* 366, no. 9483 (2005): 394–396.
"'I Tawt I Taw' A Bunny Wabbit at Disneyland: New Evidence Shows False Memories Can Be Created." *Science Daily News Release*, University of Washington, 12 June 2001, http://www.sciencedaily.com/releases/2001/06/010612065657.htm.
"Ileal-Lymphoid-Nodular Hyperplasia, Non-Specific Colitis, and Pervasive Developmental Disorder in Children" [Retraction of A. J. Wakefield et al. *The Lancet* 351, no. 9103 (1998): 637–641]. *The Lancet* 375, no. 9713 (2010): 445.

Impact of Vaccines Universally Recommended for Children in the United States. 1990–1999. Ottawa, ON: Public Health Agency of Canada, 1999.

"Invasion from Mars." *Times of London,* 14 Feb. 1949, p. 4.

"Investigating Multiple Personalities." *Geraldo.* Journal Graphics Transcripts, 10 Sept. 1991.

Jacobs, Norman. "The Phantom Slasher of Taipei: Mass Hysteria in a Non-Western Society." *Social Problems* 12 (1965): 318–328.

Janis, I. L. "Group Identification Under Conditions of External Danger." *British Journal of Medical Psychology* 36 (1963): 227–238.

Johnson, Donald Max. "The 'Phantom Anesthetist' of Mattoon: A Field Study of Mass Hysteria." *Journal of Abnormal Psychology* 40 (1945): 175–186.

Johnson, Larance. "Fact Sheet on School Crime Statistics," *School Violence Resource Center,* Little Rock, AR, 2001.

Johnston, M. "Grieving Mother Blames Cancer Vaccine." *New Zealand Herald,* 9 Jan. 2010.

Jones, Les. *Good Times Virus Hoax FAQ.* 27 April 1995, http://www.cityscope.net/hoax1.html.

Jordan, Robert Michael. "El Chupacabra: Icon of Resistance to U.S. Imperialism." Master's thesis, University of Texas, 2008.

Jory, Tom. "NBC Hopes Warning Will Avert Panic During 'Special Bulletin.'" *Syracuse Herald-Journal,* 19 March 1983, p. B6.

Judicial Watch. *Judicial Watch Investigates Side-Effects of HPV Vaccine,* http://www.judicalwatch.org/gardasil, Washington, DC, 2007.

Kapferer, Jean-Noel. *Rumors: Uses, Interpretations, and Images.* New Brunswick, NJ: Transaction Publishers, 1990.

"Key Facts About Pandemic Influenza," *Centers for Disease Control,* 17 Oct. 2005, http://www.cdc.gov/flu/pandemic/keyfacts.htm.

Kilroy, Simon. "MPs Leave Video Nasty Off Agenda." *The Auckland Star,* 9 Oct. 1985.

King, Tracy. "Viral Video Cell-Phone Scare." *The Skeptical Inquirer* 33, no. 5 (2009): 34–35.

Knightley, Phillip. *A Hack's Progress.* London: Vintage Random House, 1998.

_____. Personal communication with Robert Bartholomew, Aug. 2005.

_____. Transcript of an address to the Melbourne Press Club, 23 March 2001, Quill Awards Dinner, Grand Hyatt Hotel, Melbourne, Victoria.

Knowles, Scott Gabriel. "Lessons in the Rubble: The World Trade Center and the History of Disaster Investigations in the United States." *History and Technology* 19, no. 1 (2003): 9–28.

Knox, Ronald A. *Essays in Satire.* New York: E. P. Dutton, 1930.

Koo, J., and C. S. Lee. "Delusions of Parasitosis: A Determologist's Guide to Diagnosis and Treatment." *American Journal of Clinical Dermatology* 2 (2001): 285–290.

Koplow, D. *Smallpox: The Fight to Eradicate a Global Scourge.* Berkeley, CA: University of California Press, 2003.

Kristof, Nicholas D. "When Brad Pitt Gets More Coverage Than Genocide." *New York Times Upfront* 138, no. 2 (19 Sept. 2005): 27.

"KROQ Receives a Slap on the Wrist for Hoax." *Los Angeles Times,* 14 Dec. 1991, p. F7.

Ladendorf, Robert, and Robert E. Bartholomew. "The Mad Gasser of Mattoon: How the Press Created an Imaginary Chemical Weapons Attack." *The Skeptical Inquirer* 26, no. 4 (Jul.-Aug. 2002): 50–54, 58.

Lakshmikumar, S. T. "Power Line Panic and Mobile Mania." *Skeptical Inquirer* 33, no. 5 (2009): 32.

Leaming, Barbara. *Orson Welles: A Biography.* New York: Penguin, 1986.

Leask, J., and P. McIntyre. "Public Opponents to Vaccination: A Case Study." *Vaccine* 21 (2003): 4700–4703.

_____. "Vaccination and Risk Communication: Summary of a Workshop, Arlington Virginia, USA, 5–6 October 2000." *Journal of Paediatrics and Child Health* 38, no. 2 (2002): 124–128.

Leventhal, Todd. "The Child Organ Trafficking Rumor: A Modern 'Urban Legend.'" *U.S. Information Agency Report to the United Nations Special Rapporteur.* Washington, DC: U.S. Information Agency, 1994.

Levine, Justin. "History and Analysis of the Federal Communications Commission's Response to Radio Broadcast Hoaxes." *Federal Communications Law Journal* 52, no. 2 (1999): 274–320.

Lindley, E. K. "Thoughts on the Use of Gas in Warfare." *Newsweek* 22 (20 Dec. 1943): 24.

Lippman, Walter. *Public Opinion*. New York: Harcourt, Brace, 1922.

Littmann, Mark, and Donald K. Yeomans. *Comet Halley: Once in a Lifetime*. Washington, DC: American Chemical Society, 1985.

Loat, M. L. "Some Reasons Why You Should Support the National Anti-Vaccination League (1919)," *Wikipedia, the Free Encyclopedia*, http://en.wikisource.org/wiki/Some_Reasons_Why_You_Should_Support_the_National_Vaccination_League.

MacDonnell, F. *Insidious Foes*. New York: Oxford University Press, 1995.

"'Mad Gasser' Adds Six Victims! 5 Women and Boy Latest Overcome." *The Daily Journal-Gazette*, 9 Sept. 1944, p. 1.

"'Mad Gasser' Case Limited to 4 Suspects." *The Daily Journal-Gazette*, 12 Sept. 1944, p. 1.

Maddux, Mitchell, and Peter Pochna. "Large Candy Purchases Investigated by FBI." *Bergen County Record*, 20 Oct. 2001.

Males, M. "Who's Really Killing Our School Kids?" *Los Angeles Times*, 31 May 1998, p. M1.

Maliszewski, Paul. "Paper Moon." *The Wilson Quarterly* 29, no. 1 (2005): 26–34.

Mansoor, O., D. Sarfati, and G. Durham. "Is Confidence in Immunisation Declining?" *New Zealand Medical Journal* 111, no. 1071 (1998): 300.

Marcus, Sarah. "Panic and Fury Over Fake Television Report on Russian Invasion of Georgia." *The Telegraph*, 15 March 2010.

"Mars Raiders Caused Quito Panic; Mob Burns Radio Plant, Kills 15." *New York Times*, 14 Feb. 1949, pp. 1, 7.

Marshall, J. "We Are Ready with Gas if the Axis Turns on the Gas." *Collier's* 112 (7 Aug. 1943): 21.

Marvin, Scott. "The Halloween Radio Spoof That Shook a Nation." *Parade Magazine* (29 Oct. 1975): 4–5.

"Mattoon Gets Jitters from Gas Attacks." *Chicago Herald-American*, 10 Sept. 1944, p. 1.

"Mattoon's Mad Anesthetist" [Editorial]. *The Daily Journal-Gazette*, 8 Sept. 1944, p. 2.

"Mattoon's Phantom 'Suggestive' Fear." *Chicago Herald-American*, 21 Sept. 1944, p. 2.

McAdam, D. J. "The Menace in the Skies: I. The Case for the Comet." *Harper's Weekly* 54 (14 May 1910): 11–12.

McElhone, James F. "Bite of a Strange Bug." *Washington Post*, 20 June 1899.

"Measles Epidemic: Rising Death Rate." *The Times* [London], 31 March 1922.

"Mexicans Pray, Then Dance." *The New York Times*, 19 Feb. 1910, p. 1.

Mickle, Paul. "1976: Fear of a Great Plague." *The Trentonian*, n.d.

Mikkelson, Barbara. "Utah Evacuees." *Snopes*, 8 Oct. 2005, http://www.snopes.com/katrina/personal/utah.asp.

Milio, James, Melissa Jo Peltier, and Mark Hufnail (producers). *Martian Mania: The True Story of The War of the Worlds* (hosted by James Cameron). The Science Fiction Channel, USA, 30 Oct. 1998.

Miller, David L. *Introduction to Collective Behavior*. Belmont, CA: Wadsworth, 1985.

"Miss Smith's Poisoned Candy." *The Sun* (New York), 28 Dec. 1905, p. 2.

Mitchell, Edward P. "The Story of the Sun." *The Sun*, 3 Sept. 1883, p. 1.

"Mob Kills 15 Over Radio Station, Kills 15 After War Scare." *The Modesto Bee* (Modesto, CA), 14 Feb. 1949, p. 1.

Moore, Patrick, and John Mason. *The Return of Halley's Comet*. New York: W. W. Norton, 1984.

Moore, Toby. "Did You Hear." *The Times* (London), 7 Aug. 2006, Features Section, p. 2.

Morello, Carol. "Baby Theft Panic Cools Guatemalan Tourism, Adoptions." *Albuquerque Journal*, 17 April 1994.

Morgan, Hal, and Kerry Tucker. *Rumor!* New York: Penguin, 1984.

"Move To Have Videos Censored." *New Zealand Herald*, 28 June 1985.

"MP Pleads: Shops Bar Texas Chainsaw." *The 8 O'Clock*, 19 Jan. 1985.

Murch, S. H., A. Anthony, D. H. Casson, et al. "Retraction of an Interpretation." *The Lancet* 363, no. 9411 (2004): 750.

Murdock, Graham. "Figuring Out the Arguments." In *The Video Nasties*, edited by Martin Barker, 64. London: Pluto Press, 1984.

Murray-Aaron, Eugene. "The Kissing Bug Scare." *Scientific American* 81 (22 July 1899): 54.

"Mythical Anti-Nuclear Attack Riles Thousands of Viewers." *The Post* (Frederick, MD), 22 March 1983, p. B14.

Naremore, James. *The Magic World of Orson Welles*. New York: Oxford University Press, 1978.

"Nasty Monsters from Mars Give Radio Listeners Uneasy Moments." *Nebraska State Journal*, 31 Oct. 1938, p. 1.

"Nasty Videos 'like Peddling Drugs.'" *The Auckland Star*, 3 Jan. 1984.

Neary, John. "The Magical McCartney Mystery" *Life*, 7 Nov. 1969, p. 104.

Nelson, M., and J. Rogers. "The Right to Die? Anti-Vaccination Activity and the 1874 Smallpox Epidemic in Stockholm." *Social History of Medicine* 5, no. 3 (1992): 369–388.

New Zealand Chief Film Censor's instructions to Warner Bros Ltd., 28 Aug. 1973. [Copy obtained by the author from the film censor's office].

Newman, Kim. "Kim Newman on Ghostwatch" [Review]. *Mssv*, http://www.mssv.net/realityart/bfinewman.html.

"Newspaper Exposes Radio Hoax." *Editor & Publisher* 124, no. 17 (27 April 1991): 17.

"Night Services in Russia." *The New York Times*, 19 Feb. 1910, p. 1.

"No Gas, Not Even Madman Seen During Night." *The Daily Journal-Gazette*, 15 Sept. 1944, p. 6.

"NOAA Attributes Recent Increase in Hurricane Activity to Naturally Occurring Multi-Decadal Climate Variability." *NOAA Magazine Online*, 29 Nov. 2005, http://www.magazine.noaa.gov/stories/magl84.htm.

Norgaard, Marianne. "Driller Killer ... the Horrible, Boring Truth." *The Auckland Star*, 12 Oct. 1985.

Orent, Wendy. "We'll Survive the Bird Flu, Chicken Little." *The New Republic*, 12 Sept. 2005, http://www.tnr.com/docprint.mhtml?i=20050912&s=orent091205.

"Parisians Feared Comet Would Kill." *The New York Times*, 22 May 1910, p. 3.

Pawlaczyk, Paul. "Officials Debunk One of the Most Disturbing Katrina Stories." *Knight Ridder Tribune* (Washington, DC, Bureau), 11 Nov. 2005.

Pearson, Geoffrey. "Falling Standards: A Short, Sharp History of Moral Decline." In *The Video Nasties*, edited Martin Barker, 88–103. London: Pluto Press, 1984.

Pendergrast, Mark. *Victims of Memory: Incest Accusations and Shattered Lives*. Hinesburg, VT: Upper Access, 1995.

"The 'Perfumed City' Speaks" [Editorial]. *The Daily Journal-Gazette*, 20 Sept. 1944, p. 2.

Pierre, Robert, and Anne Gerhart. "News of Pandemonium May Have Slowed Aid." *The Washington Post*, 5 Oct. 2005, p. A8.

Pitts, M. K., S. Dyson, and D. A. Rosenthal. "Knowledge and Awareness of Human Papillomavirus (HPV): Attitudes Towards HPV Vaccination Among a Representative Sample of Woman in Victoria, Australia." *Sex Health* 4, no. 3 (2007): 177–180.

Plotkin, S., W. Orenstein, and P. Offit. *Vaccines*, 5th edition. St. Louis, MO: Saunders Elsevier, 2008.

"Pocket Monsters' Shocks TV Viewers into Convulsions." *Japan Times*, 17 Dec. 1997.

"Police Chief Says Sprayer Tales Hoax." *Illinois State Journal*, 13 Sept. 1944, p. 1.

"Police Get Two False Alarms During Night." *The Daily Journal-Gazette*, 13 Sept. 1944, p. 1.

Pompilio, Natalie. "Going for the Fake." *American Journalism Review* 22, no. 1 (2000): 29.

"Pope Not Impressed by Halley's Comet." *The New York Times*, 29 May 1910, p. 2.

"Practical Jokes" [Editorial]. *The New York Times*, 10 Nov. 1874, p. 4.

"Probe on as Protests Mark Program That Spread Panic." *Trenton Evening Times*, 31 Oct. 1938, p. 2.

"Psychiatrists Seek Animation Probe." *Yomiuri Shimbun*, 19 Dec. 1997.

"Publicity Boosts Video Nasty." *The Auckland Star*, 23 Oct. 1985.

"Quito Holds 3 for 'Mars' Script." *New York Times*, 16 Feb. 1949, p. 15.

Radford, Benjamin. "Body Part Theft: Truth Vs. Myth." *Bad Science*, 2009, http://www.livescience.com/strangenews/091222-body-part-organ-theft.html.

_____. "Candy Fears Are Mere Halloween Phantoms." *Live Science*, 25 Oct. 2005, http://www.livescience.com/strangenews/051025_halloween_candy.html.

_____. *Media Mythmakers: How Journalists, Activists, and Advertisers Mislead Us*. Buffalo, NY: Prometheus Books, 2003.

_____. "Predator Panic: A Closer Look." In *Science Under Siege: Defending Science, Exposing Pseudoscience*, edited by Kendrick Frazier, 206–212. Amherst, NY: Prometheus Books, 2009.

_____. "Sex Offenders Not a Halloween Scare." *Bad Science*, 2009, http://www.livescience.com/health/091030-sex-offenders-halloween.html.

_____. "Stranger Danger: How Real Is It?" *Skeptical Briefs*, 7 April 2006.

_____. "The Truth About Sensational Kidney Thefts." *Bad Science*, 2008, http://www.livescience.com/health/080219-bad-kidney-theft.html.

"Radio: Boomerang in Ecuador: A Mob Takes Revenge." *The Independent Record* (Sedalia, MO), 20 Feb. 1949.

"Radio Hoax Program Halted Early." *Chronicle-Telegram* (Elyria, OH), 10 Nov. 1982, p. D2.

"Radio 'Invasion' Throws Listeners into Hysteria." *Seattle Post-Intelligencer*, 31 Oct. 1938, pp. 1, 2.

"The Radio Joke That England Took Seriously." *Syracuse Herald*, 23 March 1926.

"Radio Listeners in Panic, Taking War Drama as Fact." *New York Times*, 31 Oct. 1938, p. 1.

"Radio Program Starts Riot; 7 Die." *The Independent* (Long Beach, CA), 14 Feb. 1949, p. 22.

Ragan, Steve. "Malware Then and Now — A Look Back on the Anniversary of the Melissa Virus." *The Tech Herald*, 26 March 2009, http://www.thetechherald.com/article.php/200913/3308/Malware-then-and-now-%E2%80%93-a-look-back-on-the-anniversary-of-the-Melissa-Virus?page=2.

"Realistic Dramatization of 'Invasion' by Men from Mars Causes Panic Through U.S." *Iowa City Press-Citizen*, 31 Oct. 1938, p. 1.

"Receives Poisoned Candy." *Los Angeles Herald*, 27 Dec. 1905, p. 3.

"Relax: You're Not That Tempting." *New Scientist* 174, no. 2345 (1 June 2002): 25.

Richardson, James T. "The Social Construction of Satanism: Understanding an International Social Problem." *Australian Journal of Social Issues* 32, no. 1 (1997): 61–85.

Rickard, Robert. "Whatever Possessed Parkinson?" *The Fortean Times* 67 (1992): 38–41.

_____, and John Michell. *Unexplained Phenomena: A Rough Guide Special*. London: Rough Guides, 2000.

Rosen, Craig. "KSHE, KROQ Hoaxes No Joke to FCC." *Billboard* 103, no. 18 (4 May 1991): 12.

Rosen, Edward, and Johannes Kepler. *Kepler's Somnium; The Dream, or Posthumous Work on Lunar Astronomy*. 1634; Madison: University of Wisconsin Press, 1967.

Rosenberg, Howard. "Reality Bites." *Animal's Agenda* 21, no. 5 (Sept.-Oct. 2001): 35.

Rosenberger, Rob. "*Michelangelo* Fiasco: A Historical Timeline." *VMyths*, 1 June 1992, http://vmyths.com/column/1/1992/6/1/.

Rosenblatt, Susannah, and Jamers Rainey. "Katrina Takes a Toll on Truth, News Accuracy." *The Los Angeles Times*, 27 Sept. 2005.

Rosengren, Karl E., Peter Arvidson, and Dahn Sturesson. "The Barseback 'Panic': A Radio Programme as a Negative Summary Event." *Acta Sociologica* 18, no. 4 (1975): 303–321.

Rosnow, Ralph L., and Gary Allen Fine. *Rumor and Gossip*. New York: Elsevier, 1976.

Ross, Sean, Craig Rosen, and Phyllis Stark. "Postwar Arbs Show N/T Stations in Retreat; Hoax Costs KROQ Jocks." *Billboard* 103, no. 21 (25 May 1991): 10.

"Rush to Alpine Heights." *The New York Times*, 19 Feb. 1910, p. 1.

"Safety Agent to Aid Police in 'Gas' Case." *The Daily Journal-Gazette*, 6 Sept. 1944, p. 6.

Sagan, Carl, and Ann Druyan. *Comet*. New York: Random House, 1985.

Sanders, V. "Our Army's Defense Against Poison Gas." *Popular Science* 146 (Feb. 1945): 106–111.

"Satanic Breeders." *Geraldo*. Journal Graphics Transcripts, 24 Oct. 1998.

"A Satanic Cult Survivor." *Larry King Live*. Journal Graphics Transcripts, 2 Aug. 1991.

Savely, Virginia R., Mary M. Leitao, and Raphael B. Stricker. "The Mystery of Morgellons Disease: Infection or Delusion?" *American Journal of Clinical Dermatology* 7, no. 1 (2006): 1–5.

"Scare Is Nation-Wide." *New York Times*, 31 Oct. 1938, p. 4.

Schmemann, Serge. "Soviet Furor Mounts Over Reagan's Bombing Quip." *The New York Times*, 16 Aug. 1984, p. A5.

Schlatter, Thomas. "Weather Queries." *Weatherwise* (Nov.-Dec. 2000): 36–39.

_____. "Weather Queries." *Weatherwise* (Sept.-Oct. 2002): 52–54.

Schmidt, Charles, and Tom Darby. *The What, Why, and How of the 1988 Internet Worm*. July 2001, http://www.snowplow.org/tom/worm/worm.html.

Schultz, Duane P. *Panic Behavior*. New York: Random House, 1964.

Schwartz, Marylyn. "All Fun Gone in Halloween." *Dallas Morning News*, 30 Oct. 1976, p. A1.

Scott, E. W. "Role of the Public Health Laboratory in Gas Defense." *American Journal of Public Health* 34 (March 1944): 275–278.

"Sex in the Name of Satan." *Larry King Live*. Journal Graphics Transcripts, 13 May 1991.
"Shark Attack Fatalities Compared to Hunting Incident Fatalities in the U.S. and Canada: 2000–2004." *International Shark Attack File*, Florida Museum of Natural History, University of Florida, http://www.flmnh.ufl.edu/fish/sharks/attacks/relariskhunting.htm.
Sharpe, Martin. "The Curse of the Crying Boy: Picture Is a Fire Jinx." *The Sun*, 4 Sept. 1985, p. 13.
"Sheriff's Dept. Bills KROC $12,000 for Hoax." *Los Angeles Times*, 1 May 1991, p. F2.
"Show How They Were Gassed." *Chicago Herald-American*, 10 Sept. 1944, p. 10.
Siano, Brian. "All the Babies You Can Eat." *The Humanist* 53, no. 2 (1993): 40–41.
"Sidelights of 'Mad Gasser's' Strange Case." *The Daily Journal-Gazette*, 12 Sept. 1944, p. 4.
Sidey, Ken. "Publisher Withdraws Satanism Story." *Christianity Today* 34, no. 3 (29 Feb. 1990): 34–35.
Siegel, Marc K. "Afraid of the Bird Flu? The Worse Virus Is Fear." *Fortune* 152, no. 11 (2005): 61.
Siegel, Robert. "Georgia 'Invasion' Report Stirs Panic." *All Things Considered*. National Public Radio, 15 March 2010.
Sifakis, Carl. *Hoaxes and Scams: A Compendium of Deceptions, Ruses and Swindles*. New York: Facts on File, 1993.
Simons, D., and W. R. Silveira. "Post-Traumatic Stress Disorder in Children after Television Programmes." *British Medical Journal* 308, no. 6925 (1994): 389–390.
Slemen, Tim. *Haunted Liverpool*. Liverpool: Bluecoat Press, 2000.
Smith, Ian K. "Cell Phone Scare." *Time*, 1 Nov. 1999, p. 8.
Smith, Lucinda. "Parents, Cops Quell False Rumors of 'Killer Clowns.'" *Montclair Times*, 6 June 1991. Cited in Jan. Harold Brunvand, *The Encyclopedia of Urban Legends*, 313–315. New York: Norton, 2001.
Snyder, J. "Cartoon Sickens Children." *Reuters News Agency*, 17 Dec. 1997.
———. "'Monster' TV Cartoon Illness Mystifies Japan." *Reuters News Agency*, 17 Dec. 1997.
Solomon, Alan. "A Brief History of PC Viruses." *Computer Knowledge*, 8 May 2009, http://www.cknow.com/cms/vtutor/dr-solomon-history.html.
Sottas, Eric. *Trade in Organs and Torture*. Presentation for Eurosciences Media Workshop. Geneva, Switzerland, World Organization Against Torture, 1994.
"Southern Negroes in a Comet Frenzy." *The New York Times*, 19 Feb. 1910, p. 1.
"Spray Deodorant Killed Boy." *Adirondack Daily Enterprise*, 6 Nov. 1975, p. 2.
Stardom, Brenda (pseud.). "Portuguese Teen Soap Cause for Real-life Virus Hysteria." *The BS Report*, 19 June 2006, http://www.wayodd.com/teens-suffer-from-soap-opera-virus/v/2838/.
"Statistics on Attacking Species of Shark," *International Shark Attack File*, Florida Museum of Natural History, University of Florida, http://www.flmnh.ufl.edu/fish/sharks/statistics/species2.htm.
Strayner, David, and Frank A. Drews. *Effects of Cell Phone Conversations on Younger and Older Drivers*. Salt Lake City: University of Utah, 2004, http://www.psych.utah.edu/AppliedCognitionLab/Aging.pdf.
"Study Terror in Mattoon." *Chicago Herald-American*, 18 Sept. 1944, p. 1.
Sullivan, Jim. "Radio Hoaxes Stung Bosses into Action." *Sunday Star-Times*, 28 March 1999, p. A13.
Symantec. *Wscript.KakWorm*. 13 Feb. 2007, http://www.symantec.com/security_response/writeup.jsp?docid=2000-121908-3951-99.
Szymanski, Greg. "Avian Flu May Come to America." *The American Free Press* 41 (10 Oct. 2005), http://www.americanfreepress.net/html/avian_flu.html.
Taylor, Jerry. "Police Discount Reports of Clowns Bothering Kids." *The Boston Globe*, 9 May 1981, p. 18.
"Teens Suffer Soap Opera Virus." *Reuters News Agency*, 25 May 2006, http://go.reuters.com/newsArticle.jhtml?type=oddlyEnoughNews&storyID=12254563&src=rss/oddlyEnoughNews.
Thevenot, Brian. "Myth-Making in New Orleans." *American Journalism Review* 27, no. 6 (2005/2006): 30–37.
"They Told Me I Have the Devil Inside Me." *The Sally Jessie Raphael Show*. Journal Graphics Transcripts, 14 July 1992.
Thio, Alex. *Sociology: An Introduction*. New York: Harper & Row, 1986.
Thomas, William. "Stolen Skies: The Chemtrail Mystery." *Earth Island Journal* 34–35 (Summer 2002).
"Those Men from Mars." *Newsweek* (27 Nov. 1944): 89.

"Titus Has Them Rolling in Aisle." *The Age* (Melbourne, Australia), 25 Oct. 1955.

"To All Citizens of Mattoon." *The Daily Journal-Gazette*, 11 Sept. 1944, p. 1.

Tobimatsu, S., Y.M. Zhang, Y. Tomoda, A. Mitsudome, and M. Kato. "Chromatic Sensitive Epilepsy: A Variant of Photosensitive Epilepsy." *Annals of Neurology* 45, no. 6 (1999): 790.

Tomlinson, Ray. *The First Network Email*, n.d., http://openmap.bbn.com/~tomlinso/ray/firstemailframe.html.

"Too-Real Radio Drama Gives Nation a Bad Case of War Jitters." *The Clearfield Progress* (Clearfield, PA), 3 Nov. 1938, p. 2.

Tovar, Enrique. "The Martians Cause Panic." *La Nación*, 3 March 1996.

Tucker, George. *A Voyage to the Moon: With Some Account of the Manners and Customs, Science and Philosophy, of the People of Morosofia, and Other Lunarians*. New York: E. Bliss, 1827.

"TV Movie on Asteroid Crash Causes Real Fear in Viewers." *Daily Herald* (Chicago, IL), 31 Oct. 1994, pp. 1, 6.

"Two Officials Indicted." *Times of London*, 15 Feb. 1949, p. 4.

"Two Women Believed Victims Examined at Hospital." *The Daily Journal-Gazette*, 11 Sept. 1944, p. 1.

Valentine, A., S. E. Davies, and J. A. Walker-Smith. "Ileal-Lymphoid-Nodular Hyperplasia, Non-Specific Colitis, snd Pervasive Developmental Disorder in Children." *The Lancet* 315, no. 9103 (1998): 637–641.

_____. "Retraction — 'Ileal-lymphoid-nodular Hyperplasia, Non-specific Colitis, and Pervasive Developmental Disorder in Children.'" *The Lancet*. 375, no. 9713 (2010): 445.

Victor, Jeffrey S. "Satanic Cult's Ritual Abuse of Children: Horror or Hoax?" *USA Today Magazine* 122, no. 2582 (1993).

"Video Decision Is Disputed." *New Zealand Herald*, 4 Oct. 1985.

"Video Nasties: Loose in Your Living Room?" *Grapevine*, Aug. 1985, pp. 10–17.

"Videotapes to be Classified and Labelled." *New Zealand Herald*, 13 Dec. 1985.

"'Violence' Videotape Will Be Investigated." *The Auckland Star*, 24 June 1985.

"Violent Video Seen as Prod." *New Zealand Herald*, 23 June 1985.

"Violent Videos on Agenda." *New Zealand Herald*, 18 June 1985.

Vogel, Gretchen. "Asteroid Scare Provokes Soul-Searching." *Science* 279, no. 5358 (1998).

Volk, Stephen. "Faking It: Ghostwatch." *Fortean Times* 166 (Jan. 2003).

Wakefield, A. J., S. H. Murch, A. Anthony, et al. (1998). "Ileal-Lymphoid-Nodular Hyperplasia, Non-Specific Colitis, and Pervasive Developmental Disorder in Children." *The Lancet* 351, no. 9103 (1998): 637–641.

Wallechinsky, Davis, and Irving Wallace, eds. *The People's Almanac*. Garden City, NY: Doubleday, 1975.

"War of the Worlds Revisited — Almost." *The Chronicle-Telegram* (Elyria, OH), 31 Oct. 1994, p. A3.

Watson, Ivan. "Fake Russian Invasion Broadcast Sparks Georgian Panic." *CNN News*, 14 March 2010, http://www.cnn.com/2010/WORLD/europe/03/14/georgia.invasion.scare/index.html.

"WDAF Gets Calls on 'Special Bulletin.'" *Chillico Constitution Tribune* (Chillico, MO), 21 March 1983, p. 4.

"Weird Tales of Kissing Bug." *Chicago Daily Tribune*, 11 July 1899, p. 2.

Welch, Matt. "They Shoot Helicopters, Don't They? How Journalist Spread Rumors During Katrina." *Reason* 37, no. 7 (Dec. 2005):16–18.

Welles, Orson. *The War of the Worlds*. Uncut original broadcast, 30 Oct. 1938. Metacom Incorporated, 1938.

_____, Peter Bogdanovich, and Jonathan Rosenbaum. *This Is Orson Welles*. New York: HarperCollins, 1992.

Wensing, M. "Evidence-Based Patient Empowerment." *Quality and Safety in Health Care* 9, no. 4 (2000): 200–201.

"What Radio Cannot Do." *St. Louis Post-Dispatch*, 1 Nov. 1938, p. 20.

"When You Say That, Smile." *The Commonweal* 49, no. 20 (1949): 483–484.

Whitehorn, Katharine. "Child Video Menu Hard to Swallow." *New Zealand Herald*, 5 Jan. 1984.

"Wife's Testimony Part of Poison Candy Case." *Dallas Morning News*, 14 Dec. 1974, p. A17.

Williams, Juan. "Analysis: Human Perception of Sharks." *Talk of the Nation*. National Public Radio, 15 Aug. 2001.

Wolak, J., D. Finkelhor, and K. J. Mitchellm. "Online 'Predators' and Their Victims: Myths, Realities, and Implications for Prevention and Treatment." *Crimes against*

Children Center at the University of New Hampshire. *American Psychologist* 63, no. 2 (2008).

"Wolf, Wolf." *Newsweek* 33, no. 8 (21 Feb. 1949): 44.

Wolfe, R. M., and L. K. Sharp. "Anti-Vaccinationists Past and Present." *British Medical Journal* 325, no. 7361 (2002): 430–432.

"Women Faint as Lights Go Out at Concrete." *Seattle Post-Intelligencer*, 31 Oct. 1938, p. 1.

"Worried TV Viewers Call During Drama." *Syracuse Herald-Journal*, 31 Oct. 1994, p. C4.

Yamashita, Y., T. Matsuishi, S. Ishida, T. Nishimi, and H. Kato. "Pocket Monsters Attacks Japanese Children Via Media." *Annals of Neurology* 44, no. 3 (1998): 428.

Index

ABC 20/20 9
accidental falls 177
Acosta, Jim 170
airplaning 18
Albany, New York 164
Alexander the Great 68
alligator attacks 180
Almeida, Mario 46
Altamira, Brazil 194
Alvarado, Charlie 193–94
"Amadio, Bruno" 138, 143
American Folklore Society 123
American "Kissing Bug" Scare (1899) 47–48
Amirault, Gerald 107
Amirault, Violet 107
Amiss, Dennis 72
Anastos, Ernie 40
Anderson, Hyland 85
Andrews, Nigel 70
angels 147–48, 153, 205
Angels of Mons 153
Anti-Vaccination League 199, 210–11
Arbogast, Jessie 179
Armitage, William 142
Arnold, Matthew 53
Asian Flu of 1957-58 60
Associated Press 24, 39, 41, 54, 97, 148,
Auckland, New Zealand (wasp hoax, 1949) 29
Austrian spider scare 46–47
autism and vaccination 201–2, 211
automobile accident 177

Bainbridge, William 19
Banks, John 71
Barbanell, Mauice 149
Barcelona, Spain 144
Barretto, Mario 193

Barseback Nuclear Panic (Sweden) 30–31
Bat-men on the Moon Hoax (1835) 1, 5, 79–83
Bates, Paul 68
Baxter, Gene "the Bean" 28
Bell, Art 113
Benchley, Peter 181
Bennett, Gordon 84
Bermuda 6, 90
Berry, Justin 171
Best, Joel 164
bicycle fatalities 180
Bird Flu Scare 1, 4, 10, 59–63
Blair, Mike 114
Blanco, Kathleen 55
Bock, Philip 76
Boland, Andrea 190
Bonillo, Don 143–44
The Boogie Man 70, 169
Boston, Massachusetts 6, 105–8, 126
Boston Globe 108
Bottcher, Denise 55
Boyes, Georgina 139
Bragolin, Giovanni 138, 144
Brandt, Albert 150
British Broadcasting Corporation 1, 3, 10, 13–15, 49, 52
British General Strike (1926) 13
British Medical Journal 4, 50
Brockley, Eddie 144–45
Brockley, Marian 144–45
Bromley, David 159, 161
bronchitis 210
Brookline, Massachusetts 105
Brown, Earl 62
Brown, Frederic 97
Brown, Mrs. Olive 94
Brunvand, Jan 107–8, 131
Bugs Bunny 52, 106, 160

Bull Shark 179–80
Burgess, George 180
The Burning 70
Bush, Edward 54
Butcher, Dr. Gary 62

Cable News Network (CNN) 21, 53, 55, 188
Camp Gruber refuge 122
Campbell, Terence 160
Campbell's Soup 21
cancer 177
Cannibal Apocalypse 68
Cannibal Ferox 68
Cannibal Holocaust 68, 70
Cannibal Man 68
Criminal Minds 67
Cannibal Terror 68
Canovanas, Puerto Rico 183
Cantlon, Caroline 17
Cantril, Hadley 19–20
Cape Town, South Africa 80
Capuzzo, Michael 180
Carlo, George 9, 187–89
Carroll, Sandra 165
Casablanca 16
CBS Evening News 8, 170
Cedar Rapids, Iowa 96
cell phone brain cancer scare 187–88
Cell Phone Panic 187–88
Cell Phones: Invisible Hazards in the Wireless Age 187
Central do Brasil (*Central Station*) 192
Central Park Zoo Hoax 5, 84–86
Chagas disease 48
Champaign, Illinois 97
Charles, Craig 50–51
Charleston, South Carolina 37–39
Cherry, Bob 142
Chicago, Illinois 19, 38, 48, 86, 94, 97
Chicago Daily News 94
Chicago Daily Tribune 94
Chicago Herald-American 93–97
Chicago Iroquois Theater Fire 186
Chicago Sun-Times 132
Chicago Times 86
Chicago Tribune 20, 164
China Post 102
Chippindale, Peter 136, 140
Chodas, Paul 42
Christchurch, New Zealand 47
Chronic Fatigue Syndrome 118
El chupacabra 182–186
Circus of Horrors 75
Clarke, Arthur C. 40
Clarke, David 7–8, 134–154

Clarke, J.I.C. 85
Close to Shore 180
Close-Up 208
Cole, C.E. 96
Coleman, Loren 106, 108–9
Colin, Matthew 65–66
Collier, Paul 137
Colombian Office of Human Rights 194
Columbia Broadcasting System 18
Columbus, Ohio 38
Coma 192
Compass, Eddie 54
Conan Doyle, Arthur 151
Concrete, Washington (radio panic) 17
Connery, T.B. 85
Cooperative Vitalicia Network 23
Cordes, Mr. Beula 94
Corrales, Scott 182–83
Correio Braziliense 194
Cotocollao, Ecuador 25
cowpox 198–99
Cox, Ted 41
Crestwood, Missouri 3, 32
Crimes Against Children Research Center 173
Cross, Dan 71–72
Crying Boy "Curse" 8, 134–145
Cumberbatch, Guy 68
cutaneous dysaesthesia 117
cyanogen gas 87–90

Daily Journal-Gazette 93–97
Daily Mirror 136, 140, 152, 154
Dallas, Texas 29
Darfur, Sudan 177
Dateline NBC 9, 170
Davis, Barry 141
Day, Benjamin 79–80, 83
de Bergerac, Cyrano 80
Decatur Daily Republican 86
Decatur Herald 96
Deep Throat 70
del Toro, Guillermo 192
Denham, Martin 51
Denver, Colorado 89
Department of Justice 173
Devon, England 143
Dexter 67
Dickinson, Terence 3
disc-jockey hoaxes 27–29
Discovery Channel 180
Donaldson, Sir Liam 62
Donaldson, Teresa 69
Don't Go in the Woods Alone 70
Don't Go Near the Park 70
Driller Killer 71–73

Earle, Gordon 114
Early, Pam 49
East, Paul 69
East Herringthorpe, England 139
Ebola disease 62
Edgar Bergen and Charlie McCarthy Show 18
Edinburg Courant 80
Edinburgh Journal of Science 80
Edwards, Lt. Colonel John 55
"Effort Syndrome" 118
Eichenwald, Kurt 171
Ellis, Bill 7, 123–128
Enter the Dragon 68
Epstein-Barr Virus 118
erysipelas 210
Espanola, Canada 114
El Espinazo del Diablo (*The Devil's Backbone*) 192–193
Everard, Arthur 69, 71
The Evil Dead 70
The Exterminator 69

fairies 99, 148, 169
Farrington, Rose 137
Fatal Contact: Bird Flu in America 59
Fate Magazine 149–150
Federal Communications Commission 2, 3, 19, 28, 33
Felling, Matthew 57
Fells Acres Day Care Center, Massachusetts 107
Fenner, Jerry 57
Fernicola, Richard 180
Finch, Jack 99
Fitness Life Magazine 208
Fitzpatrick, Thomas 28
Flammarion, Camille 87–88
Fleet Street 98, 136, 138, 142
Florida Museum of Natural History 180
Food and Drug Administration 165
Forsythe, Dennis 27
Fort Dix, New Jersey 60
Fort Wayne Sentinel 86
France 40, 90, 153
France, David 171
Frankel, Bernard 119
Fresno Bee 164
Fumento, Michael 60–61
Furedi, Frank 62

Galveston Daily News 85
Gardasil 206, 208–9
Gates, Bill 197
Gautier, M. Armand 87
General Medical Council 201

Georgia (former Soviet Republic) 4, 64–66
Geraldo Rivera 158
Germany 90, 193
Ghostwatch 3, 49–52
Gibb, Russ 132
Gilbert, Debbie 118
Gisborne Herald News 210
Godber, Kevin 139–140
Godstein, Steven 146
Gonzales, Domingo 79
Gonzales, Julia 185
Gonzales, Julio 185
Gonzales, Oralis 185
Goodwin, Francis 79
Goodyear-Smith, Felicity 197–211
Gori, Georgia 65
Granados, Manuel Diaz 25
Grand Guignol theatre 70, 75
Granfield, Robert 55–56
Grapevine 69
great white shark 180
Green, Sarah 50–51
Gropen, Arthur 27
groupthink 183
Grovers Mill, New Jersey 16, 18–19
Gruber, Dieter 47
Guatemala 195
Gulf War Syndrome 118

A Hack's Progress 98
Hailey's Comet Scare 5, 87–91
Hall, May 135
Hall, Peter 136
Hall, Ron 135
Hamy, Maurice 88
Handwerk, Brian 58
Hansen, Chris 170
Harper's Weekly 88
Harrisburg, Pennsylvania 39
Harrison, Kristen 142
The Harvest 192
Harvest House Publishers 159
Hassall, Peter 4, 67–76
Hatherley, Bob 142
Haunted Liverpool 143
Herring, Sen. Clyde (Iowa) 19
Herschel, Sir John 5, 80–81, 83
Hill, Clifford 68
Hill, Sandy 40
Hiss, Dr. Jehuda 196
Hitchcock, Alfred 70
Hitler, Adolf 79
hoaxes: BBC *Ghostwatch* scare 3, 49–52; BBC radio hoax 13–15; disc-jockey hoaxes 2, 27–29; great moon hoax 5, 79–

83; New York Zoo scare 5, 84–86; nuclear disaster scares 2–3, 30–33
Hogg, Lionel 99
Hong Kong Flu of 1968–69 60
Hong Kong Standard 102
"The Hook" 6, 98–100
Hooper, C.E. 18
Hooper, Paul 141
Hopkins, Anthony 76
Hora Clave 193
Horiuchi, Gerald 164
Horrie, Chris 136, 140
Houston, Texas 121
Howard, Leland 48
Hubbard, Frank McKinney 91
human papillomavirus (HPV) 206
hunting accidents 180
Huntsman, Jon 121
Hurricane Katrina 1, 4, 7, 10, 53–58, 120–122; myths 4, 53–58, 120–122

I Spit on Your Grave 70
Iggleden, Ray 99
Illinois Bureau of Criminal Identification and Investigation 94
Illinois State Journal 97
International Society for Contemporary Legend Research 123
Italy 90

James, M.R. 135
Japan 3, 6, 10, 21, 38, 44–46, 90, 195
Jaws 52, 181
Jeison, Weinis 194
Jenner, Edward 198–99
Jensen, Derek 121
Jesty, Benjamin 198
Johnson, M. Kim 115–116
Jones, Chuck 31
Jordan, Eddie 55
Jory, Tom 39
Journal of Commerce 5, 82
Journal of the American Medical Association 188
Juarez, Mexico 194
Jung, Carl 153

Kansas City, Missouri 38–39, 106
Kansas City Star 106
Kapiti Observer 211
Kaske, Sandra 137
Keelung, Taipei 101, 103
Kensit, Robert 51
Kilburn, North Yorkshire 137
Killer Klowns from Outer Space 7, 107
King, Stephen 107
King Edward VII 90

King Tutankhamen 134
Knightley, Philip 6, 98–100
Knox, Father Ronald 2, 13–14
Koc, Ahmet 195
Koch, Howard 16, 21
Koopu, Areta 72
Kramer, Keith 29
Kruger, Peter 70–74
Kyushu Island, Japan 45

Ladendorf, Robert 94
LaFave, Cheryl 107
Lance, Peter 40
The Lancet 201–2
Landers, Ann 163
Landrieu, Mary 54
Larry King Live 158, 171, 188
Larson, Melissa 195
Last House on the Left 70
Latacunga, Ecuador 24
Law, Ron 204
Law and Order 192
Lee, Bruce 68
Leitao, Mary 117
Leningor, Georgia 65
Leno, Jay 49
Leventhal, Todd 193
Levine, Justin 20
Lewis, David 60
Lexington, Kentucky 89
lightning 9, 176–77, 180
Linz, Austria 46
Lippman, Walter 26
Little Rascals Preschool Panic 107
Loch Ness Monster 148
Locke, Richard Adams 5, 79–82
Loftus, Elizabeth 160
Logo, Tony 29
London, England 1, 13–15, 17, 23, 76, 90, 95, 137, 141, 149, 151–54, 195–96
London Anarchy Hoax of 1926 13–15
Los Angeles County Sheriff's Department 28
Los Angeles Times 28, 55, 164
Lovelace, Linda 70
Lucas, William 39
Lyme Disease 118

MacKenzie, Kelvin 136, 138, 140–142
Madrid, Spain 90, 143,
Malden, Massachusetts 107
Maliszewski, Paul 83
Mallory, George 143–44
The Man in the Moone 79
Manhattan, New York 16–17
Mann, Dora 137
Marburg Virus 62

Marchand, B.M. 88
Marcus, Sarah 65
Marian apparitions 148
Marisal Sucre Air Base, Chile 24
Marsden, Brian 42–43
Marshall, Benjamin 86
Martian invasion scares: Chilean panic (1944) 2, 23; Ecuador panic (1949) 2, 24–26; United States and Canada (1938) 2, 15–22, 41
Martin, Henry 86
Martin, Jorge 183–84
Mattoon, Illinois 6, 92–97
McAdam, D.J. 88–89
McCartney, Paul 132–33
McClarence, Stephen 140
McCraw, Steve 174
McElhone, James F. 48
McKinley, Clayton 164
McMartin Preschool Panic 107
Medvedev, Dmitry 64
Megan's Laws 174
Mein Kampf 79
Mendoza, Perez 195
meningitis vaccine scare, New Zealand 201–204
Mercury Theatre of the Air 16, 18
Méténier, Oscar 75
The Mezzotint 135
Michelle Remembers 158
Mickle, Paul 60
Mikkelson, Barbara 121–22
Miller, David 19–20
Milwaukee, Wisconsin 39
Minneapolis, Minnesota 41
Minnis, Patrick 114–15
Miocene Age 180
Mitcham, Surrey 139
MMR vaccine (measles, mumps, rubella) 200–2, 210
Molotov Theatre group 75
Montclair Times 106
Moore, Sandra Jane 141
Morgellons 7, 117–119
Moriarty, Tom 29
Morley, Trevor 69
The Morning Oregonian 85
Morton, Paul 20
Most Haunted 144
murder 176, 177
Murphy, Dr. Tracy 59
Mysterious America 106

Nagin, Mayor Ray 54
National Aeronautics and Space Administration (NASA) 42–43, 114

National Anti-Compulsory Vaccinator Reporter 199
National Center for Missing and Exploited Children 173, 175
National Enquirer 154, 184
National Oceanic and Atmospheric Administration (NOAA) 58
Nelmes, Sarah 198
Neisseria meningitidis 202
New Orleans, Louisiana 4, 53–58
New Orleans Superdome 4, 53–55, 56
New York (magazine) 171
New York City 5, 16, 18–19, 21, 38, 84, 89
New York Herald 5, 84
New York Sun 5, 79, 80, 82–83
New York Times 2, 5, 9, 14, 17, 25, 55, 82, 84–85, 87, 127, 164, 171
New Zealand Herald 210
New Zealand Meningococcal Scare 202–6
New Zealand Ministry of Health 203
New Zealand Press Association 203–4
Newark, New Jersey 2, 17, 108, 165
Newark Star-Ledger 108
Newsweek 164
Night of the Bloody Apes 70
Nightmares in a Damaged Brain 70
Niman, Dr. Henry 61
Niños de Repuesto ("Spare-Parts Children") 194
Noory, George 113
Norgaard, Marianne 71
Normandy, invasion 97
North, Julian 151
Northern Advocate News 210
Northern Star 132
Northolt, Middlesex, England 49
Norwegian Institute of Public Health 205
El Nuevo Dia 183

Oamaru, New Zealand 204
Obama, Barack 4, 64
O'Bryan, Ronald Clark 163
O'Bryan, Timothy 163–64
ocean whitetip shark 180
O'Connell, Daniel 105
Okhadze, Tamuna 65
Olivier, Sir Lawrence 76
Olney, Warren 40
Oprah Winfrey Show 49, 54, 158
Orent, Wendy 61–62
Organ Snatchers 9, 193–94
Organization Against Torture 194

Paez, Leonardo 25
Paignton, England,
Paradise, Mrs. Eaton 96

Paris, France 75
Paris Observatory 88
Parkinson, Michael 49–52
Parks, Brian 137
Patriarch Ilia II 65
"Paul McCartney Is Dead" scare 132–33
Pawlaczyk, George 56
Pazder, Dr. Lawrence 158
Pearl Harbor attack (1941) 21
Pearson, Geoffrey 74–75
Pelagic Shark Research Foundation 180
Penn State University 123
Pensacola, Florida 179
Perez, Helen 167
Perry, Kevin 163
Persian Gulf War (1991) 32
Petousis-Harris, Helen 10, 197, 208
phantom clowns 6–7, 105–9
Phelps, William 98
Philadelphia Academy of Natural Sciences 48
Phillips, Mark 148
Phipps, James 198
Phoenix, Arizona 28–29
Pickrell, Jacquie 160
The Picture of Dorian Gray 135
Piehler, Chris 57
Pikachu 44–46
Piper, Richard 94
Plague 61
The Plainfield Times 86
Pokémon panic 3, 44–46
Pope Pius X 90
Port Norris station, New Jersey 17
Portland, Oregon 38
post–traumatic stress disorder 4, 49–50
The Press 211
Preston, England 137
Princeton, New Jersey 16–17, 19, 21
Princeton University 17, 19, 21
Proctor, Richard 88–89
Providence, Rhode Island 29
Psychic News 149, 151
Puente Alto, Chile 23
Puerto Rico 90, 182–85
Putin, Vladimir 64–65
pyaemia 210

Queen Victoria 134
The Queens Players 75

Radford, Benjamin 115, 147, 184
Raef, Mr. and Mrs. Orban 93
Raimi, Sam 70
Raquello, Ramon 18
Reagan, Ronald (nuclear attack scare) 3, 32

"Red Scare" 98
Redlener, Dr. Irwin 61
Reggi, Pedro 193–94
Rense, Jeff 113
Reynard, Larry 188
Rickard, Bob 148–49, 151
Rider, Mrs. George 93
Riley, Mick 141
Ripley, Derbyshire 138
Roberts, Doug "the slug" 28
Rochester, New York 150
Rosengren, Karl 31
Rotherham, England 135–36, 138–9
Rotorua, New Zealand 69
Russell, Gordon 55
Russia 4, 64–66
Russian Revolution of 1917 13
Ryder, Kevin 28

Saakashvili, Mikheil 65
St. Louis, Missouri 17, 19, 38–39
St. Louis Cardinals 33
St. Petersburg Times 53
Salem witch hysteria 96, 98, 161
Salles, Walter 192
Sally Jessy Raphael 158
Salt Lake City, Utah 121
San Antonio, Texas 121, 178
San Diego, California 29
San Francisco, California 38
San Juan, Puerto Rico 90, 182–83
San Pedro Sula, Honduras 108
Santa Lucia Cotzumalguapa 195
Santayana, George 1
Santiago, Chile 23–24
SARS disease 174
Satanic cult scare 8, 98, 157–161
Satan's Underground 159
Schlatter, Thomas 114
Scream Team 144–45
scrofula 210
Seattle, Washington 17, 38, 150–51
Seville, Franchot 138, 143–44
sexual assaults 72
The Shadow (radio show) 23
Shakespeare, William 71, 76
Sheffield Hallam University 134, 146
Sheffield Star 140
"shell shock" 118
Shone, Phil 29
Siegel, Dr. Marc 62–63
Slemen, Tom 143–44
small pox 198, 199, 210
Smith, Elsie 164
Smith, Frances 95
Smith, Dr. Ian K. 187

Smith, Lucinda 106
Smith, Maxine 95
Smith, Michelle 158–159
Smulyan, Jeff 29
Snopes.com 120
Snuff 70
"Soldier's Heart" 118
Somnium (The Dream) 79
Sottas, Eric 194
South Africa 5, 80–81, 90
South Carolina 3, 37, 117,
South Yorkshire 8, 134–135, 139
Spanish Flu Pandemic of 1918–19 4, 59–61
Spears, Britney 29
Special Bulletin (nuclear scare) 37, 39
Spiegel TV 193
"spirit photography" 146, 148, 152
Springfield, Illinois 31, 95, 97
Springfield nuclear hoax 31–32
Stanton, Bill 171–172
Steele, William 23
Stephens, Jack 56
Stewart, Martha 177
Stick It Up Your Punter! 136, 141
Stone, Tom 56
"Strawberries with Sugar Virus" 46
Sunday People 150, 152–53
Swanson, Karin 150
Swanson, Mildred 150–51
Switzerland 90
Sydney Morning Herald 99
syphilis 210
Syracuse, New York 15, 41

Taipei, Taiwan 6, 101–4
Taymor, Julie 76
Tegucigalpa, Honduras 108
Tel Aviv, Israel 196
The Texas Chainsaw Massacre 69–70
Thevenot, Brian 55–56
Three Mile Island 39
Thrillpeddlars (theatre group) 75
tiger shark 80
Timberlake, Justin 29
Time (magazine) 180–187
Times-Picayune 55
Titus Andronicus 76
To Catch a Predator 9, 170
Tobimatsu, Dr. S. 46
Today Show 171–73
Tolentino, Madelyne 182–83
Tool Box Murders 70
Totson, Kevin 164
Towaco, New Jersey 89
Toyohashi, Japan 45
Trenton, New Jersey 2, 20

Truth (Sydney, Australia) 98
Tucker, George 80
Tucson, Arizona 2, 27
Twelve Days of Terror 180

Ulett, Don 3, 32–33
U.S. Bureau of Justice Statistics 174
United States Information Agency (USIA) 193
University of Chicago 87
University of Dijon 88
University of Sheffield 134
Unsolved Mysteries 28, 106
Urbana, Illinois 95

Vampire Holocaust 68
Vancouver, British Columbia 151
The Vanishing Hitchhiker 131
Vanocur, Sandor 40–41
Van Sommeran, Sean 10
Vargas, Mrs. Luz Dary 194
Velasquez, Edwin 184
Vespertilio-homo (Bat-men) 5, 81
Vickery, Roy 139
Victor, Jeffrey 161
The Victorian 151
Video Recordings Act 73–74
Vienna, Austria 47
Violet, Louisiana 56
El Vocero 184–185
Volk, Stephen 50–51
A Voyage to the Moon 80

WABC Radio 16–17
Wakefield, Andrew 201
Walker, Bree 40
The War of the Worlds 2, 10, 16, 18, 22–23, 41
Warner Brothers 68, 160
Washington, D.C. 21, 48
Washington and Jefferson College 88
Washington Post 5, 48, 55, 87–88
Webster, Rachael 42
Weinstock, June 195
Welch, Denis 47
Welles, Orson 2, 15, 16–24, 31, 41
Wells, H.G. (Herbert George) 16–18, 23–24
West Orange, New Jersey 108
Western Morning News 142
Weston-super-Mare 142
White, Steve 29
White-Tail Spider Scare (New Zealand) 47
Wigan, Lancashire 144
Wilde, Oscar 135
Wilkes-Barre, Pennsylvania 89
Wilkinson, Alan 136, 138, 141

Winkler, Louis 21
Winn, Godfrey 152
Winnipeg, Canada 151
Without Warning (asteroid scare) 3, 40, 42
Wolak, Janis 173
Women Against Pornography 70
Women's Division of Federated Farmers 69
Woods, Poynter's 58
World Health Organization 202

Yamashita, Dr. Yushiro 45
Yeomans, Donald 42–43
Yerkes Observatory 87–88
YouTube 9, 187–89

Zenteno, Paul 23
Zinkeisen, Anna 138, 144
Zombie Flesh Eaters 70
Zombies from Beyond Space 68

www.ingramcontent.com/pod-product-compliance
Ingram Content Group UK Ltd.
Pitfield, Milton Keynes, MK11 3LW, UK
UKHW041938140426
5217IPUK00014B/542